2G SAGA
Unfolds

2G SAGA Unfolds

Andimuthu Raja

HAR-ANAND
PUBLICATIONS PVT LTD

Reprint, 2021

Published by Ashok Gosain and Ashish Gosain for:
HAR-ANAND PUBLICATIONS PVT LTD
E-49/3, Okhla Industrial Area, Phase-II, New Delhi-110020
Tel: 41603490
E-mail: info@haranandbooks.com/haranand@rediffmail.com
Shop online at: www.haranandbooks.com

Dedicated with reverence and gratitude to my parents who ploughed the field of my existence with their mettle and toil; sowed the seeds of my ethos with their simplicity and integrity; nourished the roots of my strength with their conviction and resolve; nurtured the crop of my success with their affection and tears. The harvest of my humble offerings to society is their legacy!

A. RAJA

Preface

Justice in India has often appeared to have been attacked and wounded or abused and exploited by power houses with vested interests. Yet, it has never been completely stifled or rendered impotent. It continues to retain its vitality especially in the context of our national precept of Dharma—"an ethical concept which includes the moral code, righteousness, and the whole range of man's duties and responsibilities" as Pandit Nehru so aptly described it. My tale is of a village lad, a resurgent Indian belonging to the long repressed lower social strata, who freed himself of traditional shackles but remained bound to time-honoured beliefs and native simplicity. Many of the great persons who were my ministerial colleagues would readily attest to the fact that my entrance into their cadre brought about a fresh outlook. Such an environment was fostered by my work culture and absolute sense of dedication—which to me is like oxygen. My tenacious battle is the first of its kind in the Indian political landscape. My legal war is a confrontation in the vein of the Biblical David and Goliath but I shall always preserve my faith in India's great tradition of justice.

I have compiled in this book the happenings around the 2G spectrum allocation: portraying both the challenges that I faced as well as my defiant resolve to crusade for national progress. The incidents and individuals presented in these events are in clear evidence even now, hence there is nothing for me to veil or misrepresent. Even so, this is neither an autobiography nor a ploy to make quibbling excuses. All the dramatis personae (including me) shall eventually fade from this world and may not even remain in public memory in a few years. However, in order that future administrators, politicians and citizens become cognisant of what not to do in similar situations, I think this endeavour to document history is essential. This book is an attempt to elucidate in the backdrop of the 2G case, how when relevant constitutional and statutory bodies lose their equitability and objectivity in the discharge of their duties—either due to self-interest or prejudicial external pressures—flagrant injustice, political failing and an overall repression of national interest ensues. There is no tangible loss to the nation associated with the loss of an individual; conversely, should the whole nation's good be sacrificed at the altar of an individual's selfinterest?

The Supreme Court is monitoring this case. I never asked for any clemency from the courts in the criminal case that was filed against me, but I am disturbed by the manner of implementation of the Rule of Law. Benches and galleries may vary but the Law must remain steadfast. Gandhi and Tilak embarked on agitations for the same cause but their manner of facing the law differed. When a case of sedition was slapped against Tilak he argued in court that he was not guilty; what he had written and spoken was not seditious as per the prevailing Rule of Law. Although he was convicted by the court of men, it is certain to the nation—the general populace—that his actions were justified and that he was innocent in the court of Man. Gandhi's defence was different. He accepted that he had knowingly violated the rule of law because it was wrongful and unjust. His actions were however morally right and justified according to natural law. In the 2G case, neither the rule of law nor natural law prevailed—with the exception of the provision of an actual court trial. The media hype deluded the masses into believing that there was moral delinquency while the 'arbitrating institutions' diluted legal diligence and objective, civilized jurisprudence by voicing capricious personal opinions.

I have tried to establish how right from the time of issuance of 2G licenses, arrows of suspicion and false propaganda were fired at me, with the statutory and constitutional bodies concerned setting off from a position of misinformation and remaining steeped in incomprehension. This book shall elaborate with the evidence of events and documents, how the former CAG (Comptroller and

Auditor General of India) Vinod Rai while appearing well-intentioned, has executed the functions of his office with ulterior motives and lack of objectivity. This is neither a recent observation nor just my personal viewpoint. Upon receiving CAG's Draft Report, a response report was sent on 27 July 2010 by the Department of Telecommunications (DoT). This elaborate 108-page response was compiled by many of the officers of DoT who were also included as witnesses in the 2G case. On page 100, it has been emphatically stated, "Therefore, the conclusion of the Audit regarding issuance of licenses in 2008 at 2001 prices, issuance of licenses on FCFS policy to the applicants who applied till 25 September 2007, implementation of dual technology and allotment of spectrum thereof is misconstrued and based on little knowledge of the policies of the Government and without going into detail and understanding the various recommendations of TRAI and the entire Telecom scenario in the country." Even so the CAG deliberately ignored these clarifications. Rai's report is essentially a mixture of inappropriate legal interpretations, incongruous comparisons and flippant allegations, ignoring the Government's standpoint and the concomitant laws. The few who comprehended this reality and maintained their constancy can unfortunately be counted on one's fingers. Everybody—shockingly even the Supreme Court bench—became so enthralled by the notion of a hypothesized presumptive loss figure as indicative of an actual 'scam' of huge proportion that emotion trumped over logic and—more significantly—the legal process. Vinod Rai also had the temerity to dub himself the 'Nation's Conscience Keeper' on the cover of his book titled 'Not just an Accountant' in which he dedicated a few chapters on the 2G Spectrum allocation. He in his role as CAG was the 'sutradhaar' who created the devious apparition which the media and political opposition followed. It is unfortunate that even the highest court of the country became a prey to this. I shall debunk Mr. Rai's allegations in the chapters that follow and demonstrate that issues which were paraded as pearls gleaned from the ocean of CAG's report were not even so many specks of sand. The possibility of a 'conspiracy-nexus' cannot be ruled out in this travesty of responsible and honourable jurisprudence. I will show that Rai's words and actions are:

Malicious vigilantism that makes a mockery of his constitutional responsibilities;

Disgraceful purchase of self-promotion at the cost of Truth and Integrity;

Wanton sacrifice of national progress to further perverted political goals; Corrupt commercialism couched in moral rhetoric and veiled altruism.

I am certain that reports of auditors like Shriman Vinod Rai which I will show to be mere trash shall be unanimously deemed fit for the dustbin:

When Parliamentary Democracy moves beyond cheap pandering to vote-banks;

When the nation's leaders only favour ethical means to win political mandates;

When constitutional bodies can be trusted to never overstep their defined boundaries;

When the Fourth Pillar regains its objectivity and autonomy to document the truth;

When the Judiciary's prudence will not be swayed by emotion and sensationalism;

The political adversaries of the UPA government were quite worried about UPA-2's smooth sailing. There could hence have been a deliberate plot blessed by the opposition parties to project a progressive initiative as a scam of grand proportions in order to malign and destabilize the government. Nonetheless the Supreme Court bench comprising Justices Singhvi and Ganguly thought it had no reason to doubt the credibility of the CAG and proceeded without taking into consideration all the relevant facts, policies and official documentation. That bench uttered vitriolic comments of a personal nature in open court. Former Chief Justice of India A. S. Anand has quoted, "The role of judge is that of a referee. I can blow my judicial whistle when the ball goes out of play; but when the game restarts, I must neither take part in it nor tell the players how to play ... judicial whistle needs to be blown for a purpose and with caution." The inapt conclusions pronounced at those proceedings were subsequently set right to some extent, vide the larger Constitutional Bench.

A sense of duty and responsibility drove me to pen this book and make the nation understand and beware of the political and economic disaster that would ensue if individuals or institutions are permitted to arrive at facile conclusions/decisions, on issues requiring broader consultation and deeper knowledge of various legal nuances and technical details. I have also tried to responsibly portray the consequent fallout if the journalistic world, the Fourth Pillar of democracy, sheds its accountability. Vinod Mehta the editor of 'Outlook' magazine has commented, "The increasing corporate ownership of the media landscape in India could undermine its plurality and independent functioning." It is indeed a matter of concern that the Fourth Estate is evolving into corporate commercial media houses where Truth becomes a casualty for the images that they (aim to) create and project. If the media succumbs to easy sensationalism by projecting (without proof) an individual or institution as corrupt, anti-social, criminal or terrorist, then the objectivity of journalism is diminished. I have attempted to record in the ensuing chapters the reasons for the (fleeting) success of the media in portraying me as a selfish burglar.

I take great pride in my efforts to bring technological progress to our country that was lagging behind in the wireless telecom domain by at least a decade and for being instrumental in making available Mobile, Internet, WhatsApp, Twitter, Facebook, etc., to the masses. At a time when there was insufficient understanding about 3G and WiMAX, when it was touted that spectrum required for the next generation of wireless technology was not at all available, I am pleased with my role in overcoming stiff resistance to identify the usable spectrum and in consequently making this new technology available for public consumption. Clearly the adoption of and related issuance of 2G licenses was a precursor to the subsequent roll out of 3G. My promises to the nation to bring down 2G call charges to a mere 30 paisea as also to introduce 3G technology ubiquitously, have already reached fruition. Yet, I stand blemished and cast out of any position of merit in this context. I take solace from these words of Periyar EVR, "Those in public life should not mind insults and disrespect caused while they render their service; worrying about it would only wipe away the resulting benefits of their service."

Emile Zola is one of my favourite novelists. During my college days, I read in "Letters of Anna" (*Dr. C.N. Annadurai, Founder of Dravida Munnetra Kazhagam—DMK as political party emerged from Dravidar Kazhagam—DK*) about the revolutionary campaign undertaken by Zola in the 1890s that dramatically influenced the political history of France. The seeds of my love for Zola were sown then not merely because of his brilliant writing but also because of his dedication to truth and justice. The 'Dreyfus affair' involved the wrongful accusation and subsequent incarceration of Captain Alfred Dreyfus of the French army for allegedly selling army secrets to Germany. Zola published in the front page of a Paris newspaper, an open letter to the President titled 'J 'accuse' accusing the highest levels of the French Army of obstruction of justice and anti-Semitism in the unjust conviction of Dreyfus. This forced the case to be reopened—just as Zola had intended. Dreyfus was consequently issued a pardon by the government. However, a case of libel was foisted against Zola for his writings and he was forced to seek asylum in England. He proclaimed, "I was determined that my country should not remain the victim of lies and injustice. I may be condemned here. The day will come to thank me for having helped its honour!" Regarding Zola's seeking asylum to escape imprisonment, Dr Annadurai aptly concludes, "Courage is required even to accept the title of coward."

More than 5 years have elapsed since the start of the 2G case – 15 months of which I spent in prison. On many occasions, I have been heard in person essaying my counter arguments prior to the framing of charges in the trial court. Thereafter I sent my detailed response to the Joint Parliamentary Committee, the copy of which appeared not only in the printed news but also on various web portals. Prior to my arrest, my interviews were also published five times in 'The Hindu'. I have not altered throughout, either my views or the chain of events cited. Yet, no one considered my perspective with an open mind and talked or wrote about it. I don't expect the sacrifice of a Zola on my behalf but I do despair over the fact that no individual or institution came forward to comprehend my facts and hear out my counter-arguments. I am glad however that my ambition to bring affordable 2G and 3G to the public has not been totally foiled. No nation fosters its freedom and progress without the loss of individuals or the credit that they deserve. It is saddening though that in this case it was statutory and constitutional bodies whose function it is to safeguard people's rights that caused such 'losses'. All that I have penned in this book is with a due sense of responsibility. Therefore, I have personally verified the documentary records and cross-checked facts with other individuals and experts concerned. I have only attempted to state the truth and have not sought to injure or sully anyone. I know there are those who will argue that my views are erroneous. However, my inferences are based on truth and documented facts. I have consciously steered clear of any falsifications and defamatory slurs.

I have written this book even while I was facing the charges against me in a court of law. My motivation is the conviction that it is my duty to convey my side of the story to the public, as it is they who elected me to represent their interest. I have carefully avoided reference to the legal proceedings and deposition of witnesses in the trial court as I want clear separation between the heartfelt views that I communicate here and the dispassionate legal arguments that I present in court. There is hence no doubt in my mind about the aptness of this book's release because, I believe that if I remain silent then this may be misinterpreted and distorted to further tarnish my image and consequently that of the political party to which I am loyal.

The late Arignar Anna, founder of the DMK addressed the Rajya Sabha in April 1962. That was the time when the regional DMK party gained popularity and widened its base as an alternative to Congress at the Tamil Nadu state level by emphasising the Tamil language and the Dravidian identity. That was also the time when DMK was rooting for a separate state the Dravida Nadu, due to which repressive measures were taken against DMK by the Congress-led central government. Anna said, "The fact that we want separation is not to be misconstrued as being antagonistic. Of course, I can understand the feelings that would very naturally arise in the minds of the people in the northern area, whenever they think of partition. I know the terrible consequences of partition and I am deeply sympathetic towards them. But our separation is entirely different from the partition which has brought out Pakistan." When China later attacked India, the same Anna stood strongly in favour of India's sovereignty and reinforced that DMK although a state party had in mind the greater interest of the nation. It makes me weep to think of the sullying of the intents of such a movement and its embodiment the DMK party which took both victory and defeat in its stride for 66 years upholding national interest while retaining its focus on the development and unique identity of the Tamil state.

Truth has been my guiding light and the elixir that provides me moral strength to bear the insults and strife during my protracted fight for justice. The anguish even pushed me to the brink of utter despondency. Truth safeguarded me from tipping over, but it is my party the DMK and my leader Kalaignar Dr Karunanidhi who pulled me back to a firm footing. The garlands from Kalaignar and our general secretary Professor K. Anbazhagan that graced my neck upon my return to Chennai after release from prison on bail were signs of their love and trust a symbol of our leader's tendency to nurture of me like a child in the womb. Thalapathi M. K. Stalin came in person to meet me on several occasions when I was in judicial custody as well as to my residence after I was released on bail, in order to console me and bolster my resolve. In prison as well as in court many party leaders and comrades met me lovingly and supportively out of concern for me and their commitment to the party; I will remember them fondly till my last breath. My wife Parameswari—who is herself also a lawyer—as well as my daughter Mayuri have perhaps had a more trying time than me during this period of struggle. Their love, understanding, courage and steadfast support has been my life's biggest blessing.

I am sincerely grateful to Professor SFN Chelliah, Professor Arul Jyothi John Sundar, Paran Balakrishnan, Umesh Marthi and

S.E. Rajan for their invaluable contributions in the research and transcription of this book.

The 2G Trial which is in progress from 2011 on a day-today basis as per the direction of the Supreme Court is likely to be completed in the very near future. I had kept this manuscript under wraps even though it was completed in December 2016 itself, in order to avoid unnecessary criticism and debate from various corners. I am deeply grateful to Narendra Kumar, Founder Chairman, Har-Anand Publications for his zeal to publish this book in a very short time irrespective of the court's verdict because he is personally convinced that I am on the side of truth.

New Delhi
10 May 2017 ANDIMUTHU RAJA

Contents

List of Abbreviations

ADG	Additional Director General
AGR	Adjusted Gross Revenue
ARPU	Average Revenue Per User
AS	Access Services
AIADMK	All India Anna Dravida Munnetra Kazhagam
BSO	Basic Service Operator
BTS	Basic Telephone Service
CAG	Comptroller and Auditor General of India
CBI	Central Bureau of Investigation
CPI	Communist Party of India
CPI (M)	Communist Party of India (Marxist)
CVC	Central Vigilance Commission
CDMA	Code Division Multiple Access
CMTS	Cellular Mobile Telephone Services
COAI	Cellular Operators Association of India
CCEA	Cabinet Committee on Economic Affairs
DDG	Deputy Director General
Dir.	Director
DoT	Department of Telecom
DMK	Dravida Munnetra Kazhagam
DK	Dravidar Kazhagam
EGOM	Empowered Group of Ministers
ED	Enforcement Directorate
FCFS	First Come, First Served
FDI	Foreign Direct Investment
FIPB	Foreign Investment Promotion Board
FIR	First Information Report
GOM	Group of Ministers

GSM	Global System for Mobile Communications
ITU	International Telecom Union
JPC	Joint Parliamentary Committee
LA (T)	Legal Advisor (Telecom)
LF	Licensing Finance
LOI	Letter of Intent
M(F)	Member (Finance)
M(T)	Member (Technology)
MoC&IT	Minister of Communication and Information Technology
MoF	Ministry of Finance
MoLJ	Ministry of Law and Justice
NTP-94	National Telecom Policy 1994
NTP-99	National Telecom Policy, 1999
NDA	National Democratic Alliance
PMO	Prime Minister's Office
PAC	Public Accounts Committee
PTI	Press Trust of India
S(T)	Secretary (Telecom)
SG	Solicitor General of India
TC	Telecom Commission
TDSAT	Telecom Disputes Settlement and Appellate Tribunal
TEC	Telecom Engineering Commission
TRAI	Telecom Regulatory Authority of India
TTML	Tata Teleservices (Maharashtra) Ltd
TTSL	Tata Tele Services Ltd
UAS	Unified Access Service
UASL	Unified Access Service License
USO	Universal Service Obligation
UPA	United Progressive Alliance
WLL	Wireless in Local Loop
WPC	Wireless Planning and Coordination
WTO	World Trade Organisation

CHAPTER 1

Parental Home to Public Life

During the first decade of the twentieth century when the social and economic environment of India was plagued by the curse of caste-based segregation and untouchability, my grandfather Kaliaperumal – due to a combination of his intense yearning for self-respect and his belief that an equitable livelihood was inaccessible – migrated from Velur (a hamlet in Perambalur Taluka of erstwhile Tiruchirapalli district in Tamil Nadu) to Ceylon (present day Sri Lanka) without any legal documents, in order to make a new living. This is what I heard about my grandfather from my parents during my childhood. Whenever my mother recounted memories from 50-60 years in the past, of my great grandfather Chitrambalam, my grandfather Kaliaperumal and my grandmother Unnamalai, she would always be moved to tears. She would speak of their good nature, traditional values, honest, hardworking lifestyle, and affection for their relatives and fellowmen that could be seen manifested in their sincere concern and empathetic tears. My grandfather earned the honorific 'Dharmar' due to the kindness that he showed to the villagers especially during droughts. The family's pastoral morality rooted in religious belief – as yet distanced from the ethics of urban living and scientific reasoning – was easy prey to social enslavement and consequent poverty. God and religion was their crutch and even their names reflect this hopeful immersion in the Divine. I wonder why, these simple folk, so steeped in their native setting that they rarely ever travelled – only on foot or on ox-cart whenever they did and never more than 50 kms – decided to take the leap to migrate to a far off foreign land. Perhaps scholars of the socio-economic conditions in India at that time may have answers but I think better understanding is possible through the narration of direct experiences as I was privileged to receive through my mother. She would also describe the rural socio-economic setting and highlight its basis on labour – on the human body as a tool of production. I sigh deeply when I ponder over the comparison with the present state of our family. Over the generations, my dutiful parents have at some point distanced themselves from God and religion but never have they wavered from fostering in us, the ancestral family values of dignity in labour, personal integrity and benevolence. I wistfully ponder what shape these values will take in my daughter Mayuri's generation who find the world on display on their computer screens. I once quoted to Mayuri a few lines:

"Honouring those who work with Computers, the Gen-next cares not for those who work in fields; Go and tell the present generation that Computers cannot download Rice."

Her prompt response:

"Yes, you cannot download Rice, the grain;
But you can download information, the horizon.
This is not a disavowal of farm or Rice"

While I bow in deference to the brain of this generation, I worry about its heart. In our nation's history those who used their brain often forgot their heart, while those who followed the heart were shackled from working their brain. Class and caste have been at the core of this chasm between heart and brain. This observation has always caused me great anguish. However, I am amazed that during those older times when the social stratification was extremely rigid and the chasm even more pronounced, my forefathers were progressive and nurtured their children's brain.

After saving enough through his own perseverance and the goodwill of his 'white master', my grandfather returned to India in the 1950s. He bought the same land on which he had earlier sweated fruitlessly as a farm-hand; procured strong oxen for tilling it; and upgraded the thatched hut to a firm brick-and-mortar dwelling. My grandparents migrated back to the land of their birth with the wish to return to its dust at the end of their days, but my parents stayed on in

Sri Lanka. That land of tea-plantations had workers living like a kind of slaves – being sucked dry by their masters and leeches alike. My parents and my father's younger brother Subramanian, worked untiringly to make a living amidst these folk as grocers, milkmen, cloth-traders and tailors. Then with their savings in hand and seven children in tow (clearly a time when Family Planning posters did not grace the walls of all streets) my parents also moved back in 1961. I was not yet in the picture; I was yet to be born.

While my parents were moving back, an air-mail letter addressed to them and with a black mark at its top-left corner left India and was delivered a month later in Sri Lanka. The black mark was for the sad news of my grandfather's passing away. I wonder if my grandfather during the time of such snail-paced communication would have imagined that his grandson would be instrumental in bringing 3G wireless to the country. Prior to the implementation of the Shastri-Sirimavo Bandaranaike agreement, people of Indian origin were denied citizenship as well as entry visas for Sri Lanka. Thiru M. Ayyakkannu, my mother's elder brother and a Congress MP (1957-62) pleaded my parents' case personally with the then PM Pandit Jawaharlal Nehru in order to obtain visas. My uncle was also instrumental in creating an opportunity for me and my siblings to make our mark in Government Service. Till her last breath my mother used to say that her annan (elder brother) was like Kannan (Lord Krishna) for us. My parents' regard for my uncle found expression in my marriage to his daughter Parameswari.

I was born toward the end of 1963 and was named Sathyaseelan (man of truth). Some of my friends that know this occasionally say jokingly that 'Sathyam' (truth) has fortunately still survived. During my school days, I was always surrounded by at least ten boys who would follow me around and cling to my words. I was hence given the pet-name Raja (king) by my elder sister's husband Pachamuthu who was also my teacher in school. My village plains surrounded by hills, comprised vast open stretches of dry land; grazing grounds for cattle; farmland that depended on the capricious rainfall with a select few having access to well-water irrigation; and some small Gods installed in the open at the outskirts. In such a setting, even someone owning a bullock-cart gained social prestige. These privileged folks showed-off their status by the colouring of the horns of their oxen or their bronze bells or by donating electric lights to the village temple that proudly flashed their names. In such a setting, the unfortunate 'have-nots' were steeped in illiteracy and utter poverty. It is no surprise then that my father who owned ten acres of land and had wells for irrigation was bestowed the honorific 'landlord' and addressed as such even on wedding invitations.

In 1973, after completing class five from the government-run Adi Dravidar Welfare Primary School in our village, I was admitted to a government high school in neighbouring Padalur for my further education. That place Padalur totally changed my life. Upon leaving my family and moving to hostel life, I not only gained independence but also the strength to function and think on my own. My mother who reluctantly accepted my move with a heavy heart, advised me at the bus stand before my journey, "Do not lie; do not steal; do not beg." The counsel to "Study well" came only after all that. She repeated this guidance at every instance of my journey to Padalur after holiday visits home. For her, who had not been privileged with formal schooling, the priority was that her children should become good human beings; education was secondary to that.

My ears were habituated to hearing the Suprabhatam devotional songs early every morning on the big radio set brought from Sri Lanka by my father. It was only in Padalur that I heard for the first time "Avartham Periyar" – he (E. V. Ramasamy, Founder of the social movement DK – Dravidar Kazhagam) is Periyar (the illustrious one) – in the stentorian voice of Sirkazhi Govindarajan. The gramophone player at Mayan Tea Stall introduced me to "Kallakudi konda Karunanidhi" (Karunanidhi the conqueror of Kallakudi). The influence of Periyar EVR was prominent in Padalur and its surroundings, where his Self-Respect Movement attracted many into its fold. However, at that time in my life I had little concern or understanding of Periyar and his movement.

During class six, the warden of our hostel was the very strict Rajagopal. He was such a disciplinarian that he even used to punish students who skipped bathing (due to the cold) in the morning. He would run his hands under the armpits of the students to check their body temperature. Padalur had a touring-cinema-theatre called Shanthi Thirai Arangam.

Every evening, as a routine, exactly at 6 o'clock a devotional song 'Thangamayam Murugan Sannidhanam' (The abode of Lord Murugan is golden) would be played loudly on the theatre's loudspeakers. The theatre never screened shows during the day time. One day shortly after my admission, our warden took us to the theatre to listen to Periyar EVR addressing a meeting. My father was not only a devotee of Lord Murugan but was also a keen worshipper of Lord Shiva. He used to sit in prayer on a tiger skin and recite the Skanda Shasti Kavacham. I used to sit by his side very often, observing and absorbing his activities. Pretty soon I too had memorized the prayers and even today I recite them at public forums when I speak on the subject of rationalism! That day in Padalur's Shanthi theatre, Periyar also spoke in his wizened voice on rationalism. When I came out of the theatre many books were laid out on the floor for sale at 5-10 paisa each. I bought some books with the 25 paisa that I had. When I read those books, the thoughts therein felt like pebbles being dropped in my mind's pond. The ripples were gentle but it was then that I developed the habit of reading daily newspapers at tea stalls.

A reading room named 'Anna Padippagam' was also opened around that time in Padalur. Every morning in the hostel we were required to finish our breakfast of rice kanji (rice porridge) by 8:30 a.m. and leave for the school by nine. The first bell for the Tamil tribute song would ring at 9:45. Between 9 and 9:45 every morning, I could not keep myself away from the reading room. Periodicals like Murasoli, Viduthalai, Kalkandu and later even magazines like Gokulam, reached the reading room as donations. I sensed a change inside me as I continued reading these publications. Their contents occupied my mind more than what I read in my text books at school. When I was in class eight a Tamil recitation contest was announced in our school. Sorko Chellamuthu, a trained graduate teacher who stayed in a room near our hostel gave me a booklet and suggested that I participate in the contest. The cover of the booklet had pictures of leaders including Dr Kalaignar Karunanidhi, tearfully standing by the side of the body of late Anna (Thiru C. N. Annadurai). 'Ezhuntu vaa, Em Anna!' (Rise up and come to us, our Anna) was the title of the booklet. It was an elegiac poem, a poetic obituary, composed by Dr Kalaignar Karunanidhi mourning the passing of Arignar Anna – the first non-Congress Chief Minister of Tamil Nadu after independence. I memorized the entire poem in 10 days and won first prize for reciting it at the contest. For me who had been brought up in a Congress-loyal family this poem was cathartic and it changed the course of my life. Those were the days when the rebel in me was growing. Thereafter, I never failed to win prizes in elocution contests, essay competitions and Tamil recitation meets held at our school. During my college days, the writings of Kalaignar brought me social and political awareness and gave me a sense of purpose. My eldest sister Mrs Vijaya Pachamuthu who was a post-graduate teacher in Tamil was also guiding me in honing my speeches and essays. My fondness for Tamil literature grew through her and I was even inspired to compose poems.

During the period when I was finding myself drawn to the Dravidian movement in Tamil Nadu, Emergency had been imposed on the country by the then Prime Minister Mrs Indira Gandhi. Some of our teachers at school had strong opinions against the Emergency which obviously influenced me while my parents remained oblivious of it. Whenever I pass by my old school at Padalur, I feel a sense of pride at the thought of having been the student who won the most prizes in elocution and essay-writing. Caste or other distinctions of social standing did not figure in my school life (we did not even have footwear till after class eight); there was competition but no denigration or enmity. In those days even talking to the girls was considered flagrant behaviour. The naughty delight of ogling the girls came only during the adolescent final days at school. If only our lives could be merrily lived out indulging in such simple harmless pleasures!

During the academic year 1980-81, I was nearly compelled by my family to choose Mathematics as my major with Chemistry and Physics as my ancillary subjects for my undergraduate studies at Arignar Anna Government Arts College, Musiri. Musiri which was also part of Tiruchirappalli district in those days was 60 Kilometres from my native village. Although I was enrolled for the B.Sc. (Maths) degree course, I found myself gravitating to the Tamil Association of the college and to the Dravidar Kazhagam. Additionally, the writings of Kalaignar continued to draw me towards social issues and language studies, quite at variance with the dreams of my family to see me become a big officer. His writings induced me to also read EVR Periyar, Mahatma Phule, Dr Ambedkar, Karl Marx and C.N. Annadurai. I did not have the heart to go against the wishes of my family but my awakening spirit did not let me concentrate on Maths. My professors were unhappy as I did not meet their expectations. It was their opinion that engaging in agitations on common issues, handing out pamphlets, contesting student union elections, officiating as secretary of the students wing of the Dravidar Kazhagam were not the pursuits expected of a student of maths and Sciences. In the year 1981-82, I was elected as the secretary to the 'Tamil peravai' (Tamil Union) of the college and was making my mark on the intramural stage as well as in intercollegiate elocution and essay contests. I was encouraged by Prof. Karuvai Palanichamy, the head of our Tamil department, and when I was in my final year in 1984, he compiled and published as a book, poems penned by me for various competitions, under the title Oru Suyasarithai (An Autobiography, Thirumozhi Publishers, Karur). In my preface to that book published when I was just 21, I wrote:

From the economic outlook; that
recognizes the right to property
and celebrates the right of inheritance –
From the social outlook;

that fails to look in to the inequalities
in the name of devotion -
The world of literature must be liberated!

These lines have been born now; with that thirst!

I encountered the precepts of 'division of labour' when I read Marx and Engels; when I read Periyar, Phule and Ambedkar I discovered 'division of labourers'. The notions of class and caste distinctions found in these writings reverberated in my young mind. The speeches of the late Thavathiru Kundrakudi Adigalar, 'Viduthalai' Editor K. Veeramani and other Tamil scholars who visited our college at my invitation, still ring in my ears. Clearly the sense of revolt in me was building up during this period, but I realize now that this agitation in my mind kept me from acting out impulsively and determined my future. Within the confines of my hostel and college campus, I often discussed aloud with my peers or debated silently within, "What is the purpose of education? Is it a means to earn wealth, to enrich one's personality, to serve society or is it a mixture of all these?" The letters from my home urged me to study hard, get a degree with high rank, and learn and earn from it. My readings of great leaders drove me to enrich my personality. Writings on rebellion in the cause of human rights and freedom movements led me to think about being useful to society. It was also clearly not possible for me to separate any one of these sentiments from the other. However, when the drive to be of use to society came to mind, everything else dimmed in comparison. A training camp for the students of Dravidar Kazhagam, on the subject of "Mandal Commission and Social Justice," was held in Lalgudi near Tiruchi. My focus in that camp was on the intersection of caste issues with the ideology of class struggle. It was then finally that I decided not to continue with my study of maths beyond my graduation. However, I pledged to complete my degree as if it were a bitter pill that I had to swallow to stay alive for pursuing further education suited to my newfound existential purpose. Even my approach in more recent times to the 2G situation, demonstrates how I have consistently clung to my philosophical goals while also fulfilling practical responsibilities since my very youth.

Whenever I pass by my college campus where my dreams were born, fond memories like the taste of the hostel meals and the disciplined devotion of our professors make my eyes as moist as the eyes of my then 'girlfriend' – with whom affections had alas been expressed only through our eyes – at our parting on the last day of college.

The languages of the heart
never physically articulated are
away now deprived.

Beneath thy gaze in silence even
Pacific ocean remains;
underneath its depth fathomless
lie thine affection's effervescence.

Whether it was mere infatuation or a deeper affection is still a riddle for me. That sense of mystery makes the memories so much sweeter for savouring repeatedly in rumination.

Free-spirited youth as yet unbridled by responsibilities is like an undammed river whose waters might benevolently flow to feed fertile farms, innocuously waste over barren land or malevolently sweep away a settlement. In spite of my avowed rationalism, I still yearn for that age so pregnant with possibilities.

Given my interest in Dravidar Kazhagam, I was naturally attracted to the DMK party. My exposure to DMK grew because Kalaignar the party president and Professor K. Anbazhagan its general secretary always delivered the Valedictory Address at every conference of the Dravidar Kazhagam. I clearly recall those conferences: sleeping overnight in the conference enclosure; waking up early; bathing and eating there itself; observing and absorbing everything till the very end of the event; and returning to my village with notes of all the highlights. During my final year in college, Tiruchi Siva, (presently Member of Parliament) DMK enrolled me in the DMK Students Wing, of which he was the State Secretary.

I reluctantly continued my BSc and immediately thereafter applied for a degree course in Law, without informing anyone. My family wanted me to continue with Mathematics for my post-graduation. Hence to keep them placated I also applied for that program. Entrance tests for admission to the Law degree course had been introduced for the first time in 1984-85. The admission process took a lot of time due to some legal cases, but eventually I was successful in securing admission to the Madurai Law College. My preference was Madras or Tiruchi Law College so I was a little disappointed. I was not really familiar with the Southern districts having only visited some tourist spots. Finding a place to stay was a big challenge as the college did not have any hostel facility. I eventually managed to get a room near the college. Our college hours in Madurai were only pre-noon, so it took me a while – months in some cases – to get to know my fellow students. It was not only shocking but also unpleasant for me to note the eagerness of some of these friends to find out the caste of their fellow-students by peeking into the college registers. After a while I found some like-minded friends whose outlook and ideologies had no room for caste distinctions.

During that period the Tamil Eelam movement spearheaded by the LTTE (Liberation Tigers of Tamil Eelam) and other military outfits was in full swing. I got introduced to some of these activists. When Dhileepan of LTTE succumbed to his fast unto death in protest against the mission of IPKF (Indian Peace Keeping Force) into Sri Lanka, there were many demonstrations and rallies in which my college friends also participated. In Madurai Law College also, my speeches and writings earned me laurels. Most significant was the first prize in an inter-college elocution contest. At the prize distribution function held in Madurai's Yadavar College the award was given to me by someone who already held a place of high regard in my mind due to his writings, speeches and captivating voice. Yes, it was the great Dr

Kalaignar Karunanidhi himself! That day in his presence, hearing his brilliant speech, earning his praise, and feeling his touch will remain one of the fondest memories of my life. "A starving lion once hunted down an elephant in a forest. Its prey fell to the ground on its left side. This was considered a slight to the lion's valour, so the lion walked away from the prey and starved to death. This is how noble men behave: they will not resort to ignoble actions no matter what is at stake." Such quotes by Kalaignar from ancient Tamil literature (in this instance Naladiar, 300 AD) would always enthral me. I had never imagined that I would someday find myself sitting at his side on the same stage, but I certainly wished for my association with him to grow.

After completing my law course, I registered at the bar as an advocate in the year 1988. Even this did not satisfy my family as they considered this of little significance compared to their dreams for me to become a big officer. They thought that the lawyer's profession could not guarantee social status or good income, and even if it did, it would take a very long time. I practiced law for just seven years, of which two were spent as an apprentice. Valluvan Nambi my senior advocate, guided me in the preparation of pleadings, structuring of presentations and arguments, and finalization of drafts. An unfortunate accident and ensuing health issues of Nambi led to his creating a career opening for me and thus enabled me to become a full-fledged lawyer. Even during my short law career, my competence and potential for success were acknowledged. This brief courtship with the law profession has stood me in good stead in my political career, especially right now when I am battling the 2G case.

Science has brought about many miracles in today's rural life which long back in the 1980s were just dreams. Those were the days when pregnant women had to be taken to hospitals on bullock carts and often one or the other, or even both would not return alive. People would fall dead from accidents while digging wells; others would succumb to snake bites before they reached the hospital. Telephones were brought in on trucks laden with tin-sheet telephone poles fixed first only at our village post office. Even then there was the many hour or day long wait for a trunk call connection or dead phone lines for a considerable part of every month. It took a longer period before phone connections at homes started becoming available. My family had to wait until 1989 for this privilege. That was the year when my elder brother Dr Ramachandran (Indian Forest Service) who had advised me to pursue a career in politics and spent all his savings to further it without any expectations, procured a phone connection in our village house to enable us to speak to our parents. As a senior official in government service, his experiences had led him to the conclusion that political power is the key to all powers. Hence, he advised me to seek a career in politics. His support and motivation is one of the key factors for my entering the political arena and achieving a level of success there. In the same year, I registered as a lawyer in the Perambalur – our district HQ – Bar Association. In order to travel the distance of 10 kilometres between my village and the Perambalur court, I got my first scooter, set up an office from my own savings and procured a phone connection. It is amusing to recall that I also installed a 'number lock' in order to secure the long-distance STD (standard trunk dialling) facility. I remembered this sorry state of affairs in the area of Telecom when I became the country's minister in charge of that portfolio. I had experienced first-hand the tribulations of people in villages, where telecom services remained either impossibly out of reach or lagging behind by decades by any worthwhile standard of comparison.

Thiru Murasoli Maran was my mentor in politics. On his death, I wrote a dedication titled,

"Thirst for Knowledge; Desire for Idealism" in a commemorative volume published by the Tamil magazine 'Kungumam'. I tried to document for posterity Thiru Maran's clarion call at the World Trade Organization (WTO) summit in Doha – where he was speaking in the capacity of Union Minister for Commerce and Industry – for safeguarding the rights of developing nations lest the WTO tried to become a World government of its own. Here is an excerpt from my conversation with him in this context.

Me: "When so many nations are oblivious, as if blind to their own nakedness in the WTO, how does this impending danger strike you?"

Thiru Maran: "When racism reared its head, we opposed Aryan supremacists and continue to do so. When language was thrust upon us, we opposed Hindi and continue to do so. When religion maligned our devotion, we even defied God and continue to do so. Steadfast against all hegemony is the path of Periyar and Anna. Hence I follow that path and oppose the dominance of USA's 'commercial baby', the World Trade Organization."

I have been moulded in this ideology and am incapable of suffering injustice or oppression. This 'inability' is my true identity and my pride. My response to the entire 2G situation reflects this identity.

All individuals involved in the 2G case were motivated by their ego as was I. My ego springs from my ideology and leads me to take certain assertive, well-intentioned and swift (some have dubbed them hasty) steps. Labelling these sincere actions as unfair or lacking transparency is irresponsible and libellous. I have been used by some influential persons for their political motives and ignorant beliefs. I have also been put to use to shatter the over-confidence of some mavericks. I have been both blamed and lauded, for causing either the great fall of some or the grand success of some others. Periyar was once asked, "Is it religious code to conclude that 'one who contemplates evil shall be ruined?" He replied, "It is Nature's code that the one who will be ruined contemplates evil." In the 2G spectrum issue those who had evil in their hearts and hatched conspiracies will perish. This is an assertion of my faith not a curse – I do not believe in such notions. To quote Kalaignar in this context, "hiding Truth is like hiding seed in the soil." That seed will germinate and emerge from the ground. This is my unshakable faith in the impermanence of evil and artifice.

My siblings and I approached our ailing 75-year-old father Thiru Andimuthu a day before his demise (in 1997) and asked him, "What is your message to us before you depart?" He said, "Your own thoughts decide your life. What else can I add?" Ten years later when my mother Thirumathi Chinnapillay Ammal was in the hospital for cardiac surgery, she called us all and told us, "Have the will in life to become a great person. In case you are unable to achieve that, have the resolve to at least be a good person." Although the blessings and instructions of others cannot decide one's life they can certainly provide invaluable guidance. I feel deeply grateful for my parents' simple but truthful advice that motivated us siblings to follow a righteous path. In these times when the joint family system is rapidly disappearing, when parents die, 'e' (Tamil word for flies) throng their bodies whereas their children remain engrossed in 'e'-mails in foreign lands. My parents who dreamt only for the sake of their children, and gracefully lived and died in fulfilling those very dreams; as also my brothers and sisters born alongside me who showered me with their love and affection impressed upon me the value of human relations which is permanently engraved in my psyche. I acknowledge that materialism also governs human relations and accordingly accept the potential conflicts as also the possible solutions that it brings. Even then, I am of the view that more than the luxury, status and fame that material wealth can give in social life, the gentler sentiments of kinship that bring happiness, sense of security and solace have greater strength. If money could grant or take away hunger, sleep, tears, laughter and happiness, then all men on this earth shall become machines. Human relations are essential for the heart to continue beating until some marvellous mechanical key is invented to turn the heart's beat on. When I was imprisoned in the 2G case, the strength of these relations and the encouragement they gave were key factors that kept me whole.

CHAPTER 2

Onward to Parliament

My career as an advocate commenced in 1988 but was interrupted in 1996 when I contested parliamentary elections for the first time. That was also the year of my marriage to Parameswari, the daughter of my uncle who had enabled my parents to return from Sri Lanka to their motherland. When Vaiko (Thiru V. Gopalsamy) left DMK in 1993, a slot opened up in the party for a young person. Our party leader Kalaignar Karunanidhi blessed me with that opportunity to contest elections from Perambalur constituency based on the recommendation of the district secretaries Thiru S. Siva Subramaniam (former Rajya Sabha MP) and Thiru K. N. Nehru (former minister). When I won the seat, and entered parliament at the age of 33, I was not only in awe of the Chamber that manifested our country's democratic machinery but was also feeling very grateful to the DMK for its culture of enabling even common people from the nation's hinterland like me to come into the fold and become a member of parliament. During that brief period when there was a non-Congress, non-BJP coalition government at the centre, I got the opportunity to speak only once but had the privilege to listen to others frequently.

On 19 March 1997, I recorded my maiden speech in the Lok Sabha when participating in the discussion on the general budget. I said, "As one of the youngest members of this House, I seek your permission to submit my views on the budget as my maiden speech ... It is my duty to express my gratitude to our beloved leader Dr Kalaignar M. Karunanidhi, the chief minister of Tamil Nadu, by whom I was inducted into the ideology of Thanthai Periyar and Arignar Anna during my school days, and by whose blessings I stand before you today." I welcomed the budget on behalf of the DMK, appreciating the importance given by the finance minister P. Chidambaram to establishing infrastructure for irrigation, energy, transport and communication. I pointed out that developing infrastructure alone cannot make a nation self-sufficient and emphasized that schemes for alleviating poverty must also succeed. I further stated that these poor who are denied their basic and rightful needs are the ones working tirelessly to produce the wealth that brings perpetual comfort to the elite few. My thoughts were well received by the honourable members of that august house. Except in rare instances the Indian Parliament best exemplifies the respect given to everyone's point of view in our Democracy.

By the time that I learned the ropes and was in a position to perform efficiently in office, the government was toppled and another election was thrust upon the nation in 1998. I contested again but had to face defeat this time. In 1996, the people of Tamil Nadu were angry with the then Chief Minister, late Jayalalitha for poor administration, amassing disproportionate assets and creating a repressive environment. The courts have recently also passed a guilty verdict against Jayalalitha and her co-conspirators in the disproportionate assets case. It was unexpected that so much public anger and disillusionment would water down so soon under the newly established political alliance. In 1999, another general election was thrust upon the country as a result of the apparently 'healthy alliance' between Jayalalitha and Subramanian Swamy which directly led to the fall of Vajpayee's government at the Centre. That was the time when the Honourable PM Vajpayee quoted out of desperation while campaigning, "those were my sleepless nights." I not only contested elections for the third time and won, but was also inducted on behalf of DMK as a Minister of State in the Union Council of Ministers. Omar Abdullah, former Chief Minister of Jammu and Kashmir and I were the youngest members of the Council. I was also fortunate then to have the opportunity to interact on an almost daily basis and benefit from the advice of late Thiru Murasoli Maran, who was then the parliamentary party leader of DMK and the minister of Industries and Commerce in the Union Cabinet.

I was assigned to the Ministry of Rural Development. 75-year-old Sundarlal Patwa, who was earlier the CM of Madhya Pradesh, became the Cabinet Minister. This senior politician had started his career with Jan Sangh but then moved to BJP and worked steadfastly till the party came to power. There was a big generation gap between us and our ideologies were poles apart. Only the Cabinet Minister is empowered to decide on the distribution of powers and the work allocation to the Ministers of State. At that time there was another Minister of State in the same Ministry of Rural Development, Subash Maharia from Rajasthan. The departments of Land Resources and Drinking Water Supply were allocated to me, while Maharia had the departments of Poverty Alleviation and Rural Sanitation. The primary function of these departments was the distribution of allocated funds proportionately among various states and supervising the implementation of several schemes. In 1998, when the coalition led by BJP was in power a new formula for allocating funds to Rural Development projects was adopted, as were the guidelines to be followed by state governments to apply for these funds. Accordingly, it was decided to gradually reduce the funding to the better performing States and increase allocation to the States that were lagging behind or were not implementing schemes successfully.

At that time, our party leader and CM of Tamil Nadu Dr Kalaignar Karunanidhi accompanied by the officials of the state government, came to Delhi to participate in the meeting of the National Development Council (NDC). After the NDC, the CM called me to point out that the new funding guidelines were not only against the interest of states like Tamil Nadu but they were also akin to punishing them for being efficient in their timely implementation of schemes. He wished for this anomaly to be remedied. The officials who accompanied the CM provided me the details of the reduced fund allocation under various heads for that financial year. Their concerns were pertaining to departments not under my purview. We Ministers of State were not empowered to function and take decisions independently. Although I got the opportunity to respond to queries in Parliament, I knew that many others did not open their mouths even once during their whole tenure. There were many ministers who completed their five-year tenure just travelling in special red-beaconed cars, sitting in plush air-conditioned office rooms and occupying VIP seats in special enclosures during national celebrations like Republic or Independence Day. However, I felt that I could not sit by idly but must do something about the justified complaint from Tamil Nadu. Every year in every ministry there used to be unused funds either after having met planned expenses or due to the inability to fully implement certain schemes. Generally, this corpus could be carried forward to the following year. I learned of this when I discussed the matter with some officials and colleagues without raising it to the Cabinet Minister lest it lead to any discomfiture. They gave me all this information only verbally and also suggested that these budgetary savings could be redirected to states in need. I felt that my request would be blocked if made directly only to the Cabinet Minister. I hence, prepared an official note backed by data and details and sent it to the PM Vajpayee. As a matter of protocol, I also sent a copy to the Cabinet Minister.

One day, after question hour in Parliament, an officer conveyed to me that the PM wanted to see me in his office. When I met the PM, the note that I had sent him was present on his desk. He said, "I have read your note. I have given suitable instructions to Brajesh Mishra, my Principal Secretary to discuss with the Secretary of your ministry and then to arrive at a fair decision after consultation with your Cabinet Minister." That kind gesture of the PM to call me in person in spite of his busy schedule furthered my respect for him. Towards the end of that week, Sundarlal Patwa announced a modified guideline that the states making progress will not be subject to a cut in their fund allocation and that the special privilege for backward states would be extended only after monitoring the timely implementation of sanctioned schemes. Being my senior Patwa could have chided me for having gone over his head; instead he gave me the charge to implement the new policy and the opportunity to field Question Hour in both Houses of Parliament. His magnanimity and grace impressed me and it would be no exaggeration to state that it motivated me to perform better in my role thereafter. Needless to say, the CM and officials of Tamil Nadu were very pleased and Thiru Ko Si Mani the Honourable Tamil Nadu Minister of Rural Development hosted a special lunch for me at the Secretariat.

I continued in the Ministry of Rural Development for only a year. In September 2000, following a Cabinet reshuffle, I was moved to the Ministry of Health and Family Welfare. Dr C.P. Thakur from Bihar was the Cabinet Minister. He was a famous researcher in the field of medicine with a first-place gold medal M.B.B.S Honours, M.D, M.R.C.P and F.R.C.P degrees. He had revolutionised the concept of treatment of Kala-azar (black fever or leishmaniasis) and was recognised as an international authority in this field. Upon assuming office, he issued orders that all files needing his review would be routed through me. He would consider all my notes in the files before taking any final decisions. In November 2001, while I was touring my constituency, I was seriously injured in a road accident and taken to a hospital in Tiruchirapalli. I recall with sincere gratitude that Dr Thakur arranged an Army (ambulance) Helicopter with the approval of the PM to have me airlifted to Apollo Hospital in Chennai. Shatrughan Sinha became the next Cabinet Minister of the Health Ministry in the subsequent Cabinet reshuffle. It was only then I had the opportunity to interact frequently with the popular film star and I found out how open-minded he was. In the beginning, he used to have me sit by his side during question hour in Parliament (11 am to noon) and often ask my opinion. He issued an internal order that I should participate in all the review meetings held in the Health Ministry. In a few months, he gave me almost the entire responsibility for handling question hour.

A list of 20 oral questions would be circulated with the names of the honourable members who had posed the query. In order to facilitate supplementary questions, responses to the oral questions would be kept in the lobby in the morning, well in advance of the meeting of the House. During the session in the House not more than six or seven questions would get their turn. If some questions were of significance, then the number would not even cross four as many supplementary queries would be asked. It was the general practice for ministers not to prepare themselves beyond question number seven or eight. Strangely, on 4 December 2002, the number of members in attendance in the Lok Sabha was very low. Many members for whom questions had been listed were not present. Shatrughan Sinha was present for replies with me at his side. Unexpectedly question number 15 got its turn and it was pertaining to the Ministry of Health. Sinha nervously started reading the question and there were ripples of laughter in the House as many members thought that the Minister would not be prepared and would fumble. However, I got up and replied as I had been doing for some time during question hour at that point. I was able to provide complete and appropriate responses as I had responded to a similar question earlier in the Rajya Sabha. There was thunderous applause in the House and I also received the appreciation of the honourable speaker Manohar Joshi. Sinha was even more exuberant and embraced me in the lobby and expressed his appreciation. Even the PM praised me a few days later as he had watched the live telecast of the proceedings from his office. Having noticed me on a number of occasions, answering queries with a lot of supporting scientific and medical information, he started addressing me as 'doctor' in jest.

In September 2002 when PM Vajpayee went to Maldives on an official tour, he took me along as part of his delegation – a privilege normally reserved only for Cabinet Ministers. When introducing me to Abdul Gayoom, the President of Maldives the PM said, "He is my young boy in the Council of Ministers." Gayoom raised his eyebrows, held my hand in a very firm shake and remarked, "Oh! I thought he is an officer." I representing India and Ahmed Abdulla the Health Minister of Maldives signed an agreement in the presence of both Heads of State to carry out extension work in a hospital established in Maldives by India in memory of the late Mrs Indira Gandhi.

Let me recount another touching incident of that period. In July 2002, I got my first opportunity to pilot a Bill – the Indian Medical Council (Amendment) Bill – in the Rajya Sabha and field the consequent debate. The Chairman of the Rajya Sabha and Vice

President of India, the Honourable Krishna Kant was in the chair. On 27 July when the Bill was taken up for discussion, some members of the House participated and then the session was adjourned. After two holidays, the House met again on the 30th to continue discussing the Bill. However, Krishna Kant was no more. He died of heart attack the very evening of the day when I had introduced the Bill. On the 30th when I started to respond to queries, I had the chance to pay tribute to him, "When I moved this bill last Friday, our Vice President and Honourable Chairman of this House, Shri Krishna Kant was in the Chair. He heard me on that day and then adjourned the House for lunch. I take this opportunity to express my condolences on his sad demise. His role as Parliamentarian, and above all, as a Statesman, will inspire us of the younger generation." On several occasions Krishna Kant had invited me to his chamber, offered me tea and provided encouragement. I also vividly recall the times when he had raised queries from the Chair to me during Question Hour.

In the beginning of 2003, Shatrughan Sinha was shifted to the Shipping Ministry and Mrs Sushma Swaraj who was already the Minister of Parliamentary Affairs took over his portfolio as well. She knew of my performance in Parliament and had affection for me, frequently addressing me as beta (son). She too entrusted me the charge of handling Question Hour. The PM as well as Mrs Swaraj had noticed multiple situations when I had to quote that the Primary Health Centres and all National Programmes for Disease Eradication are not implemented by the Centre but by State Governments with major funding from the Union Government because as per our constitution 'Health' is in the State's list of responsibilities. It was common to find House members dissatisfied with this response and on many such occasions Mrs Swaraj would step in and provide further clarification in support of my statement to placate the inquisitor.

One day during a debate I mentioned casually that no National Institute for Health had been established by the Centre since the Nehru era. Upon hearing this Mrs Swaraj decided to open more such institutes. We took this up repeatedly with the PM and the Finance Minister until finally an announcement could be made about setting up 6 AIIMS (All India Institute of Medical Science) in Patna (Bihar), Raipur (Chattisgarh), Bhopal (Madhya Pradesh), Jodhpur (Rajasthan), Rishikesh (Uttaranchal) and Bhubaneswar (Odissa). Orders were also issued to set up similar institutions at a cost of Rs. 100 crore by upgrading various existing medical college hospitals including the one in my constituency of Tiruchirapalli. I had the opportunity to make this announcement in Parliament. Later on when Anbumani Ramadoss became the Union Minister of Health the plan to upgrade Tiruchirappalli was changed to Salem. I have cherished memories of the cordial relationship that I enjoyed at both personal and official levels with PM Atal Behari Vajpayee, Sundarlal Patwa, C.P. Thakur, Shatrughan Sinha and Sushma Swaraj during the tenure of the National Democratic Alliance. In December 2003 T.R. Baalu and I had to resign from the Council of Ministers as directed by our party DMK due to political differences with the BJP. Yet, Mrs Swaraj in appreciation of my performance not only hosted a farewell lunch at Hotel Ashok but also felicitated me with a memento. As heartening as it was to note such gestures and values in the Centre in Delhi irrespective of political differences or party alliances, it was saddening to see cheap and crude behaviour at some State levels frequently.

In 2004, pursuant to the victory in the general elections of the United Progressive Alliance (UPA-1) coalition led by Dr Manmohan Singh, I assumed office once again on behalf of DMK, but this time around as Minister of Environment and Forests. I gratefully took my charge, thanking our leader Dr Karunanidhi and the DMK party for entrusting me with the great responsibility of such a vital Ministry at my young age. Environment was not only an important portfolio but also one that needed to be handled with a nuanced scientific outlook. It would not be an exaggeration to state that Mrs Indira Gandhi was the first leader who created awareness in our country of the importance of environment issues and their role in governance. Our environmental scientists were worried that India was lagging behind in this domain by 25 years or so. Although the Indian Forest Act of 1927 enacted during British rule was in place and had been amended from time to time, in the backdrop of emerging issues as well as the impact of International Treaties and Commitments, Mrs Gandhi saw that it was necessary to implement the Forest Conservation Act in 1980. She stated in Parliament when this legislation was enacted, "We do not have exclusive right to do with the Globe as we want; rather it is an asset that has been entrusted to us by our forefathers to deliver safely to our future generations." It was through this legislation that the Air (Prevention and Control of Pollution) Act and the Water (Prevention and Control of Pollution) Act of 1981 were also enacted and were later brought under the aegis of the Environment Protection Act, 1986 during Rajiv Gandhi's regime. I took charge of the Environment Ministry knowing well its historical background as well as the international situation in which India needed to play a leadership role among developing nations. I had the responsibility to evolve a position regarding environment policy for more than 60 developing nations. Over the course of 15 or more foreign summits including the 10th Global Conference on Climate Change of Buenos Aires in 2004, the 11th Global Conference of Montreal in 2005, the Conference on Environment and Sustainable Development of Sydney in 2006, the Conference of the Environment Ministers of Asia-Pacific of Japan in June 2006, the Conference of the Environment Ministers of G-8 Nations of Germany in 2007, I handled the reins carefully and courageously to affirm India's leadership and continued commitment to environmental matters. In all these forums, the other developing nations were keen to understand India's stance on Climate Change and Carbon Trading as they thought the standpoint of a country of India's size and significance would also be a safe bet for them to adopt. After every foreign visit, I would write detailed reports for submission to the PM and I also had discussions with him on certain occasions.

Though my role as the Environment and Forests Minister demanded that I focus on measures to preserve natural resources and ensure sustenance of the Earth, I was well aware that the growth and development of the country could not be left by the wayside in lieu of environment considerations alone. As a developing nation, India needed firm focus in continuing to develop new technologies, industries and infrastructure. When I realized that a comprehensive environment policy for India had not been established even in 2004, its necessity became apparent to me.

Despite the fact that laws were in place to conserve natural resources like water, land, air, wildlife and to preserve bio-diversity, I understood that the non-existence of a comprehensive National Environmental Policy akin to the ones established by developed nations – covering legislation and all related factors – was a significant handicap for India. The immensely knowledgeable Pradiptha Ghosh was the Secretary to the Ministry at that time. The task of establishing a comprehensive National Environment Policy was undertaken at the end of 2004 by holding discussions with legal experts; environmentalists and NGO's including CII, FICCI, TERI; various state governments and their ministers; and other stake-holders. Seminars were organized while also holding extensive consultations via websites until the project was completed with the successful ratification of the policy by the Cabinet and the Parliament in June 2006. To this day this policy document is considered a template for adoption by developing nations and I am proud of my role in its creation.

Article 48(A) of our constitution deals with environment related issues and there have been many judgments passed by the Supreme Court on its basis. The National Environment Policy 2006 gives a policy form to these judgments. Till 16 May 2007 while I remained in the Environment Ministry, necessary updates were made to the Coastal Zoning Regulations and Impact Assessment for developmental schemes. Similarly, there were many legal inadequacies and hurdles for curbing and taking action against poaching and smuggling of rare wild animals and endangered species. In spite of having the Wild Life Protection Act, there were many problems in enforcing it. In addition to the involvement of organized criminal gangs, international crooks were also at work and the union government was well aware of this. In the State Ministers Conference, I proposed the creation of the Wildlife Crime Control Board under the Wildlife Protection Act to enable the states and the centre to consult and have an investigating body to identify crimes and punish offenders, which was accepted and successfully implemented.

CHAPTER 3

The Cat is Out of the Bag

In May 2007, upon the resignation of Dayanidhi Maran, I was asked by my party leadership to take charge of the Ministry of Communications and Information Technology (MoCIT). MoCIT comprises three major departments viz. Telecom, Information Technology and Department of Posts. Let me first highlight some of my initiatives and achievements in the Departments of Posts and Information Technology. Roughly 12,000 post-offices around the country were fully computerized. When Jyotiraditya Scindia joined the Ministry as Minister of State, we took efforts to identify and modernize more than 500 Post-offices to wear a new look and offer better services through computerization under the scheme 'Project Arrow'. I also take pride in the fact that we released commemorative stamps honouring eminent personalities from several fields including the release in Chennai, on 17 September 2007 of stamps honouring Dr C. Natesan, Dr T.M. Nair and Sir Pitty Thiyagarayar, great heroes of the Dravidian Movement. It was at the behest of Kalaignar Karunanidhi (the then CM of Tamil Nadu) that Tamil was finally officially declared as a classical language by the Central Government even though Tamil had already been hailed by linguistic scholars as one of the great classical languages of the world, alongside Latin, Greek, Hebrew, Chinese and Sanskrit. A moment of great privilege and honour for me was to release a special commemorative stamp into the hands of Kalaignar at the Classical Tamil Conference in Coimbatore. I also dutifully led the initiative to introduce the National e-Governance Programme under the aegis of the Department of Information and Technology which was also inaugurated by Kalaignar at a function in Chennai.

The first and foremost duty of a Minister is to familiarise himself with the administrative structure, policies and goals of the Ministry. Accordingly starting from the day after taking charge, I had the Ministry officials brief me in detail. My background in Maths, the Sciences and Law as well as my prior experience in several ministries reduced my startup time to function effectively in the Telecom Ministry. Additionally, Sreedhara, the Additional Secretary who was also the Member (Technology) in the ministry helped me extensively in learning curve. I spent a lot of time carefully studying the National Telecom Policy 1994 and 1999 (NTP-94, NTP-99), Unified Access Service License (UASL) Guidelines 2005, Indian Telegraph Act, Indian Wireless Telegraph Act, recommendations from Telecom Regulatory Authority of India (TRAI) and related Cabinet decisions. Very soon, Sreedhara was impressed with my ability to respond during Question Hour and would ask how I was managing to convey more information than had been provided to me by my staff. I explained to him that a Minister needs to know the objectives behind the Ministry's charter and policies; only then is it possible to extrapolate from provided information, take a holistic approach and make sensible decisions. I established strategic goals for the ministry to empower people in the lowest rungs of our socio-economic ladder with Telecom and IT facilities akin to what is available in developed countries. I announced this in media interviews, which were widely published in newspapers.

The Department of Telecommunications (DoT) under the MoCIT, is the custodian of wireless spectrum. Spectrum is a Radio Frequency or Electronic Magnetic Wave band, used as the medium for specifically manufactured electronic devices to implement wireless communication. It is a finite natural resource that cannot be increased. However, its usage does not cause it to be depleted or exhausted; hence there is no extinction factor as in the case of other natural resources like Iron, Petroleum, Coal, etc. The International Telecom Union (ITU) has the responsibility to classify the bands of wireless spectrum for various types of usage, by ascertaining the technology that would best suit the band. For instance, the police department of every state is specifically assigned 700 MHz spectrum. Accordingly, wireless equipment for Wireless Radio, Cell Phones, TV and Radar devices are also manufactured exclusively for relevant spectrum band specification. The Wireless Planning and Coordination (WPC) Wing of the DoT was created in 1952 based on the Indian Wireless Telegraph Act 1933. WPC is the national nodal radio regulatory agency of the government responsible for planning, regulating and managing the limited sources of Radio Frequency (RF) transmission and associated satellite resources. All information about the spectrum classified in a particular band and the extent of allocation to service providers or to the Defence department is governed by WPC. 2G alludes to second-generation wireless telephone technology which came into commercial use from 1991. Radio signals on 2G networks are digital compared to analogue in all prior networks. 2G's primary benefits are digital encryption of communication; significantly higher efficiency of spectrum utilization enabling greater penetration; and provision for data services like SMS, MMS and internet. Although 3G and 4G have also become available now, 2G networks – along with related advancements 2.5G (GPRS) and 2.75G (EDGE) – are still in use in most parts of the world even as some developed countries are in the process of shutting down 2G and repurposing that spectrum. Clearly in our nation's scenario where connectivity for the masses – especially in the rural hinterland – has been so lagging, 2G must be considered a basic infrastructural requirement akin to roads or railway lines that should be broadly available to the common man. The fundamental flaw in all evaluations of the 2G saga is omission of this principle. The ability to interconnect our country's vast population is essential for enriching the quality of life and for enabling social inclusion of the poorer sections of our society. If the government focused solely on profit in this context, then those purely financial gains would come at a heavy societal cost.

The licensing framework has been an integral part of India's telecommunication law. The Indian Telegraph Act of 1885 empowers the government to grant license to any person to establish, maintain or use a telegraph. However, until the early 1990s the government maintained complete monopoly in the provision of telecom facilities. In 1991, the government first allowed private telecom companies to manufacture telecom switches for telephone exchanges and then in 1992 DoT invited bids for licenses for cellular service across the four metros – Bombay, Delhi, Calcutta and Madras. In 1994, a broader perspective was adopted in order to increase teledensity by expanding private sector participation. The National Telecom Policy (NTP 1994) was thus established detailing criteria for private sector participation as well as a roadmap for the future of Indian telecom with key objectives like making telephone connections available on demand, the provision of world-class services at reasonable prices, wider geographic penetration and adoption of telecom facilities, etc. A very significant aspect was the inclusion of foreign direct investments (FDI) – in fact this was a mandatory condition for a corporation's eligibility – as it was obvious that the Indian telecom operators did not yet possess the requisite technical or financial wherewithal. This drove the need for a regulatory body and accordingly Telecom Regulatory Authority of India (TRAI) was established on 20 February 1997 by an act of parliament. TRAI's objective is to implement a transparent policy environment that would foster quick and sustainable growth of the telecom sector. TRAI regularly issues orders and recommendations on subjects like tariff, interconnections, "Direct to Home" (DTH) services and mobile number portability. In 2000, the Telecom Disputes Settlement Appellate Tribunal (TDSAT) was constituted through an amendment of the 1997 TRAI Act. The primary objective of TDSAT is to strengthen the regulatory framework by freeing TRAI of adjudicatory and dispute settlement functions. Any dispute involving parties like licensor, licensee, service provider and consumers are arbitrated and resolved by TDSAT.

In 1992, two operators were licensed for each of the four metros. In 1995, 21 regions divided into 3 circles (A, B, C) on the basis of revenue generation potential were defined for licensing outside of the 4 metros:

Metros: Delhi, Mumbai, Kolkata, Chennai

Circle A: Gujarat, Karnataka, Tamil Nadu, Andhra Pradesh, Maharashtra

Circle B: Haryana, Punjab, Kerala, Rajasthan, West Bengal, Uttar Pradesh (West), Madhya Pradesh, Uttar Pradesh (East)

Circle C: Bihar, Northeast, Assam, Orissa, Himachal Pradesh, Jammu and Kashmir Based on an auction, two licenses were awarded in each circle in order to avoid monopoly of any single service provider in a circle. Fostering healthy competition in order to deliver better value to the public has always remained a guiding principle in India's Telecom policy framework. A total of 34 licenses were issued for a ten-year term. The licensees had to pay an annual license fee which was agreed during the auction. There was no spectrum allocation built-in, hence the government levied additional charges for spectrum usage. The tariffs fixed by DoT were the same as for the metro licenses which at that time of low teledensity especially in the non-metro circles were bound to be untenable. Consequently, by 1998, six of the service providers defaulted on their service fee obligations. TRAI studied this in 1999 and reported the following reasons for the financial failure of the telecom operators:

- Heavy capital investment for setting up infrastructure, which remained underutilized
- Actual number of subscribers was much lower than projected
- The average revenue per user (ARPU) was lower than the operator's costs
- Significant finances of the operators were needed to pay the license fees and operational charges

This financial failure and TRAI's findings directly led to the formulation of NTP-99 which allowed migration of the licensees from a Fixed License Fee Regime to a Revenue Arrangement Scheme (with effect from 1 August 1999). Under the new scheme the license fee was a proportional tax (set at 15%) on the service provider's revenue. The operators also had to pay a spectrum usage charge. Alongside this, the government introduced itself as a third operator in each circle.

In 2001, licenses for basic telephone services using Wireless in Local Loop (WLL) were issued – notably, this was the first time that first-come-first-served (FCFS) process of issuing licenses was adopted. Additionally, bids for a fourth cellular operator – beyond the three already in play – were invited in Jan 2001. The auction carried out in 3 stages issued licenses at 17% fee on revenue in addition to an entry fee. In September 2003, PM Atal Bihari Vajpayee constituted an empowered group of ministers (GoM) on telecom issues. Their resultant recommendations were approved by the union cabinet in October 2003 and became an addendum to NTP-99. This led to the introduction of the Unified Access Service Licensing (UASL) regime. UASL "permitted an access service provider to offer both fixed and/or mobile services under the same license, using any technology."A GoM was also constituted to recommend an efficient pricing formula for spectrum and for the freeing up of spectrum by the ministry of defence. The country was divided into 23 service areas, 19 telecom circles and 4 metro circles under UASL. The license fees were two-fold: migration fee – equal to the amount paid by the fourth licensee in 2001 – for conversion from the legacy Cellular Mobile Telephone Service (CMTS) license to UASL; annual usage fee – 10%, 8% and 6% of adjusted gross revenue for circles A, B and C respectively. A telecom licensee is eligible for 4.4 MHz of spectrum. When Pramod Mahajan was the Telecom Minister, this allocation was raised to 6.2 MHz in 2001, which remained the base allocation till the end of my tenure.

In spite of all these attempts to fillip the Telecom Sector, at that time in 2007 when I stepped in, the overall mobile phone consumer base was just 23.4 crores; the call rate was almost ₹1 per minute; and there were a mere 7 telecom providers in the country. I recalled the abysmal state of telecommunication in and around my native place and was convinced that although progress had been made and market-friendly policy changes had been rolled-out there was a long way to go before the common man in India had viable and reliable means of being connected. I decided to grab the bull by the horns and promptly convened a review meeting of the Telecom Department with the aim of getting to know the number of service providers/operators using 2G Technology and the quantum of spectrum allotted to them in proportion to the total spectrum available. The ministry officials probably did not expect this level of investigation from me so quickly and I could sense their hesitation and perplexity in responding to my queries. I was very disappointed with their replies. In all my prior roles, I had no need to compete with anyone personally in order to deliver on my duties and initiatives. However, in the DoT my efforts were met with resistance and animosity from some sections. It was becoming clear to me, while the general public, government institutions and the Judiciary remained oblivious, that resources under the purview of the Telecom Ministry were being selectively almost gifted away and that there appeared to be a nexus involving 4 or 5 Telecom companies. These Telco's lobbied and influenced ministry officials to render policy decisions in their favour, get requisite government approvals and consequently reap huge profits. Even though there was no clause in the existing license agreements mandating increase of spectrum allocation from the base 4.4 MHz, the allotment was raised by 1.8 MHz in the first stage (in 2001) and then gradually again by 2 MHz - that too without any upfront fees – on the basis of subscriber volume (subscriber base) until it reached 10-12 MHz in most cases.

The exact quantum of 2G spectrum remaining unallocated was never disclosed in the past by the DoT officials. The reason cited for this was that the availability of spectrum can be identified periodically only through extensive coordination – between various wings of the DoT including the Telecom Engineering Centre (TEC) – and collating the fragmented information. Instead of taking up this activity at one go, the officers learnt the trick of 'discovering' unallocated spectrum through 'coordination' only at times when some existing provider expressed the need for additional spectrum. I was amazed that my predecessors in the ministry permitted this. This tracking and documentation of available spectrum is not a big technical or logistical challenge that would take years to complete. Once I issued stern instructions to the staff, information of the availability of around 35-40 MHz of unallocated spectrum came to the open in Nov 2007. All those financial wizards who made so much noise of the (apparently) big loss to the government in the spectrum allocation, never bothered to take account of the real loss – not only financial but also in terms of service penetration (teledensity) – when so much available spectrum was being kept hidden. In fact, on 11 January 2006, then Telecom Minister Dayanidhi Maran had observed in a letter to the PM: "The one major bottleneck is the availability, not allocation of spectrum for Telecommunication services and particularly thereafter vacation of Spectrum occupied by the Defence Services. It is therefore necessary that the proposed GoM should focus its attention on this aspect of vacation of spectrum by the Defence." This shows that information about the availability of spectrum might have been hidden even from the Telecom Minister at that time forcing him to seek this intervention for repurposing spectrum from the defence department.

Telecom companies like Airtel, Aircel, Vodafone, Idea were operating with GSM (Global System for Mobiles) technology whereas TATA and Reliance were operating with CDMA (Code Division Multiple Access) technology. Globally, GSM is more prevalent than CDMA. GSM originated from an industry consortium whereas CDMA technology is largely owned by chipmaker Qualcomm. This made it less expensive for third parties to build GSM equipment. GSM adoption spread rapidly also because in 1987, Europe mandated the technology by law. Since 2006 itself, Reliance's Anil Ambani was seeking permission for GSM in addition to CDMA. The existing GSM providers including Airtel's Sunil Mittal were indirectly but belligerently intent on disallowing this demand from the CDMA operators. The GSM operators ganged up to form COAI (Cellular Operators Association of India) while the CDMA operators formed AUSPI (Association of Unified Telecom Service Providers of India) in order to lobby their respective causes. The members of COAI had the upper hand and the commercial grip because of their existing shared infrastructure. The business-war between these two groups had been a chronic administrative headache for the Telecom Ministry.

On 26 April 2007 (prior to my taking charge as Telecom Minister on 16 May) a letter with a reference note was sent to TRAI requesting an updated set of holistic recommendations for wireless services. All the relevant ministry officials had approved this note of the SO (AS-II) which clearly stated, "Further processing and examination of the existing UASL applications/new UASL applications received in future will be carried out after receipt of the recommendation of TRAI." I signed in that file eventually but had not been involved in its initiation. Consequently, in August 2007 TRAI released its 200-page report of recommendations which was published on the Telecom Ministry's website on the 29th of that month. In his preface to this report Nripendra Mishra Chairman of TRAI quoted, "It had become essential to seriously consider the issues like 'who should be the best judge to determine the spectrum price?' and 'what is the most transparent mode of spectrum allocation?'. The Authority while making recommendations has made attempts to introduce market forces to maximum in the decision making. As a Regulator, we are concerned with maximising the welfare of the consumers, healthy growth of Telecom and financial viability of Telecom companies." The other core facet of TRAI's recommendation related to the need for a 'level playing field' as highlighted in the preface, "It is obvious that a lot of developments have already taken place in the sector and the Authority while accepting the legacy and level playing field has to fall back on modular building approach." The report further stated, "In a developing economy, the regulator has not only to address the social good or consumer interests but also has to play a catalytic role in development." The key recommendations made were:

- There should be no cap on the number of access providers in any service area
- Existing UAS licensees may be permitted to expand their existing networks by using alternate wireless technology i.e. a UAS licensee who is presently using GSM for wireless access may be permitted to use CDMA and vice-versa
- Spectrum for the alternate technology, CDMA or GSM (as the case may be) shall be allocated subject to availability after payment of prescribed fee

- BSNL and MTNL being incumbent operators shall be permitted usage of alternative technology and allocated the requisite spectrum without paying the prescribed fee
- For the purpose of payment of license fee and spectrum charges, the stream wise revenue of different technologies shall be considered
- Enhanced Subscriber linked criteria for spectrum allocation:

GSM subscriber base criteria (millions of subscribers)

Service Area	2x6.2 MHz	2x8 MHz	2x10 MHz	2x12.4 MHz	2x15 MHz
Delhi/Mumbai/	0.5	1.5	2	3.0	5
Chennai/Kolkata	0.5	1.5	2	3.0	5
A	0.8	3	5	8	10
B	0.8	3	5	8	10
C	0.6	2	4	6	8

CDMA subscriber base criteria (millions of subscribers)

Service Area 3rd carrier 4th Carrier 5th carrier 6th carrier (2x3.75 MHz) (2x5 MHz) (2x6.25 MHz) (2x7.5 MHz)

Delhi/Mumbai/0.5 2 3.0 5 Chennai/ Kolkata 0.5 2 3.0 5

A	**0.8**	**5**	**8**	**10**
B	**0.8**	**5**	**8**	**10**
C	**0.6**	**4**	**6**	**8**

These recommendations were discussed and unanimously accepted by the Telecom Commission headed by the Telecom Secretary. Nripendra Mishra had also his considerable experience as Telecom Secretary in DoT during the period of 2004-2006. The consultation paper floated by him earlier as Chairman, TRAI to finalise the recommendations and subsequent vast deliberations thereon with various stakeholders were commendable both technically and scientifically. Inspite of the political change in the entity of Central Government, he has been accommodated as the Principal Secretary to the PM Narendra Modi. However, TRAI's recommended figures were not agreeable to COAI. They argued that the technical factors and data that TRAI had relied on were faulty and partisan in nature, resulting in very high subscriber base criteria which would lead to losses for them. COAI's other major bugbear was dual technology licensing which the government had enabled through UASL. In 2006, when Dayanidhi Maran was the Telecom Minister, the Reliance Group, which already had CDMA, applied for permission to operate GSM, and their application was considered for the grant of consent and allotment of GSM spectrum. Legally, once UASL had been implemented, there should have been no impediment to a licensee for operating these two technologies simultaneously. However, possibly in order to have a statutory safeguard, Dayanidhi Maran referred this to TRAI for their recommendation. TRAI in their latest recommendation had re-affirmed that technological neutrality is inherent in UASL and accepted granting the permission to CDMA operators for GSM also, upon collection of an additional entry fee of ₹1650 crore (the prevailing fee for a new licensee). However, COAI remained firm that dual technology should not be permitted. They had apprehensions about the competition and threat to their business as existing CDMA operators (like Reliance or TATA) could start their (GSM) operation immediately upon being allotted the spectrum since they had adequate infrastructure and technical facilities all across the country. So, they tried by all means to keep the government policy favourable to them and avoid the threat of competition even though it would quite naturally have benefited the public.

After posting of the TRAI report on the government websites, officials of different wings of the Telecom Ministry separately started their proceedings for submission to the Telecom Commission. Alongside this process, debates were raging in the media and a number of letters were being received in this context, addressed to me or to the PM. Some letters were from COAI and AUSPI but additionally others were from MPs and leaders like Chandrababu Naidu and Amar Singh. Their views either supported or opposed one or the other between the COAI and the AUSPI. Without malice towards the MPs/leaders, I must opine that the content and motivation for these letters was provided to them by representative of one or more of the constituent telecom companies. The heads of these companies also started calling on me which started getting prominent mention in the news. Anil Ambani and Ratan Tata of AUSPI as well as T.V. Ramachandran and Sunil Mittal the key executives at COAI came to meet me to discuss plans for the future of Wireless Telecom in India.

Karthi Chidambaram who is an acquaintance called me up one day during the middle of September 2007 and told me that his friend Sunil Mittal (of Airtel) urgently wanted to speak with me that very day, since he was going abroad later in the night. I was having dinner at 'Tamil Nadu House' in Delhi, with a senior Minister of the DMK who was on an official visit when the call came. The social and industry standing of Mittal, the substantial share of COAI in the Telecom sector and Karthi Chidambaram's recommendation made me agree to meet him at 10:30 pm in my camp office. At this meeting, Mittal said that the TRAI recommendations did not give adequate protection to foreign investors who had invested in their Indian partner companies using GSM and also did not ensure provision of additional spectrum for their future expansion. He argued that foreign companies had invested several thousand crores in their Indian telecom partners with an eye on future returns and that allowing new players to enter the scene would be detrimental to them and the overall health of the telecom sector in India. He complained that TRAI's recommendations were against the growth of the GSM providers but were in favour of the CDMA providers. He stated that TRAI had not weighed appropriate scientific and technological considerations while recommending the 'subscriber linked criteria' for additional spectrum allocation. He boasted of his position of influence in the telecom sector as also his personal political clout. He claimed that COAI was used for very cordial relations with all my predecessors in the ministry and he expected "similar cooperation" from me as well which seemed to me extreme my contemptuous and cynical. I urged him to take a broader perspective saying, "At the same time when considering your contribution, investment, and the future interest of the Indian telecom sector, the Government cannot ignore the recommendations of TRAI. So, please extend your cooperation to the Government to resolve the situation amicably and ensure a level playing field."

Referring repeatedly to his business acumen, considerable resources and political influence, Mittal kept trying to emphasise his apprehension that the ministry may yield to his competitors and wrongly dilute his position even if the move had the premise of being legally and procedurally valid. He was perhaps attempting to alert me from being misled and convinced by others, or perhaps he was attempting to coax me before someone else could. I was keen on ensuring an environment conducive to the amicable enforcement of TRAI's recommendations, so I continued the dialogue. "Do you fear that somebody will buy me? Let me assure you that there might be a price for me but I don't think there is anybody in this world rich enough to pay it." This got Mittal on the defensive and he denied any intention of implying that. He reiterated his comment about cordial relationship with the ministry and concluded that, "they were prepared for any kind of cordial relationship." The underlying allusion seemed easy to comprehend and I made it clear to Mittal that I was not for such one-sided cordiality when what was needed was an objective and neutral atmosphere for the good of the nation. He took leave saying, "Let me come back to you after discussing with the other companies. Please do not take any decision until then. Let me meet you after my return from my foreign tour." I agreed to this. Contrary to my expectation and his earlier assurance Mittal did not follow-through on his promise of a subsequent meeting. I briefed the PM about this meeting with Mittal as well as Karthi Chidambaram's role in arranging it and ensured that he understood the tenor of this key stake holder and industry leader. In the same month, Anil Ambani of Reliance also met with me to speak on behalf of AUSPI. He sought permission for GSM in addition to CDMA and placed AUSPI's point of view that the members of COAI should not continue to be granted additional spectrum beyond 4.4 MHz at no cost. This irreconcilable difference between the two groups of Telecom providers was well known to the PM and also to senior ministers like Pranab Mukherjee, H.R. Bhardwaj and P. Chidambaram. I mention these names specifically because they had a role to play in the 2G saga. Anil Ambani and Ratan Tata had further meetings with me along with executives of their companies to discuss the way forward. They did not oppose the TRAI report or push any alternative suggestions but only stressed that the recommendations should not be diluted. Since the Telecom Ministry had already accepted TRAI's recommendations on subscriber base criteria, I went ahead and gave my approval to it on 18 October 2007 – which was also reported in the media. To my disappointment, COAI, which was determined to stall the course of these recommendations, wrote more than 10 letters of grievance to the Telecom Ministry. Then on 23 October 2007 they filed a case with TDSAT without any advance notice or specific discussion with my office in spite of all the earlier assurances of attempting to work collaboratively. The media got more fodder for sensationalism in the pre-existing context of the animosity between COAI and AUSPI.

At this point, Farid whom I had met a couple of times along with Sam Pitroda regarding some new technology, requested me to grant yet another appointment to Sunil Mittal and his brother Rajan Mittal as they wanted to meet me to find some amicable solution. I was puzzled by what their reason for meeting me now might be after having already filed a case with TDSAT. However, in order to try and make some progress, I agreed to meet with them. Even during that meeting which took place in the end of October 2007, Sunil Mittal was insistent that TRAI's recommendations must be scaled back – in fact he demanded the subscriber base criteria should be halved – and that dual (GSM and CDMA) technology should not be permitted.

I: "How can I as a Minister reject a report of TRAI based on scientific facts without any basis? Either the recommendations must be sent back to the Authority or must be reviewed through due process. Then the base criteria could be reduced if it is deemed viable. Since the recommendations have already been accepted by the Department of Telecom, there is nothing I can do now."

Mittal: "In that case, do not allot any spectrum or issue new license till the case is resolved."

I: "When there is no stay order in the case how can I stop allocation?"

Mittal: "Is it not reason enough that the case is pending?"

I emphasised: "Even after giving additional spectrum to all your companies (COAI), considerable amount of Spectrum has been identified for new providers at this point. So, it is just not possible to suspend all this at this stage."

I admired the confidence – even though it had shades of smug conceit – of Sunil Mittal who probably believed that the Telecom Sector's governing bodies were obliged to pander to an industry player of his stature. I was also thinking of his breach of trust given his earlier assurance to me of a follow-up meeting.

The conversation was not heading in the direction of compromise or agreement. T.V. Ramachandran, one of the Executive Officers of COAI had met with me and our department officials on several occasions before and also after my meeting with the Mittal's. In all these meetings held either with COAI or with Sunil Mittal – who in anyway controlled COAI – their stance was either to force a change in the policy decisions of the government or to put them on hold. At no point, were they willing to concede anything or scale back their demands. This sort of bullying to try to control the workings of the government was not acceptable to me. I murmered a couplete in Thirukural "Azhukkaaru, avaa, veguli, innachchol - naankum
Izhukkaa iyandrathu aram"

"Envy, greed, wrath and uncouth words
These four avoided is virtue"

Since the Ministry had approved the TRAI recommendations, the pending application received from Reliance seeking additional Spectrum in GSM was accepted. When Reliance immediately paid the ₹ 1650 crore fee, they earned the right to get an allotment of additional 4.4 MHz spectrum. On 19 October 2007, a Press release was issued explaining in detail the Government's decision to grant permission for dual technology. COAI put forth its arguments to TDSAT challenging this decision and claiming that the approval for dual technology was legally flawed, "In order to benefit the said one set of operators TRAI admittedly went beyond its terms and references and suo motu and without consultations made some very arbitrary and ad hoc recommendations ... DoT thus has acted with undue and seemly haste in a bid to advantaging one set of operators over the others, thus denying equal opportunity and level playing field to GSM operators." Clearly the corporate war that I alluded to earlier is not my exaggeration but is something that COAI referenced openly.

As I have already explained, the Telecom landscape in India has attempted to take major strides since the early 1990s in order to bridge the gap with the developed world. Needless to say, every stakeholder in the ecosystem has had to learn and adjust according to circumstances. Differences of opinion and legal disputes have plagued the course even as the technologies, business/operating models, government policies, regulatory framework and official procedures have matured. For example, even at the time of the first telecom bids in 1992 the rejected bidders had appealed to the Courts for what they claimed was an unclear and arbitrary selection process. This litigation (although rejected by the Supreme Court) delayed the rollout by 3 years. In the following auction, a single provider had the highest bid in 9 circles and the government was forced to intervene by making the provider choose 3 circles as it was certain that the company would be hard pressed to shore up the finances to pay license fees for 9 circles. Similarly, there have been instances when the government has taken steps to either reach an amicable settlement with petitioners or convinced them to withdraw their cases. In the current instance of COAI's TDSAT appeal, there was so much obstinacy and hype that a compromise solution became infeasible. When COAI's case before TDSAT came up for hearing on 12 November 2007, Vahanvati the Solicitor General appearing on behalf of the government raised objection to the granting of a stay order and then the court adjourned the case until 12 December 2007. When a case is filed, normal procedures could be stalled while the matter is 'pending before the court'; and the situation could get much worse and take years to be resolved if the petitioner obtains a stayorder from the court. Hence following my direction, the Telecom Ministry's steps were carefully orchestrated to ensure that COAI would not obtain such a stay-order. It is not unusual or unthinkable for individuals or companies to go to Court either to challenge the decision of the Government or to appeal against it. However, there must be sufficient grounds for such a challenge. The Tribunal (TDSAT) and the Delhi High Court not only upheld the actions of the Telecom Ministry but also levied a fine on COAI for filing a case without sufficient grounds.

Sunil Mittal wrote a letter to the government dated 1 November 2007 stating, "I have been running what has been universally acknowledged as a highly efficient mobile operation under the Brand 'Airtel' for the past 13 years. Despite having one of the lowest allocated spectrums amongst its worldwide peers, Airtel is not only the largest mobile operation in the country but the 10th largest operator in the world. Sir, we would not claim to be experts in our sector, but can certainly claim some degree of knowledge to challenge the absurd proposed spectrum allocation which has been put forth by TEC.... In the meanwhile, please ensure that no spectrum is allocated which may compromise the legitimate right of the existing operators." The wording of that letter reaffirms Mittal's sense of entitlement and his belligerent posture. He audaciously expected the government to believe that his knowledge was so superior to that of TRAI and TEC as to dub their recommendations as absurd. I also balk at what he refers to as "legitimate right". As an erstwhile lawyer, I can only assess 'right' as something that has been granted by Law. The right Mittal refers to is not based on any Law; it was not granted by any policy document of the government or in any clause of the license or in the written agreement issued to his corporation. But the members of COAI had a 'big brother' attitude and felt they deserved special privileges. The letter made flippant remarks about policies in other countries ignoring the fact that TRAI had reviewed and discussed the methods followed by various foreign countries in its recommendation. Since COAI was not in agreement with the TRAI report on spectrum allocation, TEC made another recommendation in October 2007. I am not exaggerating when I say that this report from TEC which recommended an even greater increase in the subscriber base criteria made the COAI tremble. TEC officials explained that their report had been prepared scientifically with appropriate technical inputs. In spite of all the due diligence and care taken by TRAI and TEC in formulating their recommendations, due to the importance of the issue and these rumblings from key stake holders I ordered the constitution of another special committee – headed by Bandyopadhyay, Additional Secretary of Telecom Department along with Dr Baskar Ramamoorthy of IIT Chennai and Dr Ajit Kumar Chaturvedi of IIT Kanpur – on 6 November 2007 to review the situation. In addition to the expert members one representative each from COAI and AUSPI were also included in the committee. As the committee proceeded with its work, COAI probably realized that their arguments would not stand the test of a methodical scientific review. Hence, 2 weeks prior to the release of their report, COAI withdrew from the committee. Thus, COAI continued with their stand of 'only what we say is correct and the government must accept it,' having first alleged that TRAI's recommendations ratified by the Telecom Commission were flawed, then calling the report of the specialized technical body (TEC) of the Telecom Department absurd, and not cooperating even with the special committee of experts, setup to redress their complaints. I could have accepted and implemented the Bandyopadhyay Committee's report received on 18 December 2007 which made recommendations that were even less favourable (much higher counts in the subscriber base criteria) to COAI than the prior recommendations of TRAI and TEC. However, I remained objective and did not display annoyance or spite for Mittal's behaviour towards me, for the complaint to TDSAT, or for their inflexibility even in the face of multiple cycles of methodically conducted reviews.

After deliberation with the Telecom Department officials, with this sense of balance in mind, it was decided to find an interim arrangement for implementing the Bandyopadhyay Committee Report, while continuing to engage with stakeholders to arrive at a more amicable solution. I passed an order with the following interim measures:

- Spectrum would be allocated based on the TRAI recommendations dated 28 August 2007.

- Additional Spectrum beyond the contractual obligation (of 6.2MHZ) would be allocated in multiples of 1 MHz as per the provider's eligibility.

I am not so naive as to assume that industrialists and wealthy individuals cannot influence the administration of the country and the actions of political parties. As long as they do some good to the nation this is perhaps acceptable. The situation becomes unacceptable when self-interest outweighs public-interest. This has always been my pragmatic approach to my responsibilities as a public servant and elected representative of the common man.

The cartel mentality and the battle lines between COAI and AUSPI had become very apparent to me now. '**Only when there is Competition, the tariff would come down; and the subscriber base would increase'** is the National Telecom Policy (NTP-99). '**If there is competition our investments may have no protection; our business margin would reduce; so, there should not be competition**' is the stand of COAI. Adherence to the National Telecom Policy was not only my duty but the underlying principle of public good was also my moral imperative. As I pondered over this and reviewed COAI's petition to TDSAT, I couldn't help mumbling to myself, "the cat is out of the bag." But still I remained faithful to the lines Tamil Sangam literature,

"Muraiyenappaduvathu Kannodaathu Uyir vawwal"
(Rendering impartial justice lies in protection of lives)
"Setramum uvagaiyum seyyathu kaakkum yemankol"
(Righteousness lies in keeping balance against hatred and desire)

In the midst of all this political drama, a much more dramatic event of a very personal nature took place. On 15 September 2007, my mother passed away. Although I do not believe in religious rituals, I stayed back in our native village for a few days for the sake of my siblings. Even at the time of my father's death when I was expected to shave my head clean as per the Hindu tradition, I was not ready for it. Similarly, after my mother died, I did not agree to perform any rituals. My rationalism asserts that there is no life after death, whereas the rest of my family believes in the afterlife. When Lord Buddha preached, “There is no soul”, He was asked, “Where does life go after death then?” His reply was in the form of a question, “Where does the light go after a lamp is put off? ” I firmly believe that ‘action’ is life and ‘inaction’ is death. I returned to my work in Delhi by the end of that month.

Chapter 4

2G Saga Unfolds

By 24 September 2007 we had already received 167 applications for telecom licenses. A.K. Srivastava, the Deputy Director General (DDG-AS) made an official note on that day, "It is felt that it may be difficult to handle such large number of applications at any point of time. Therefore, it is proposed that we may announce a cut-off for receipt of UASL applications so that no new applications will be received after the cut-off date till further orders. We may give a reasonable time to all who wish to submit new UASL applications so that the decisions may not be challenged. The reasonable period may be, say 15 days. Therefore, we may announce 10 October 2007 to be the cut-off date for receipt of new UASL applications till further orders." This file was first sent to Sridhara, the officer in-charge of the License Branch (Additional Secretary) and with his signature it was sent to the Secretary (Telecom) and then finally sent to me for my approval. I read it carefully and called the Secretary (Telecom) and the DDG-AS to my chamber to discuss the matter. We conferred on the number of applications already received and the expected number of applications and then recorded the observation, "In view of large number of applications pending and to discourage speculative players, we may close receiving applications on 01 October 2007, i.e., one month from the date of TRAI's recommendations." I then signed on the file. Accordingly, a Press Note was issued by the ministry, which appeared in the newspapers on 25 September 2007, setting a deadline for new applications as 1 October 2007. Our decision to change the deadline from 10 to 1 October was validated when a staggering count of 575 applications for 22 circles from 46 companies were received!

A problem of plenty (of choice) is certainly good for public benefit but it was bound to pose challenges in terms of processing logistics for the ministry. The Department was of the opinion that there was inadequate spectrum available at that time in order to fulfil all the applications. Therefore, on 24 October 2007 a Brief was drafted with two proposed alternatives (File No. 20-100\2007 A S -1) for processing the applications. Nitin Jain, the Director of the License Branch sent the file to DDG-AS.

Alternative-I: DoT proposes to process the applications on FCFS basis in chronological order of receipt of applications in each service area as per existing procedure. LoI may be issued simultaneously; number will vary based on the availability of spectrum to be ascertained from WPC wing.

Alternative-II: Certain number of LoIs about 2 times of applicants as proposed in Alternative-I may be issued in each area in phase–1 as it is expected that only serious players will deposit entry fee.

When Sridhara, who is also the Member (T), received the file back, he came along with DDG-AS to my chamber for a discussion. Sridhara said that he had a contrary view on Alternative-II and made two points: limiting the number of licenses in each circle based on number of applicants, might be contrary to the 'no cap' principle advocated by TRAI; the date 1 October was announced as the last day to receive applications **till further orders** in order to avoid setting any sort of **final** date which also might seem to be contrary to 'no cap'. UASL 2005 Guidelines did not stipulate that requisite spectrum should be available in order to issue licenses, because a UASL license could be applicable to either wireless (GSM / CDMA) or to land-line operations which requires no spectrum. The Ministry had also never followed a practice of issuing licenses considering the quantum of spectrum available on a particular date due to which in the past, there had been instances where Telecom companies had to wait even over a year in some cases for spectrum allocation even after being issued licenses. Hence, Alternative-I on limiting the number of licenses on the basis of spectrum availability seemed unviable. It was consequently suggested by the ministry officials, that it would be better to come up with a third alternative where a 'cut-off' date is fixed on the basis of some notional projection of applicants who would actually complete the licensing process and the spectrum required for them.

Alternative-III: LOIs to all those who applied by 25 September 2007 (the date on which the cut-off date for receipt of applications were made public through press) may be used in each service area as it is expected that only serious players will deposit the entry fee and seniority for license/ spectrum based on

(i) the date of application (or)

(ii) the date/ time of fulfilment of all LOI conditions.

After reading this brief and accepting their view, I made the following addition in my own handwriting in the file, "Alternative IV: Any other better approach which may be legally tenable and sustainable for issuance of new licenses," wrote, "approved as amended" and then signed the file. On 25 October 2007, D.S. Mathur Secretary (T) noted again in the file, "The opinion of SG may be obtained as per the draft approved by the MOCIT. However, the attention of MCIT may be drawn to NTP-99, paragraph 3.1.1...The policy has stipulated that availability of adequate frequency spectrum is essential for entry of additional operators. Hence, the options to issue LOIs / licenses to all 575 applicants do not stand in the light of this provision. NTP 99 was approved by the Union Cabinet and only the Cabinet can effect a change in the Policy." On 26 October 2007, my approval was obtained on the final draft of the file and it was forwarded to the Law Ministry asking for their review and opinion on which alternative would be procedurally tenable. The Joint Secretary (Law) returned the file to DoT with a request for additional reference documents and clarifications. While DoT was in the process of collecting the requested documents, suddenly the same Joint Secretary called Srivastava DDG (AS) over the phone and asked for the file to be sent back to the Law Ministry. It is strange that such a phone call was made instead of following the usual protocol of file movements. The file was sent back by DoT as requested. It was placed before the Law Minister H.R. Bharadwaj who then surprisingly made the observation (without providing any reasons), "... in view of the importance of the case and various options indicated in the statement of the case the issues to be considered by Group of Ministers." The file was received by Nitin Jain Director (AS) who then discussed it with Sridhara Member (T) and Srivastava DDG-AS before forwarding to me. When this file reached me, I wrote, "Please discuss" and forwarded it to the Department. No officer who had reviewed the file in the Law Ministry, including the Law Secretary, said that this issue should be referred to the GoM. All that they sought was to examine some additional documents. Therefore, within the Telecom Ministry the Director, DDG-AS and Member (T) opined in a discussion with me that the Law Minster's comment was 'out of context' and pointed out the relevant provision in the Transaction of Business Rule in support of their view. They also affirmed that the advice of the Law Minister was not binding as it was made without any consultation even within the Law Department itself and did not imply a rule but was only a personal opinion. It is important to note here that this tag of 'out of context' was not my fabrication but the informed opinion of ministry officials. Nitin Jain, the Director who examined this file on 2 November 2007 was of the same view and noted, "The matter was discussed with DDG(AS) and Member (T) who had in turn discussed it with Hon'ble MOCIT. It was discussed and felt in the meeting that the proposed advice was out of context. It is therefore, advisable that we may follow the existing policy for grant of new licenses as suggested by the Secretary (T) in the meeting chaired by the Hon'ble MOCIT. DoT has till now been following a process of First Come First Served basis for grant of UASL. In view of the TRAI recommendations of no cap on number of operators, large number of applications was being received in the DoT. Therefore, it was decided that no more applications shall be received after 01.10.2007 till further orders. Till the cut off date of receipt of UASL applications were received from 46 companies for 22 service area ... in order to avoid any legal implications of cut-off date, all the applications received till the announcement of cut-off date in the press i.e 25-9-2007 may be processed as per the existing policy."

I signed the file on 2 November 2007 with the note reiterating the agreed course of action, "Approved; LOI may be issued to the applicants received up to 25 September 2007. Even after I signed the file on 2 November 2007, the Secretary (Telecom) who was out of station at that time, upon his return noted in the file that a further discussion should be held and an Officers' Meeting was accordingly convened on 6 November 2007. The Secretary (Telecom), The Additional Secretary (Telecom), Member-Technology, DDG-AS and Director attended the meeting. Mathur, the Secretary (Telecom) opined that the provisions 3.1.1/3.1.2 of NTP 99, the Cabinet decision of 2003 and Guidelines for UASL 2005, should be addressed into the files. In the file (No.20/100/2000-AS-I) that recorded the proceedings of that meeting it was clearly documented, "Secretary (T) has desired to examine whether LOI can be given without assured availability of spectrum." The file was sent for my approval again on 7 November 2007. Even at that time, no one even mentioned, let alone recorded in the files, any objections in relation to the cut-off date of 25 September 2007. Para 3.1.1 of NTP-99 deals with spectrum based Cellular operations which says adequate spectrum is essential for new entry of additional operators. Para 3.1.2 of NTP-99 deals with fixed landline which says the number of players can be added as recommended by TRAI. When the Cabinet on 31 October 2003 approved the UASL regime these two services were merged and the option of choosing the type of services was made open by amending the NTP-99 as follows "License for United Access (Basic and Cellular) Services permitting license to provide Basic and / or Cellular Service using any technology in a service area." On the other hand the UASL Guidelines 2005 says "Licenses shall be issued without any restriction on the number of entrants for the provisions of the Unified Access Service in a service area." Hence, there was a legal anomaly whether availability of spectrum is essential to issue licenses since the UASL was silent on this issue and to some extent inconsistent with UASL guidelines.

Right from the beginning my view was that there cannot be any restriction to consider all the 575 applications when the UASL guideline imposed no such restriction. My belief was that only those companies who have the requisite entrepreneurial zeal and wherewithal would pay such a big entry fee (₹ 1650 crore) and hence was personally somewhat wary of imposing a cut-off date. However, in practical terms spectrum is needed for the new operators as the entire telecom sector has migrated to Cellular system and therefore I was convinced by the Secretary (T) and other officers to fix a cut-off date. Even when Gadhvi MP raised a question in the Lok Sabha on 26 November 2007, I had clarified, "It is true that earlier when the National Telecom Policy was declared in 1999, there was a categorical observation in the Policy that wherever the licenses are issued, it must be in accordance with the availability of spectrum. In other words, if the spectrum is not available, the Government should not give new licenses. It was referred to the Group of Ministers in the year 2003 wherein the unified access license policy came into existence. The paragraph 11 of the Guidelines which were approved by the Group of Ministers and were also placed before the Cabinet said that the licenses shall be issued without any restriction on the number of entrants for provision of unified access services in the service area. The Government is sticking to it." Under these circumstances, at my instance, the availability of spectrum was reviewed up front and listed down. As a follow-up, measures were taken up to identify and free up spectrum for allocation including the efforts to reclaim spectrum from the Defence Department. The officers of the Licensing Branch were in constant touch with the applicants who had applied till the cut-off date and were also obtaining additional information in writing where required. All parties concerned were clearly aware of the cut-off date and it was never a secret. None of the Telecom companies that had applied complained to any institution that they did not know anything about the cut-off date or that matters had been hushed up.

After having signed the file, on 2 November 2007, I wrote a letter **(Annexure-I)** to the PM in order to apprise him of the events and decisions taken in the department in relation to the 2G licensing/spectrum. The details furnished in my letter were as follows:

1. 575 applications for licenses were received.

2. Opinion sought from the Law Ministry about the method established by the Telecom Ministry to process those applications.

3. The Law Minister (not the Ministry of Law) on his own without any legal basis made an observation recommending the matter to be placed before (the already in-session) GoM.

4. When that observation of the Law Minister was considered under the policies, rules and procedures adopted by the Ministry, it was decided that it was 'out of context'.

5. It was decided then on the basis of the availability of spectrum and the quantum of spectrum that would become available soon, to consider in the first phase all applications received until 25 September 2007.

Co-incidentally, a letter (Annexure-II) from the Prime Minister's Office addressed to me was also simultaneously on its way and delivered at 7 pm on the same day to my 2A, Motilal Nehru Marg residence. Upon reading the letter it becomes apparent that its contents match the representation by COAI in this context. What is also noteworthy is that it was only on 5 November (three days later as noted in the PMO records) that both the Joint Secretary (Telecom) and the Director (Telecom) working in the PM's Office were shown the PM's letter to me as well as my letter addressed to him. This makes me wonder whether this letter was indeed drafted by the PMO. The key topics highlighted in the annexure of the PM's letter were:

1. Enhancement of subscriber-linked spectrum allocation criteria

2. Permission for CDMA service providers to also provide service in GSM and be eligible for spectrum in the GSM Band

3. The processing of large number of applications received for

fresh licenses against the backdrop of inadequate spectrum to cater to overall demand

4. In order that spectrum use efficiency gets directly linked with correct pricing of spectrum consider:

i. introduction of transparent methodology of auction, wherever technically possible

ii. revision of entry fee which is currently benchmarked on old spectrum auction figures

5. Early decision on issues like rural telephony, infrastructure sharing, 3G, Broadband, Number Portability and BWA on which TRAI had already provided recommendations

Out of the five topics mentioned above, on the first four, the decisions of the Government were filed in the records after obtaining the recommendations of TRAI, their acceptance by the Telecom Commission and my approval of it. It is still a puzzle to me as to what could have prompted the PM to send that letter to me. With all due respect, I am of the opinion that such a letter bearing the PM's signature should never have been sent. It is just not expected for the PM to get into the nitty-gritty of the operational functions, procedures and guidelines of a ministry. If such information is required by the PM, as per usual procedure, a Minister or a Secretary would be called upon to explain in person or else a report in writing would be sought from the ministry. In order to provide explanations and information to brief the Prime Minister, a Joint Secretary or an Additional Secretary from every Ministry is available in the PMO in order to contact the departments concerned whenever required. On behalf of the Ministry of Telecom Mrs Vini Mahajan, a Joint Secretary performed this function. However, no such follow-up had occurred with the Telecom Ministry through her prior to the PM's letter.

The covering letter sent by the PM stated, "I would request you to give urgent consideration to the issues raised with a view to ensuring fairness and transparency and let me know of the position before you take any further action in this regard." I felt wounded by the use of words like "let me know of the position before you take any further action" and "ensuring fairness and transparency" and concluded that the PM had been led to believe that there was something amiss in the functioning of my Ministry. It was not as if I had personally issued some edicts. The decisions had been taken by TRAI and the Telecom Commission and I had performed the subsequent due-diligence in concert with the ministry officials to provide the final stamp of approval. The Prime Minister in his letter had asked whether it would be possible to issue new licenses without adequate spectrum availability. The letter also contained the COAI's argument that TRAI had not substantiated its recommendation in a proper manner with regard to the subscriber-linked criteria for additional spectrum allocation to existing service providers. The basic reason behind COAI raising these issues was that they were keen to expand their monopoly as in some states they already enjoyed spectrum to the tune of 10 -12 MHz instead of their legitimate share of 4.4 MHz. COAI had on one hand moved the Tribunal challenging the policy decisions of the Government but had failed to get an interim stay order in its appeal to the Delhi High Court. On the other hand, it was apparently also knocking at the doors of the PMO for intervention. Realising that the letter from the PM appeared to doubt the credibility of my actions, I decided to immediately write a response. I showed the draft of my response to the letter of the PM, to Sridhara, whom I had called in to verify my facts. After making certain corrections pointed out by Sridhara, I sent that letter **(Annexure-III)** to the PM around 10 pm on the same night. Till date, no one has proved that the details in my reply letter were untrue or uncorroborated by the department files. Instead of verifying whether the contents of my letter were correct, those sitting in judgement only raised questions like "how can the Prime Minister's advice be ignored?" In fact, the PM had not provided any specific instructions in his letter; he had merely stated that "a number of issues relating to allocation of spectrum have been raised by telecom sector companies as well as in sections of media." When the PM himself had not claimed to have given any advice, it is such a sham to claim that I had ignored the PM's advice. It would be childish to posit that simply because a letter has come from the PM it is somehow legally binding. I am well aware of the PM's powers, duties and responsibilities. Furthermore, the PM can transact any business assigned to him only on the basis of the Cabinet decisions, policies framed by the Parliament and the laws and procedures of relevant institutions. The PM cannot take action based purely on the advice of a third party, particularly when such advice is contrary to the existing policies and rules. The PM must reject such advice or consult with his ministers in order to properly evaluate it.

I had a meeting with the PM later in the month of November in order to further discuss the matter contained in our letters along with details of the existing rules and regulations that were followed and related precedents. I explained everything in detail to him citing the observations in the department files. I pointed out to him that the enhanced subscriber base criteria recommended by TRAI was central to the concerns raised by COAI. I also explained that COAI's brief to him was a ploy to procure additional spectrum only for them while ensuring that it was not distributed either through new licenses or on the basis of dual technology operations to CDMA operators like Reliance. The PM understood the motives of COAI and asked me to explain more about the enhanced subscriber base criteria. I then stated that the Wireless Planning and Coordination (WPC) wing of the Telecom Ministry had discovered the availability of a considerable quantum of unallocated spectrum. I added that even after distributing the additional spectrum desired by COAI and to providers adopting dual technology, there would still be spectrum left over for new licenses. The PM expressed his surprise because he had been repeatedly misinformed that spectrum was not available. Not only the PM but also the Parliament and the general public were never informed about the availability of spectrum until I took over as the Telecom Minister. No initiative had been taken to use this spectrum optimally to increase teledensity and generate additional revenue for the government. The Prime Minister shifted in his seat, looked askance at me and asked, "Is that so? I have been told that the impediment to the growth of Telecom sector is the non-availability of spectrum. Only on that basis, a GoM has been constituted to release band-width from the Defence Department. How is it possible to have that much of spectrum available for distribution to so many?" I emphatically stated that a stealthy ploy had been stage-managed in the Telecom Ministry to obfuscate the availability of spectrum and to gather the scattered spectrum only when the time came to assign additional spectrum and increase the monopoly of the existing service providers. "If that is so, why not issue licenses? And what is the problem for COAI in that?" he asked. Concluding that it would be difficult to make the PM fully understand all the technical details in that short conversation, I decided to use an analogy, "In 1985, when I was studying Law, I travelled by Jawa-Yezdi motorcycle. That vehicle gave a mileage of only 20 Kms per litre and with a lot of noise and foul emission. But now bikes like 'Hero Honda' are available, which run 80 kms to the litre with significantly less noise and emissions that meet today's stringent pollution control standards. These benefits have emerged because of technological innovation and upgrades. The petrol driving the vehicles is the same and has in fact become costlier so who should be allocated the petrol now, Jawa or Hero Honda?" The PM understood the truth and the strength of my arguments. The number of consumers that can be connected by 1MHZ of spectrum differs from one technology to the other. New technology has now arrived to provide connectivity to two or three times the number of consumers who could be connected in the past. This new technology would require additional capital expenditure (Capex) and operation expenditure (Opex) to rollout. But COAI was insisting that it would continue with the old technology to avoid expenses while demanding additional spectrum from the government at no cost. Unless the existing companies upgraded to the improved technology, no additional spectrum should be allocated, was effectively the stand of the Telecom Ministry. I had approved this stand and it was also included in the affidavit filed by the Ministry before TDSAT.

The initiatives I was taking under the circumstances, the forces working against me and the way in which the Ministry and I handled the situation comforted the Prime Minister. He wished me success in my efforts. He also agreed with me when I stated, "Some in the Cabinet are supportive of COAI in this issue and some are against it. Corporations are trying to thrust their views not only upon me but also on some senior Ministers." Without hiding anything I disclosed to the PM the facts related to my discussions with Sunil Mittal and to all those who had approached me in this context to plead their cause. I also explained to him the intent of my first letter to him on 2nd November. I pointed out the unfounded observation made by the Law Minister, to refer to the GoM, the Telecom Ministry's proposals on the method of processing the applications for licenses, when he had only been asked to provide an opinion on suggested modalities framed by the Ministry for the issuance of licenses after ascertaining the required spectrum availability. I further explained that there was no need for another GoM as per the Transaction of Business Rules and reminded him that the existing GoM on spectrum was constituted with specific terms of reference to look into the vacation of 2G/3G spectrum by the Defence and other Ministries. Based on the constitutionally defined Rules of Allocation of Business and Transaction of Business, the Telecom Ministry is fully empowered to issue Telecom Licenses and to allocate spectrum for those licenses. The personal opinion of the Law Minister was not tenable under these rules as the issuance of license and allocation of spectrum were not matters for Inter-Ministerial consultation. The

PM, who is also the final decision maker regarding constituting the GoM, was in agreement with my stand and might have later discussed this with the Law Minister, H.R. Bhardwaj. At a later date, after the end of a Cabinet meeting, Bhardwaj spoke to me, admitting that the stand of the Telecom Ministry was correct as per the rules and that he was in agreement with it. Bhardwaj also revealed to me that he had become aware only later that licensing and spectrum pricing matters had been dropped from the terms of reference of the GoM. I could understand from Bhardwaj's reply that somehow, he had developed a misunderstanding around the Telecom Ministry's file for issuance of licenses and hence he had written that contrary observation (suggesting referring the matter to GoM). A Minister is well within his rights to ignore or reject suggestions or observations from Ministerial colleagues, even if it comes from a senior (either in age or administrative hierarchy), when it is inconsistent with the rules of transacting parliamentary business. The ruckus created around this later on and labelling me as an unfair law-breaker (even though I was following all the rules) was obviously orchestrated for the benefit of vested interests. The Prime Minister after listening to my explanations patiently and carefully made it clear to me that his letter was motivated by the news in the press about wrongdoings in the Ministry and the apprehensions raised by the COAI. I got his approval to go ahead with the process as indicated in my letters. I subsequently asked the Ministry officials to expedite the issuance of licenses. During this period, in one of the cabinet meeting which I could not attend due to my parliament work, Kamal Nath the then Union Minister raised the issue of spectrum allocation for new and existing operators and suggested to constitute a GOM. His suggestion was seconded by P. Chidambaram. However, the Prime Minister asserted that, there is no need for the GOM as he was directly dealing with the issues in consultation with Telecom Minister. This was revealed to me by T.R. Balu and Oscar Fernandes.

On 22 November 2007, the Telecom Secretary D.S. Mathur received a letter from the Finance Secretary Subba Rao, "The purpose of this letter is to confirm if proper procedure has been followed with regard to financial diligence. In particular, it is not clear how the rate of ₹ 1650 crores determined in 2001 has been applied for the license given in 2007 without any indexation let alone current valuation. More over in view of the financial implications, the Ministry of Finance should have been consulted in the matter before you had finalized the decision." This letter was duly considered in the Ministry in a proper manner based on NTP-99, UASL Guidelines and Cabinet decision-2003. The Ministry's decision was to make no change to the entry fee structure in light of the TRAI recommendation. This was clearly explained in the ministry file which was also signed by Mrs Manju Madhavan, the Member (Finance) attached to the Telecom Ministry and holding the rank of Additional Secretary in the Finance Ministry. Since the file was put up to me with the unanimous decision of all the officials in the Ministry, I concurred with them and gave my approval. Thereafter a letter conveying this decision was sent to the Finance Secretary on 29 November 2007. The technical explanation, commercial strategy, resultant social outlook and the targets cited by TRAI for its recommendation not to increase fees from the 2001 levels were entirely based on NTP-99. There is hence no scope for narrow cost benefit analysis; merely increasing revenue was not the priority in the overall scheme of things. It is generally appropriate for the Finance Ministry to have a focus on augmenting revenue; however, the law itself permits deviation from this general principle in order to further socio-economic goals. In an administrative structure, delegation and separation of powers is not only requisite but also inviolable. So, when it has been legally decided already as per law that a regulatory authority (TRAI) would oversee an area which the Finance Ministry would otherwise have, the Telecom Ministry is wholly justified in pointing out to the Finance Ministry that it is overstepping its bounds when seeking explanations regarding telecom license fees. Accordingly, and as directed by the Telecom Secretary, Nitin Jain, Director, Access Branch prepared a reply on 27 November 2007 and it was sent to Srivastava, DDG-AS, "The Government has taken a conscious decision not to bring changes in the existing policy and not to invite bids for entry fee for grant of UAS licenses as all the pending applications are in terms of existing UASL guidelines. If such changes are made at this stage then there may be litigations. Moreover, the cost of offering the service, if increased, may consequently lead to increased tariff and low tele-density, thereby defeating the government objective of achieving 500 million telephone connections by 2010."

After the file was endorsed by the DDG, it was sent to D.S. Mathur, Telecom Secretary who then sent it on 27 November 2007 to Mrs Manju Madhavan. Since it was a file related to entry fee, Mathur had carefully annotated the file "may please see and advice." On receiving the file Mrs Manju Madhavan, discussed it with D.S. Mathur and then sent it back to Telecom Secretary on 28 November with her approval noting that it was "discussed". Then the Telecom Secretary forwarded the file to me and I gave my assent to the explanations given by the Ministry. Neither before that nor after that had I provided any personal view or opinion on that matter. I was not even aware of the letter from the Finance Ministry or the reply to that letter or the details in the file until the file was sent to me. The letter based on that file was sent to the Finance Ministry stating that the entry fee may not be increased. Generally, if there is a denial or non-acceptance to a reply sent by a Ministry, it is a practice for the Secretary to that Ministry to state the appropriate reasons after due verification and annotate 'your opinion/stand is wrong; unacceptable'. If not, it must be resolved after sending it either to the Prime Minister or the Cabinet Secretary. Such a rejection did not come to the Telecom Ministry either from the Finance Minister or from the Finance Secretary. Not only that, the Finance Secretary who received the letter from the

Telecom Secretary on 29 November 2007, sent it to the Finance Minister on 30 November 2007. The Finance Minister Chidambaram had written on it, "please examine carefully portions marked on the margin." In the margin, the documents NTP-99, Cabinet decision-2003, UASL 2005 and TRAI recommendation were marked as sought for perusal. In fact, it was only in those documents sought by Chidambaram that the appropriate information with regard to entry fee was recorded in detail. As per Chidambaram's note, on 12 December 2007 an Office Memorandum came to the Telecom Ministry from the Finance Ministry asking for copies of the 2003 Cabinet Note and Cabinet Decisions. Accordingly, those documents were sent on 13 December 2007 with the approval of Mathur. Thereafter there was no letter or memo on that subject either from the Finance Ministry, Prime Minister or the Cabinet Secretary. Later on, towards the end of a Cabinet Meeting, Chidambaram mentioned to me that the reply from the Telecom Ministry had been received. Thereafter there was no disapproval, or rejection of the contents of the ministry's letter, nor was there any contraindication even after 10 January 2008 when the Letters of Intent for the new UASL licenses were issued.

In order to finalise the Draft Letter of Intent (LoI), the policy file to issue licenses was prepared by Shah Nawaz Alam, a Director of the License Finance wing. After being endorsed by the Deputy Director General of the License wing (DDG-LF) and the Advisor Finance, that file was sent to Mrs Manju Madhavan on 30 November 2007. It was she who accepted the decision for not revising the Entry fee and gave approval to send the reply to the Finance Secretary in another separate file justifying this on the basis of TRAI's recommendation. On 30 November 2007, the Finance Minister himself saw the documents sent to the Finance Ministry in which Mrs Madhavan had given her approval without reservation. However, surprisingly and quite incoherently on the same day (30 November), in the file meant to finalise the Draft

Letter of Intent (LOI) Mrs Madhavan wrote, "Since the rates have not been revised and the finance secretary has raised the issue, I am of the view that this should be examined in depth before any further steps are taken." The file containing that noting was sent to me through the Telecom Secretary. It would have been fair had D.S. Mathur as the head of the Telecom Commission sent back that file to Mrs Manju Madhavan asking her the reason for the baseless change in her stance within a day. I believe that he did not do so because it was perhaps he who had prompted her to write such a noting! When the file was sent to me, I wrote, "The matter of entry fee has been deliberated in the Department several times in the light of several guidelines issued by the Ministry and Recommendations of TRAI. And, accordingly the decision was taken that entry fee need not be revised. On the above lines Secretary (T) has also replied to the Finance Secretary's letter dated 22.11.2007." I never allowed my legalistic stand and the logical truth to be diluted anytime for anyone. Had Finance Ministry really intended to increase the Entry fee, Mrs Manju Madhavan could have utilized two appropriate opportunities. One when she attended as a Member the meeting of the Telecom Commission convened on 10 October 2007 to consider the TRAI recommendation. The second, when the reply letter to the Finance Ministry was being prepared on 29 November 2007 and when upon request additional documents were sent to the Finance Ministry. On both occasions, she was in agreement with TRAI's recommendation about not changing the Entry Fee and was also fully engaged in getting my approval. But suddenly she changed her stand even without consulting the Finance Ministry and wrote contrarian views in the file – presumably, to oblige somebody. During the time when the processing of applications for the issuance of licenses was in progress there were many such attempts of interference. On 22 November 2007, the Financial Express (Mumbai) carried a news item, "New Telecom licenses as per existing policy.... COAI has also said if Letters of Intent are issued to all prospective licensees, it would seriously hamper investors' confidence. This would be absolutely incorrect, arbitrarily illegal and untenable for the Government." It is no surprise that COAI had gone to the Finance Ministry when their attempt to put the efforts of the Telecom Ministry on hold through the PMO had also failed.

UASL Regime consists of Entry Fee, License Fee and Spectrum Charge. All these three even though inter-related are fundamentally different. Entry Fee is a non-refundable fixed amount charged to a telecom provider when they sign-up for a new license; License fee and Spectrum Charge are both linked to adjusted gross revenue (AGR) but Spectrum Charge is levied (in addition to License Fee) only on revenue from wireless services. TRAI did not increase the entry fee to ensure a level playing field for both existing and new telecom providers. As per the Cabinet decision taken in 2003, entry fee must be determined based on the recommendation of TRAI. The Telecom Commission which included Mrs Manju Madhavan unanimously decided based on that Cabinet decision not to implement any indexation to increase entry fee. This was not my sole decision as minister! Paragraph 2.73 of TRAI 2007 recommendations explains this, "The allocation of spectrum is after the payment of entry fee and grant of license. The entry fee as it exists today is, in fact, a result of the price discovered through a markets based mechanism applicable for the grant of license to the 4th cellular operator. In today's dynamism and unprecedented growth of telecom sector, the entry fee determined then is also not the realistic price for obtaining a license. Perhaps, it needs to be reassessed through a market mechanism. On the other hand spectrum usage charge is in the form of a royalty which is linked to the revenue earned by the operators and to that extent it captures the economic value of the spectrum that is used. Some stakeholders have viewed the charges/fee as a hybrid model of extracting economic rent for the acquisition and as to meet the criterion of efficiency in the utilization of this scarce resource. The Authority in the context of 800, 900 and 1800 MHz is conscious of the legacy i.e. prevailing practice and the overriding consideration of level playing field. Though the dual charge in present form does not reflect the present value of spectrum it needed to be continued for treating already specified bands for 2G services i.e. 800, 900 and 1800 MHz. It is in this background that the Authority is not recommending the standard options pricing of spectrum, however, it has elsewhere in the recommendation made a strong case for adopting auction procedure in the allocation of all other spectrum bands except 800,900 and 1800 MHz." This clearly illustrates that TRAI was well aware of the notion of 'market price' or 'present value' in the context of growth in the telecom sector.

When TRAI has given its recommendation so clearly and decisively, there was no necessity for either the Telecom Ministry or the rest of the Government to go chasing phantoms in assessing 'market value'. The next paragraph 2.78 of the report stresses the importance of level playing field for telecom providers and the growth of rural teledensity. "As far as a new entrant is concerned, the question arises whether there is any need for change in the pricing methodology for allocation of spectrum in the 800,900 and 1800 MHz bands. Keeping in view the objective of growth, affordability, penetration of wireless services in semi-urban and rural areas, the Authority is not in favour of changing the spectrum fee regime for a new entrant.... Any differential treatment to a new entrant vis-a-vis incumbents in the wireless sector will go against the principle of level playing field." In conclusion, paragraph 2.79 explains how spectrum auction is not plausible. **"It is therefore recommended that in future all spectrum excluding the spectrum in 800, 900 and 1800 MHz bands should be auctioned so as to ensure efficient utilization of this scarce resource.** In the 2G bands (1800 MHz / 900 MHz / 1800 MHz), the allocation through auction may not be possible as the service providers were allocated spectrum at different times of their license and the amount of spectrum with them varies from 2 x 4.4 MHz to 2 x 10 MHz for GSM technology and 2 x 2.5 MHz to 2 x 5 MHz in CDMA technology. Therefore, to decide the cut off after which the spectrum is auctioned will be difficult and might raise the issue of level playing field."

Newspapers were continuously publishing reports relating to spectrum allocation. How can it be justified to give away spectrum in 2007 at the same price as it was in 2001? Can the 2001 price of land per ground in Delhi or Mumbai be applicable in 2007 also? The people who subscribed to such sensationalism were not just common folk but learned people, parliamentarians, economists, politicians, journalists, and surprisingly (or rather tragically) even judges. At a first glance these questions may appear to be valid, but there is a need to understand the legal, commercial and technical reasons for TRAI's recommendation to not increase the entry fee in order to avoid imbalance between existing operators and new players. The UASL Regime was devised in such a manner that license fee would be collected in terms of percentile of revenue share that would increase every year over the one-time entry fee of ₹1650 crore, apart from the spectrum (usage) charge. When the license fee increases on the basis of revenue share it should be deemed that the entry fee also increases progressively. The telecom policy and related guidelines aim to ensure that entry fee does not become a barrier for new telecom providers thus fostering competition; and links government revenue (from license fee and spectrum charges) to the telecom provider's revenue thus fostering business growth and service penetration (teledensity).

In the first week of December 2007 I had another meeting with the Prime Minister. During that discussion, I explained the background of the TRAI recommendation and its legal interpretations. I handed over copies of the Finance Ministry's letter (22 November 2007) and the Telecom Ministry's reply letter

(29 November 2007). After going through the letters, the PM gave me a good suggestion, "There is nothing wrong in your effort to prove that you have legal justification for every action of yours. I know well that some of the Ministerial colleagues have a partisan view on this issue. On one side the pendency of judicial proceedings, on the other side the insufficient understanding within the Cabinet and the media's attempts to depict as if a very big irregularity was taking place; so, you send me a note after examining the ways to resolve this issue which is considered to be a complex one after holding talks in detail with both Pranab Mukherjee, the Chairman of the GoM on spectrum and Vahanvati, the Solicitor General who is appearing in these cases, enabling us to find a right course of action." He also spoke to Pranab Mukherjee in my presence over the phone to facilitate my follow-up. When I was taking leave of the PM I told him, "When we overcome this complex issue with so many hurdles, we would be able to reduce the Telephone Tariff drastically and the teledensity would increase from 30 percent to 65 percent within a year. My wish is that 3G service should be started within the next two years. After that, 2G service must be made available free of charge creating an atmosphere where there would be 'no cost to talk'. Some countries have already begun to offer 2G service free of charge." The PM conveyed his best wishes for the success of my efforts.

Subsequently, I met Pranab Mukherjee in his office and explained to him with relevant documents the details of the discussion that I had with the Prime Minister. I also apprised him that I would soon be meeting the Solicitor General Vahanvati. I held talks with Vahanvati, in the second week of December 2007. I requested him to prepare a brief note on the stand taken by the Government in the cases filed by COAI and the procedures to be adopted in the issuance of new licenses and dual technology. In the same week after the note was prepared, I again met Pranab Mukherjee in his office along with Vahanvati. As the Chairman of the GoM on Spectrum, Pranab Mukherjee who had adequate information and knowledge about the documents started the discussions with questions related to the additional spectrum demanded by COAI, the dual technology request of the CDMA companies and the new licenses. Vahanvati walked us through his note in about fifteen minutes touching upon the unwarranted litigation by COAI while elaborating the legal position in offering dual technology as also the procedures to be followed in the issuance of new licenses and related allocation of spectrum. Once Vahanvati left, Pranab Mukherjee conferred further with me and then told me that he would be sending a note directly to the PM but also asked me to inform the PM myself, highlighting the steps to be taken in the light of the discussion we had just completed.

Accordingly, on 26 December 2007, I wrote to the PM a detailed letter **(Annexure-IV)** including an annexure with extensive details about the subscriber base criteria for the additional spectrum to be given to existing companies, dual technology, new licenses and allotment of spectrum. This letter was subsequently incorporated as a reference document into the policy file workflow related to issuing new licenses. In the context of processing of large number of applications received for fresh licenses against the backdrop of inadequate spectrum to cater to overall demand, I reiterated the fact that DoT would continue to implement first come first served (FCFS) policy and that the UASL licensing and spectrum allocation is a 3-step process:

1. Issuance of LoI's

2. Issuance of UASL Licenses: "The First-cum-First Served policy is also applicable for grant of license on compliance of LOI conditions. Therefore, any applicant who complies with the conditions of LOI first will be granted UAS license first. This issue never arose in the past as at one point of time only one application was processed and LOI was granted and enough time was given to him for compliance of conditions of LOI. However, since the

Government has adopted a policy of 'No Cap' on number of UAS License, a large number of LOI's are proposed to be issued simultaneously. In these circumstances, an applicant who fulfils the conditions of LOI first will be granted license first, although several applicants will be issued LOI simultaneously. The same has been concurred by the Solicitor General of India during the discussions."

3. Grant of wireless license: "The First-cum-First Served policy is also applicable for grant of Wireless License to the UAS Licensee. Wireless License is an independent license to UAS license for allotment of Radio Frequency and authorising launching GSM / CDMA based mobile services. There is a misconception that UAS license authorises a person to launch mobile services automatically. UAS license is a license for providing both wire and wireless services. Therefore, any UAS license holder wishes to offer mobile service has to obtain a separate Wireless License from DoT. It is clearly indicated in Clauses 43.1 and 43.2 of the UAS License agreement of DoT"

Pranab Mukherjee also sent a note from his side to the PM as he had assured me. When I met the Prime Minister later on, I learnt that Mr. Pranab Mukherjee's note and my letter were reviewed together in the PM's office in the first week of January 2008. The PM said that during that meeting he had been fully briefed on this matter. He also said that the Finance Minister had expressed the view that more revenue has to be earned from the existing telecom companies that had been granted excess/additional spectrum. I reminded him of my perspective that I had already conveyed to him in our earlier meeting about some companies having spectrum up to 10-12 MHz, much beyond the license agreement and that too free of cost. I assured him that I would speak to the Finance Minister in this regard very soon. I don't intend to imply that I had obtained approval on the files from the PM for every single step. There is no need for that as per the rules and government procedures. I am only re-emphasising that the PM had been kept fully aware of all my actions. Not only was there no resistance from him but he had also explicitly conveyed his support to my efforts. It is alarming and unfortunate that the letters between me and the PM were later subjected to critical scrutiny and unwarranted speculation by the media, CAG and the Supreme Court.

Subsequent to my meeting with the Prime Minister and with his concurrence, I followed up with the ministry officials to expeditiously execute the process of issuing licenses. As early as on 15 October 2007, a committee had been formed by the Secretary to the Telecom Ministry to scrutinize the applications received until 25 September 2007 for their eligibility. The files were forwarded to me for final sign-off with the fully qualified recommendations – to accept or reject the application – of the officers of various wings (Finance, Legal and Technical) within that committee. I found the decisions taken by the officers to be correct during my review for sign-off. I found no cause to write in any file to accept an application rejected by the committee or to reject any application accepted by it. This file that contained the proposal for the issuance of LoI's as mooted by DDG (AS) was approved on 7 January 2008 by Member (T) and Member (Finance) and was sent to Siddharth Behura, Secretary (Telecom). After it was duly signed by him and Member (T), Behura wrote a postscript, "If approved, a press release may be issued, draft of which is placed at flag 'x'". I signed the file after reviewing all the details and making the note, "approved: pl. obtain SG's opinion since he is appearing before the TDSAT and High Court." Thereafter, my Private Secretary R.K. Chandolia came back to me and pointed out that there was a difference in the Press Note and the decision recorded in the file. I reviewed the file and the press note again. A particular sentence in the press note was not present either in the guidelines, in the files, in the letter written by me to the Prime Minister or in the note prepared by the Solicitor General or in the department files. That sentence was, "However, if more than one applicant complies with LOI condition on the same date, the inter-se seniority would be decided by the date of application. "It was clearly a new stipulation introduced by the Secretary (T) – who incidentally also became an accused in the court case. That new stipulation had never been agreed in the ministry, discussed with Pranab Mukherjee the Chairman of the GoM or shared with the Prime Minister. On the same day (7 January 2008), I wrote in that file,"'X' is not necessary as it is a new stipulation" and signed after deleting that sentence. Since the file contained reference to that press note, I wrote below the already written note using the same pen just above my signature, "Press release approved as amended." After my correcting the press note, when the file was sent to the Secretary (T) he forwarded it to the Solicitor General who wrote in it, "I have seen the notes. The issue regarding new LOIs are not before any court. What is proposed is fair and reasonable. The press release makes transparency. This seems to be in order." I also signed off on 9 January 2008 in the separate files regarding the eligibility of companies. After completing this due process, Letters of Intent for the licenses were issued by the Ministry to the eligible applicants on 10 January 2008. That very day many of these applicants fulfilled the conditions mentioned in the LoI while just a couple of applicants completed their formalities the next day. After the issuance of LoI and the fulfilment of requisite conditions by the applicants, the Ministry completed the job of signing the actual licenses.

As agreed with the Prime Minister, I had a discussion on 30 January 2008, with the Finance Minister P. Chidambaram (in the presence of Finance Secretary Subba Rao), about the ways and means to earn additional revenue from spectrum usage. Chidambaram provided some valid suggestions. It was decided that an approach paper be prepared and discussed in the telecom department to arrive at a decision which would then be sent to the Telecom Commission for its approval. Accordingly, an Approach

Paper was sent to Subba Rao by the Telecom Secretary Behura on 8 February 2008. In paragraph 4.2 of that Approach Paper under the heading 'Fixed price for spectrum beyond 6.2 MHz', two options were suggested:

Option – I: For this purpose, it may be desirable to index. the entry fee of ₹.1650 crores in the year 2003-2004 (for initial spectrum 4.4 MHz) i.e. 375 crore per MHz for inflation, potential growth of Tele density and revenue etc. approximately. If we take an inflation of about 5% per year for 4 years upto 2007-2008 which would mean about 20% compounded inflation till 2007. Therefore additional charges can be levied at 20% of Rs. 375 cr. for 1 MHz spectrum i.e. 425 crores.

This option is not favoured in view of the low value of the spectrum.

Option – II: The service area wise AGR figures as per MHz for the year 2003-2004 and the anticipated figures were calculated and is given at Annexure-I. It may be seen that there is an increase of about 3.5 times, on the figures of 2007-2008 when 2003-2004 is compared. It is for consideration to charge 'x' times of base price of Rs. 375 Cr. Hz, where 'x' is to be decided. This will be charged to existing as well as new entrants. Those who decide not to pay be asked to surrender the excess spectrum beyond 6.2 MHz.

It was upon my insistence that the second option in the Approach Paper – a new revenue plan – was proposed for levying an additional spectrum charge on the basis of AGR for Telecom companies using spectrum beyond 6.2 MHz. While sending this Paper to the Finance Secretary on 8 February 2008, Behura noted, "I have sent a copy of the 'approach paper' to MOCIT and also discussed with him. He has desired that based on the above, Telecom Commission meeting may be called at an early date in order to take appropriate decision."

When the Prime Minister's role in the 2G case was questioned in the Supreme Court by Justices Singhvi and Ganguly, the opposition parties had cleverly furthered the illusion that the Prime Minister was also tainted since the Government had crouched back instead of advancing compelling arguments in his defence. The contents of my letters and the way in which the Prime Minister conducted himself in this matter in no way constituted any administrative lapses on criminal acts. In fact, the PM was disturbed when I explained to him the exploitation by the cartel in the telecom sector. He wanted the hidden spectrum to be made available for public use. The patronage shown by him to me in relation to 2G licensing and spectrum allocation was totally justified and correct as per policy and law. My anguish is that the Government headed by him did not back him up. His concern for national interest to be foremost is proved beyond doubt by the support and mentorship he had provided for every step I took. I have had the privilege of hearing from the PM about his humble beginnings and have also witnessed the colossal intellectual and moral stature he has achieved. I do not know why he could not muster the resolve even though truth was on his side, to stand against the verbal abuses of the opposition, unwarranted criticism of the 2G Bench and the staged outbursts of the biased media. That one action – or rather inaction – has caused so much damage to his reputation. As Lord Jeffery so aptly states, "A good name, like good will, is got by many actions and lost by one."

CHAPTER 5

The Inquisition

Needless to say, this expedient execution by the Telecom Ministry came as a shock to COAI whose aim was to halt the processing of applications and further issuance of licenses. Within a few days after issuing LoI's, COAI filed a case in the Delhi High Court on 14 January 2008. Newspapers affiliated to the opposition or attempting to ingratiate themselves with the COAI, went ahead with the task expected of them: they raised questions as to why so many licenses were issued on a single day in an apparently hasty and non-transparent manner; they spread gossip as if spectrum was being allocated at a huge loss to the exchequer; they made allegations that I had personally manipulated the cut-off date (advancing it from 1 October 2007 to 25 September 2007) in order to favour some companies. Even in the counter affidavit to COAI's case, filed on behalf of the Telecom Department it was clearly stated, "Further, with regard to grant of letter of intent (LOI) for UASL to the pending applicants, government has issued certain clarification to put at rest the confusions being created by some of the petitioners through a press release, before issuing the LOIs on 10 January 2008 to receive the LOI, but for a formal announcement and convenience of the applicant and the petitioners and other interested parties, respondent again issued a press release stating the venue and time in the afternoon. However, there was no need for such announcement through press release as per the past practice. After ensuring that all the applicants who were to receive the LOI have assembled at the designated venue, the Government issued the LOIs to the recipients. To make the process smooth, government took appropriate action well in time including security arrangement through in-house CISF. A copy of the signature sheet is annexed herewith and marked as enclosed at Annexure – R/A-2." However, once this media blitz started even the respectable and objective newspapers seemed to cave in and buy into the sensationalism, proving right the Tamil saying, 'Erumbu oora kallum theyum' (mere ants can chafe even a stone).

The press carried news like "loss of several thousand crores of rupees due to allotment of spectrum instead of auction"; "some companies got spectrum at a cheaper rate and sold it at a huge profit"; "pre-dated licenses were issued without anyone's knowledge"; "the first come first served rule was not applied"; etc. At the height of it on 11 February 2011, the Times of India published a report that I had ₹ 3,000 crore apparently received as kickbacks and followed-up with another article on 2 March stating that the money was held in some banks in Mauritius and Seychelles in the name of my wife. I am certain that none of these journalists ever bothered to validate any of the facts or study the national telecom regulations. Lord Tennyson once said,"A lie which is also a lie may be met and fought with outright; but a lie which is part of truth is a harder matter to fight." The claim that the Government incurred a loss of thousands of crores of rupees is not true, but it gained the appearance of truth due to the (seemingly logical) supposition that licenses should be issued in 2008 for a higher entry fee than that fixed in 2001 or that auctioning 2G could have earned as much money as in the 3G auction. "What was the reasoning behind keeping the entry fee unchanged? Was there really a loss to the exchequer? Are 2G and 3G the same in terms of commercial utility and value? Is the socio-economic situation in 2010 (at the time of 3G auction) the same as in 2008?" These questions were however not being asked. This confusion of the facts and underlying truth led to a furore. I do not say that my actions and decisions are beyond inspection or criticism but there must be positive intent behind it, not vicious mudslinging with ulterior motives. Unfortunately, among the many who got carried away by the hype were some Government agencies starting with the Central Vigilance Commission (CVC). On 11 October 2007, Arvind Kejriwal wrote a letter to the CVC, "The Ministry of Communication and IT is continuing to allocate new Spectrum for existing operators and new entrants – using its first come first served policy in the near future ... thus causing a loss of thousands of crores of rupees to the exchequer.... No wonder DoT has received more than 500 applications by companies who hardly have the ability to install a nationwide project which could easily cost upwards of Rs. 25,000 crores within the first four years.... It is critical that CVC uses its powers to inquire into the current policy and specifically about the question of why an open, transparent auction process cannot be followed in the upcoming 2G and 3G auction." On 17 October 2007, 'Common Cause', an NGO also wrote to the CVC, "It has been reported that the Department proposes to accept the recommendation of TRAI for continuance of old policy of allocation of Spectrum at a pre-determined price on a FCFS basis." On the same day, 'Common Cause' sent a similar letter to the Telecom Secretary D.S. Mathur. What is noteworthy here is that the letter **referred to news reports** and **not to verified facts from authentic sources**. The very same 'Common Cause' filed a case in the Supreme Court later in 2010, based on which charges were filed against me. It is also striking that Kejriwal's letter and the NGO's letter were written in the same week when the Telecom Commission headed by D.S. Mathur had accepted the recommendations of TRAI (to not change the Entry Fee fixed in 2001). Neither letter found fault with TRAI nor stated that first come first served basis had not been employed before. Strangely it was only the ministry officials, like Mathur who **even without soliciting my approval or inputs**, were responding to those letters directly and citing Government policy and Telecom Commission recommendations. As I had pointed out earlier, NTP-99 had recommended not to auction 2G Spectrum as had TRAI. However, when some people pressured the Constitutional bodies insisting that the Government should auction 2G spectrum, these bodies dove into misguided, ill-framed and ill-executed 'investigations' that even went to the extent of alleging a fantastical presumptive loss figure of ₹1.76 lakh crore. It is indeed disappointing that the Government remained fairly inert and oblivious to the damage that would ensue.

On 19 November 2007, K.S. Rama Subban, Secretary to the CVC wrote a letter to Mathur, "The Commission has received some references regarding allocation of Spectrum by the Department of Telecommunications.... The commission has also desired that the department should make a presentation on the policy of the Department on Spectrum, date for which will be intimated subsequently." That letter was read and considered by all the officers concerned including the Telecom Secretary, Additional Secretary (Member-Technology) and Wireless Advisor. Consequently, that team got busy preparing the presentation asked for by the CVC. In advance of that presentation Mathur wrote a letter on 18 December 2007 stating, "I may mention that the Spectrum has been allotted in line with the conditions of the respective Telecom Service licenses for various service providers and keeping in view the objectives of the New Telecom Policy 1999 (NTP-99).... It may be added that the annual Spectrum revenues have increased from ₹ 25 crores in 1997-98 to more than ₹ 2,000 crore in 2006-07, the total contribution to the national exchequer by the telecom sector as license fee, spectrum charges, service tax, etc. is of the order of ₹ 25,000 crore in the financial year 2006-2007 and major part of this is contributed by mobile services." It is evident that until that time, the Telecom Secretary was confident that there were no policy deviations or any irregularities as suspected by the CVC. Mathur, who was superannuated on 31 December 2007, had signed off on all the above files and been party to all the policy decisions related to the LoIs in his capacity as Telecom Secretary. The only piece of action that he missed was the final administrative task of actual issuance of the LoI's which happened on 10 January 2008, post his retirement. Yet, in the subsequent court proceedings he pleaded ignorance and declared that he had nothing to do with the issuance of LoIs given his retirement date. He was possibly (?) instructed as prosecution witness to make statements which contradicted his own prior decisions but shifted blame onto me – which also says a lot about the CBI's impartiality and integrity. Jean Paul Richter, German novelist famous for his humours works has aptly said, "A timid person is frightened before a danger, a coward during the time and a courageous person afterward." Siddharth Behura who took over from Mathur as the new Secretary to the Telecom Ministry, sent to CVC on 7 January 2008 the detailed responses prepared by the Ministry, to the additional queries raised by them. It was distressing but not a surprise to me that the CVC's questions were reaching the press even before they reached us in the ministry.

The very first query of the CVC was not related to the auctioning of spectrum; it pertained to how the first come first served rule had come about and would that not be putting a cap contrary to TRAI's recommendations of issuing licenses with 'no cap'. The Economic Times dated 4 January 2008 carried a news item, "CVC-questions DoT's spectrum policy – says First Come First Served Policy appears to be in conflict with TRAI's recommendation 2003." T.K.A. Nair, Principal Secretary to the Prime Minister upon reading this article wrote to Behura asking for relevant details. Behura sent to Nair a copy of the responses already sent to the CVC. This is another evidence of the fact that the PM's Office was monitoring this matter and following up on it, proving false the allegation that the PM was misled or kept in the dark. The presentation to the CVC was made on 7 February 2008 by the Telecom Ministry and the following explanations were provided:

What was the reason for not auctioning this additional spectrum?

Response

- The New Telecom Policy (NTP) – 99 stipulates that modern telecom services be made available to public at affordable tariffs.
- To keep the tariffs to affordable (low) level, no upfront/initial/one time charges were levied for the spectrum and only the spectrum usage charges have been levied.
- The TRAI has also not recommended auction of spectrum for 2G (existing) mobile services.

Why additional 'entry fee' or 'spectrum enhancement charge' was not levied from the existing operators? This has led to substantial financial loss to DoT.

Response

- As per the UAS license agreement, there is no provision for charging additional entry fee for the use of the spectrum in the frequency bands 900 and 1800 MHz.

- However, the additional spectrum usage charge is being levied based on the quantum of allotted spectrum.
- The annual spectrum revenue have increased from Rs.25 Crore in 1997-98 to more than Rs. 2,000 Crore in 2006-07. For three quarters of 2007-08 Rs. 2,440 cr. 2008-09 (expected) Rs. 2,806 cr.
- The total contribution to the national exchequer by the telecom sector as license fee, spectrum charges and service tax, etc. was of the order of 25,000 Crore for the financial year 2006-07 and a major part of this is contributed by mobile services.

DoT issued as many as 22 licenses in December 2006 on the entry fee determined in 2001 auction. Why did DoT continue to issue licenses based on the old entry fee? Did DoT make any attempt to determine the fresh valuation of the license?

Response

- TRAI in its recommendation dated 27 October 2003 on Unified Licensing had discussed 3 alternatives for entry fee payable for migration to UASL regime including entry fee based on bidding. However, they recommended that the existing entry fee of the fourth Cellular Operator would be the entry fee in the new Unified Access Licensing Regime {Paragraph 7.15 to 7.19}
- TRAI further recommended that BSOs would pay the difference of the fourth CMSP's existing entry fee and the entry fee paid by them and that the migration from Basic Service to UAS regime would be on a voluntary basis and those WLL (M) players who do not wish to migrate to the full mobility regime, would only be required to pay the fee for WLL (M), with mobility strictly within SDCA, being recommended in line with TDSAT's direction {Paragraph 7.26} i.e. Service providers were to be given choice to migrate to the new regime or maintain the present position.
- TRAI further recommended that the Government to publish terms and conditions of authorization, e.g., nominal entry fee, Universal Service Obligation (USO), security conditions, etc.
- Accordingly, the entry fee was finalized for UAS regime in 2003. It was decided to keep the entry fee for the UAS license same as the entry fee of the fourth cellular operator, in line with TRAI's recommendations, which was based on the bidding process in 2001.
- However, wherever there was no fourth cellular licensee, the entry fee was fixed equal to entry fee being levied for Basic service license. For West Bengal, entry fee of Rs. 1 Cr was finalized subsequently based on TRAI's recommendation after re-reference.

- Once again in its recommendations dated 28 July 2007, TRAI discussed the issue of entry barrier / entry fee as below:
- Ensuring a potential competition in the market would mean no barrier to entry. Needless to say, competitive market provides the greatest benefits to consumers. Low or nil barriers to entry facilitate a high degree of innovation. [Paragraph 2.19}.
- Placing artificial entry restriction in the form of a licensing policy may not be appropriate at this stage. {Paragraph 2.28}
- The entry fee as it exists today is, in fact, a result of the price discovered through a markets-based mechanism applicable for the grant of license to the 4th cellular operator. In today's dynamism and unprecedented growth of telecom sector, the entry fee determined then is also not the realistic price for obtaining a license. Perhaps, it needs to be reassessed through a market- mechanism. {Paragraph 2.73}
- However, no specific recommendation in respect of entry fee for UASL was made in the recommendations. Accordingly, the Government has taken a conscious decision not to bring changes in the existing policy and not to invite bidds for entry fee for grant of UAS licenses as all the pending applications are in terms of existing UASL guidelines.

Even after this briefing, the CVC sent another letter on 28 March 2008, "The Commission after considering the matter has desired that the Department of Telecommunication may furnish its comments on the enclosed questionnaire within one week." 11 questions were enclosed with that letter. This was received much after 122 LoIs had already been issued on 10 January 2008. Questions regarding the auctioning of spectrum, subscriber-linked criteria for allocation, TEC Report of the Technical Wing of the Telecom Ministry on that allocation, Dual Technology permission, the method of 'first come first served' and the cut-off date decided by the Ministry to issuc licenses were referred in this latest set of questions. The Telecom Department responded to all queries and also referenced auctions held in countries like USA and New Zealand pointing out the license cancellations that followed the auctions as the financial terms proved to be unviable to the telecom providers.

Right from October 2007, when the CVC initiated its enquiry the Telecom Ministry sent suitable explanations and replies whenever asked. Finally, on 12 October 2009, when it was still unable to arrive at a clear decision on the explanations provided by the Telecom Ministry, the CVC sent a letter to the Central Bureau of Investigation (CBI) stating that grave irregularities had been found in the issuance of licenses. Till that day and even while the CVC was sending queries to the ministry, no officer had recorded in any file the opinion that licenses should not be issued or spectrum should not be allocated, nor had anyone advised me as such. Instead, the ministry had only expedited the licensing and spectrum allocation process since they were all confident that their action was legal and legitimate. Of the six 'irregularities' listed in that letter from CVC to CBI, five were related to 2G.

1. It is seen that the entry fee which was decided in the year of 2001 was adopted for the licenses issued to the new entrants in the year 2007 especially when the telecom sector was growing leaps and bounds and becoming highly vibrant. This is duly established by the huge profits reaped by M/s. Swan and M/s. Unitech in off loading their shares.

2. There is no mention of FCFS policy in the guidelines issued by DoT on 11 November 2003.

3. As per the policy of DoT, issued vide press release dated 10 January 2008 under which an application received first was to be processed first thereafter, if found eligible, was granted LoI and then whosoever complied with the conditions of LoI first was to be granted UASL license. However, it is seen from the list of new UASL licenses issued since 2003 that certain applications which were received later were processed first and granted LoI, disregarding the applications which were received earlier

4. (Not related to 2G case)

5. On the one hand TRAI recommended that no cap be placed on the number of accesses service providers in any service area, while on the other hand DoT restricted the number of service providers by issuing press release stating that new application for UASL would not be accepted after 1. October 2007.

6. The absence of lock in period on off loading of stakes enabled them to offload their stakes at a very early stage. The issue which

requires detailed scrutiny was who were the real stakeholders in Swan and Unitech. The possibility of hidden beneficiaries of the vast margins that were created is not ruled out and warrants an open investigation.

Along with that letter signed by Vineet K. Gopal, a Direct Inquiry Report (DIR) was also sent as an annexure. The report mentioned, "A number of complaints received in the Commission regarding FCFS policy in respect of allotment of UASL by the department of Telecom.... A number of questionnaires were sent to Department regarding clarification sought on FCFS policy. As the replies received by the Department were not specific, the Commission decided to conduct a direct enquiry in this case on 17 June 2009." The CVC stated that the reason for initiating the enquiry was due to its receiving several complaints specifically about the first come first served (that is without auction) method. What were the details of these complaints? Who wrote them? Were the complainants knowledgeable about the relevant guidelines? Were they complaining in public interest or to protect some vested commercial interests? The CVC did not raise these questions nor did it forward the complaints to the Telecom Ministry for investigation and clarification. Even in the FIR filed by the CBI on 21 October 2009 as per the directions of the CVC, the column for name of the accused was filled as "unknown officers of the DoT and unknown private persons and companies" and for complainant was filled as just "source" – a meandering CVC inquiry was leading to a vaguely constructed CBI investigation based on an 'orphan' complaint! The FIR filed under provisions of the Indian Penal Code and the Prevention of Corruption Act also stated that ₹ 22,000 crores was the revenue loss to the Government on the basis of the reported capital generated by Swan and Unitech through the shedding of shares.

On 22 October 2009, CBI conducted raids in the Telecom Ministry office in Delhi and in the offices of the Telecom companies that had been newly issued licenses. The press asked me about the raids and I told them, "The decision on issuance of licenses and allotment of spectrum were taken in accordance with NTP-99 and

TRAI recommendations; any administrative irregularities in implementation are found, let the law take its own course." After seeing this interview on TV Sharad Pawar, the Union Minister of Agriculture called me and inquired about the goings on. Immediately, I went to meet Pawar and explained things in person. He advised me to meet the Prime Minister and explain the situation to him also. Accordingly, the same evening I met the Prime Minister in his office in South Block at around 7.00 pm. T.K.A. Nair was also present. People will find it hard to believe that the PM was quite surprised when I told him about the CBI raids. I reminded the PM of my earlier consultations with him, Pranab Mukherjee's note, discussions with the Attorney General, etc. and sought his guidance on how I should respond to the media. After coming out of the PMO, I gave sound bites to NDTV, CNN-IBN and Times Now, "I did everything in accordance with policy and the recommendations of TRAI in consultation with the PM." I also gave a lengthy interview to PTI on 27 October 2009 stating, "I have been saying that the issuance of license and allotment of spectrum have been done in accordance with Telecom Regulator TRAI's recommendations, in consultation with the PM after the clear approval of the Solicitor General of India who was appearing before the Tribunal.... All my predecessors followed the same procedure as did I. There is no deviation in terms of legal rules and procedure. There was an implied stagnation or some sort of cartel. I wanted to bring competition in accordance with TRAI norms, so competition might have created some storm. Let it be investigated. "I remained steadfast in my legally justified stand in the Parliamentary proceedings (Question Hour) and in the interviews given to the press. In parallel, the CAG's team had also been conducting an audit on the 2G licensing and spectrum allocation process. The constitutional charter for the CAG clearly states that it is not meant to play a role in questioning or defining government policy, "The CAG has the mandate to scrutinize transparency in procurement and the way in which things have been done, acting like a watchdog. If a watchdog is not allowed to criticize, then what kind of parliamentary accountability will you ever get? Its reports are based on records and policies of the government placed before it. It is not expected to frame an alternative policy, but we must understand that the CAG can certainly test the present policy and the way it is being implemented. That is certainly within its mandate. It can certainly go into the question [of] whether the government of the day has correctly and in an accountable manner carried out a pure process of execution." However, in the 2G audit CAG Vinod Rai had strong opinions (and perhaps external motivation) against the policies implemented and hence orchestrated the actual investigation, the framing of the report and the media interactions in such a biased manner as to sensationalize the situation and rile up the public – and unfortunately as a consequence even the Supreme Court. When Rai subsequently wrote a book 'Not Just an Accountant – The Diary of the Nation's Conscience Keeper' he focused heavily on the 2G saga. F. Scott Fitzgerald made the brilliant observation, "You don't write because you want to say something, you write because you have something to say." I for one do not believe that Rai had something (of consequence) to say.

On 27 July 2010, the Telecom Ministry responded to the draft report submitted for review by CAG. As the CBI had already taken possession of all the related documents on 22 October 2009, it was not possible for the ministry to provide fully vetted responses with supporting documentary evidence. However, the Telecom Ministry highlighted to CAG, "It may be noted that response of the Department is based on the recollection of the concerned officers dealing with the subject and whatever records available in the department in the absence of the files, which are in the custody of CBI. Since the documents are not available with the Department, the Department reserves the right to modifying the responses after the relevant files / records are received back from the CBI." Between 7 April and 6 October 2010, CAG was sent 5 or 6 correspondences in writing by the Telecom Ministry. Additionally, direct replies were provided on two or three occasions through conferences held between the CAG and DoT. On 20 May 2010 an 'exit conference' was also held between the CAG's team and the DoT officers for discussing the audit findings in the draft report and the minutes were formally signed-off **(Annexure-V).** There are some key highlights worth noting in these minutes:

1. Loss due to non-revision of entry fee from 2001 to 2008: audit team agreed that the word 'loss' needs to be substituted and the views of DoT need to be incorporated in the audit report.

2. Flawed implementation of FCFS: audit team said that the phrase 'flawed' will be substituted.

3. Issue of license to ineligible operators: audit team agreed that in light of the explanations provided they will revisit the observation.

4. DoT suggested and the audit team accepted that another sitting should be held for the audit team to get a better understanding of the different issues involved in the issue of licenses and allotment of spectrum in order to facilitate reconciliation of the position of audit queries and DoT's replies.

The CAG field audit team was clearly in agreement that their draft report needed to be modified in light of DoT's clarifications but still the follow-up meeting that they had promised was never scheduled and Rai chose to ignore these points when releasing his final report. In spite of all the communication and clarifications from the ministry, CAG also eventually went ahead and obtained some documents directly from CBI thus further compromising the Telecom Ministry's ability to respond holistically to all the audit findings/allegations. Even the professional courtesy and expected due process of seeking TRAI's viewpoint was not observed prior to the release of the CAG report.

The CAG published its report on 8 October 2010 and stated under the heading, 'Why did we decide to do an audit on issuance of license and allotment of Spectrum now?', "Issuance of 120 licenses in first one day and at a price discovered in 2001 has drawn the attention of Media, Parliament and informed Members of the civil society.... This department had been receiving innumerable references from Members of Parliament and other sources repeatedly, questioning the allocation process and the price fixed for such allocation. The claim in each such reference is that ineligible applicants seem to have been granted licenses and at a price which appeared far below what has been perceived to be the appropriate market price in 2008." The report was prepared giving conscious and undue weightage to media reports and the letters of the Members of Parliament instead of to the relevant policy documents and official Ministry files. CAG's report towards the end of the second chapter mentions, "We place on record our sincere appreciation for the cooperation of the DoT, Ministry of Finance and CBI in facilitating our audit." I am anguished that those lines have not been taken into consideration by any of the Jurists and the Legal experts who believed that DoT had flouted authority, undermined due process or refused to cooperate. Under Section 8 of the CVC Act, CVC can send its Inquiry Report to the CBI for further investigation. CBI received a reference from the CVC to ascertain whether there was any criminal conspiracy; but who gave sanction to CAG that the CBI meant for investigating the criminal conspiracy in the issuance of license could be allowed to assist them in their audit? Where is the sanctity of articles of responsibility and separation of duties between CVC, CBI and CAG – the 3C's as Rai dubs them in his book? If we take a step back and analyse the charges reported in the charge-sheet of the CBI, violations pointed out by the CVC and the observations of the CAG, Supreme Court and JPC we can see that they have all had their own disjointed perspectives while making their investigations, inquiries, observations, judgments and charges about the 2G Spectrum allocation. 'I got the impression from the first day that the minds were closed and views are determined' (The judiciary I served – Justice Jagmohan Reddy). Either the way in which the Court proceedings were conducted or the apathy and malaise of the Government in the timely furnishing of adequate and appropriate information to Courts became the cause for a case to be filed against me. What is strange is that the order of the Tribunal and the proceedings in the High Court that upheld the decisions taken in the Ministry were not at all considered as related relevant documents at any point of time during the course of their proceedings either by the CVC, CBI, CAG or the Supreme Court. An important point to be noted here is that many of the points on which CAG, CBI and the Supreme Court took the stand that these were in violation of law, had already been duly considered just and correct by both the Tribunal (TDSAT) and the Delhi High Court. On issues where there are different views amongst the constitutional and statutory bodies, framing charge and filing a case without resolving these differences and reaching a decision is clearly improper and at variance with rightful jurisprudence. It can be easily surmised that the documents they submitted to support their claims that corruption and irregularities had occurred, are mostly irrelevant, tangential (read out of context) or based on hearsay (media reports) and that they have attempted to reach conclusions without considering the truly relevant documents (policies and official files). There are also a number of contradictions amongst the findings of these institutions. Let me present my arguments categorized by the alleged violation.

I. ENTRY FEE AND SPECTRUM AUCTION

CAG refers to paragraph 7.39 of TRAI's 2003 recommendations, "The Induction of additional mobile service providers can be considered if there is adequate availability of spectrum.... If Government ensures availability of Spectrum then in the existing licensing regime, they may introduce additional players through multi-stage bidding process as was followed for the 4th operator." Having pointed this out CAG further states, "... This issue was neither deliberated in TRAI in its recommendation (2003) nor at the Telecom Commission nor by GoM on Telecom matters in 2003..." "Even in their report TRAI has recommended for two-stage implementation of the UASL Licensing regime in which first phase was migration of BSOs and CMTs to UASL and the second phase was regarding new UASL licenses. This second phase was to commence only after the receipt of fresh recommendations from TRAI within six months. Therefore, the issue of non revision of entry fee for new licences/operators was not discussed in any forum Telecom Commission, TRAI, GoM or Cabinet." Thus, according to TRAI categorises two different methods of licensing. The first one was implemented immediately. The second one was not implemented as TRAI did not provide its recommendations for the issuance of new licenses. So, CAG made an intellectual leap to conclude that for such licenses entry fee was never fixed by the Cabinet. On 31 August 2010, DoT in its explanation to the CAG clarified "In this regard, it is clarified that while recommending so, TRAI believed that acceptance of its recommendations by Government will take time as it would require the approval of the Cabinet and if during that intermittent period, Government decides to issue more licences, it should continue through multi-stage bidding in the then existing licensing regime of CMTS licences as was followed for 4th cellular operator. Since Government decided to migrate to UASL regime immediately within 4 days of TRAI's recommendation, this recommendation became redundant as no licences were issued between recommendations of TRAI and acceptance of them by the Cabinet." Additionally, TRAI's 2005 recommendation, "The basic objective of Unified Licensing is to ensure the easy entry of the operator into the Indian Telecom sector, and therefore, the intention is never create any barrier in the form of high entry fee but at the same time the level playing field issue among various operators is a very important regulatory aspect.... Keeping all these aspects in mind, authority does not consider it necessary to make changes in the entry fee proposed in its draft recommendation" is conveniently ignored by CAG. On 14 November 2003, the then Chairman of TRAI Pradip Baijal wrote to the Telecom Secretary that the license fee for the revised UASL applied to migrated existing cellular and land-line operators would also be applicable to new licenses **(Annexure-VI)**. But Rai in 2010 asserted that the Chairman's letter was not valid or legally binding because it was a decision taken by the Chairman in his personal capacity without due process. Even if we accept CAG's view for the sake of argument, two questions arise. First, did TRAI ever question this recommendation while 51 licenses were being issued between

2003 and 2007; why is there no reference to this in the TRAI recommendations of 2005, 2007 and 2010? Second, how did this issue never surface between 2003 and 2007 even in the context of CAG's routine yearly audits?

On 26 March 2008 TRAI wrote a reply to the questions raised in a letter by MP Laljan Basha stating categorically that it did not make any recommendation to change the Entry Fee, "Keeping in view objective growth, affordability, penetration of wireless services in semi-urban and rural areas and the principles of level playing field and opportunity of equal competition between the incumbents and new entrants, the authority recommended the same entry fee as was taken from the 4th Cellular Operator for grant of CMTS /UAS license in year 2001.... TRAI has repeatedly held the view that the telecom services and spectrum should not be treated as a source of revenue for the Government." Even after the case filed by the CBI was taken up for hearing by the Trial Court, on 20 August 2011, TRAI wrote a letter to CBI saying that it did not recommend auction methodology or any increase in the entry fee. The CAG having decided that "Audit reiterates that specific value of 2G spectrum could have been discovered only through an efficient market drawn process," had developed illusions of grandeur that he could mandate government policy. The Supreme Court simply endorsed CAG's argument and hence objective jurisprudence fell by the wayside. The erroneous view of the CAG – about the migration for UASL on the basis of NTP-99 and about the recommendations of TRAI on spectrum auction made in 2003 – as also the consequent observations of the Supreme Court Bench were sought to be ratified by the Union Cabinet. Therefore, as recommended and approved by the Union Cabinet, on 12 April 2012, a Presidential Reference was filed before the Supreme Court. The Presidential Reference disapproved the of views held by CAG and the Supreme Court Bench; instead, it accepted entirely the recommendations made by TRAI on 27 August 2007. Rai continued to skirt constructive discussion on the matter and kept wailing about 'spectrum auction'. It would perhaps have been in the public's better interest to investigate Rai's motivation to rush into this 'hunt' while almost blatantly ignoring the decisions and recommendations of TRAI, the Union Cabinet and the Telecom Commission! Even after TRAI's explanations refuted the views expressed in the CAG's report, Rai was not willing to correct his stand. It is ironic that such a person lays claim to the badge of 'Nation's Conscience Keeper'.

CAG in his report has observed (paragraph 3.2.5), "... in regard to the fixation of entry fees for new licensees, prudent principles of governance would have required DoT to engage in further inter-ministerial discussions particularly with the MoF. The fact that this was not done despite repeated advices from MoF does give scope for creation of doubt, on the validity of the decision taken to fix the entry fee for new licenses at 2001 levels." Let's be clear that there was no official correspondence or minister-level contact after the Telecom ministry furnished the documents sought by the Finance Ministry on 12 December 2007. No one had submitted any statement/affidavit referring to any such document evidencing that the Finance Ministry's advice had been ignored or violated at the time when CBI was recording statements. **Why did CAG not write to the Telecom Ministry to get a response, if they had found that the Finance Ministry had taken a contrary stand in their file?** How can a Constitutional authority so evidently rely on just hearsay? CAG also stated in his report (paragraph 4.3.1) that if there are different opinions about a particular issue among more than two Ministers, then the issue must be referred to the Cabinet or a GoM. The Cabinet Secretary is responsible for implementing the Transaction of Business Rules. K.M. Chandrasekhar was the Cabinet Secretary at the time when I sent the files to the Law Minister and also when I wrote to the PM mentioning that the Law Minister's observation was out of context. On 18 October 2012, in his evidence before the Joint Parliamentary Committee, K.M. Chandrasekhar said, "I went through all D.O. letters received from the Telecom Department from June 2006 till December 2009. We went through it with a fine-tooth comb and there is not any reference in any of them about any departure from the Transaction of Business rules or established policy of the Government. "What prompted Rai to insist that the advice of the Law Minister was 'countermanded' and that the matter should have been referred to the GoM even after the Telecom Ministry had adequately explained things to him in detail and when D.S. Mathur, the Telecom Secretary and Chandrasekhar, the Cabinet Secretary had never stated so?

In his book Rai writes, "It may be recalled that in the entire run-up to the issuance of licenses, DoT stood by its viewpoint of not permitting any change in spectrum pricing, which had been arrived at in 2001 for allocation of 2G spectrum in 2008, and blocked attempts by the Prime Minister and the Ministry of Finance to engage in a review of the pricing formula."

Let me also elaborate here on entry fee and the spectrum pricing formula. These were among the recommendations approved on 31 October 2003 by the then union government and presented after a discussion in the Cabinet Committee on Telecom headed by the Finance Minister:

❖ The Department of Telecom and Ministry of Finance would discuss and finalise spectrum pricing formula, which will include incentive for efficient use of spectrum as well as disincentive for sub-optimal usages (paragraph 2.1.2(3))

❖ DoT may be authorised to finalise the details of implementation with the approval of the Minister of Communication and IT in this regard including the calculation of the entry fee depending on the date of payment based on the principle given by TRAI in its recommendations. (paragraph 2.4.6 (ii))

The most important thing here is to understand the difference between '**entry fee**' and '**spectrum charges**' as per the Cabinet decision. As per paragraph 2.2.2(3), spectrum pricing formula must be determined after discussing with the Finance Ministry. According to paragraph 2.4.6(ii), Entry fee must be fixed by the Telecom Ministry in accordance with the recommendations of TRAI. The Finance Ministry had raised comments about revision of the entry fee and I have already explained what happened next as well as the follow-up action that I took to draft an approach paper and convene the Telecom Commission to decide on means to maximize revenue from spectrum charges.

But, Rai cites as the reason for his conclusion the decision taken to remove the subject 'spectrum pricing' from the terms of reference for the Group of Ministers on Telecom sector constituted in February 2006. D.S. Mathur was the one who had drafted that plea and Dayanidhi Maran had written to the Prime Minister accordingly. This is why the PM intervened and removed 'spectrum pricing' from the GoM. Ironically, the same D.S. Mathur had become a witness for the prosecution in the 2G case. When I made the sound and legally valid point that raising entry fee was not in the ambit of the Finance Ministry I was charged with ignoring the advice of the Finance Ministry.

The very same people who had argued that no one outside the Telecom Ministry, including the Finance Ministry can intervene in spectrum pricing, even if the Finance Ministry could logically be thought to have a role in it, became CBI witnesses in the case against me. Yet the CBI did not bother to question the change of heart of such officials as D.S. Mathur and Mrs Manju Madhavan. I came to know that D.S. Mathur had at one point explained to the Public Accounts Committee (PAC), that he was the one who had insisted that Mrs Madhavan should write the note in the file. It was only this note (which I have already elaborated upon) contradicting her own decision from just a day prior that provided the thread to the CAG to spin his yarn claiming that Raja had ignored the Finance Ministry's advice. Unfortunately, neither the Prime Minister nor the Finance Minister came forward to explain this, or to back my legitimate position. It needs to be remembered that even on 11 May 2010, TRAI gave its recommendation that 2G spectrum in 800, 900, and 1800 bands must not be auctioned and also stated, "It must be noted that the decision to award licenses at ₹ 1650 crore is essentially a policy decision. While revenue generation is no doubt significant, NTP-99 underlines the need for providing Telecom services at affordable rates. That the low telecom tariffs in this country have fuelled the rapid growth of telecom services in the country, and have helped different sections of society to access these services, is widely acknowledged." This recommendation of TRAI came after the 3G auction in 2009. Clearly, TRAI had all the facts and experiences at hand to substantiate its recommendation. What other response can I provide for the utterly biased presumption that 2G should have been auctioned like 3G?

Mathur who retired towards the end of December 2007 was the Chairman of the Telecom Commission which on 18 October 2007 approved the recommendations of TRAI. After participating in the Telecom Commission's meeting on that day, he wrote to the CVC that all the actions taken till then were appropriate and valid. Mathur's contribution and the role in deciding the entry fee, determining the cut-off date, adopting FCFS and deciding the seniority of TATA Teleservices to get Dual Technology were not only significant but also valid. Yet buckling under the pressure from CBI, he changed even his justified view regarding observations on decisions taken in the DoT files. One can deny a verbal quote but how can one disavow what he has written in official government records. He also sought to distance himself from the licensing activity, using the hollow argument that he was not in office on 10 January 2008 when the LoIs were issued. The issuance of Letter of Intent and the signing of licenses were the culmination of the policy decisions that had been approved by him. Mathur was a talented official, but he was inconsistent and succumbed to outside pressures. While I recall thankfully his civilized behaviour of expressing regret while talking to me in the court premises after his deposition as a prosecution witness, I must also express my anguish that a senior officer like him would stoop to such levels.

Vinod Rai asserts on page 89 of his book, "It needs to be emphasised that even the 10th Five Year Plan document on spectrum policy mention that 'spectrum pricing' needs to be based on relative demand and supply over space and in time in a dynamic manner (with) opportunity cost to reflect the relative scarcity of the resource in a given situation. Thus, the action of the DoT to take a price discovered in 2001, when the sector was still nascent, and apply in passage of seven years in spite of changes in market conditions and in a face of contrary advice from the PMO, Finance and Law, certainly does not pass any test of transparency." In the 10th plan document, six important principles are put forth as guidelines for framing

Spectrum policy (Box 8.5.7). The first principle advocated is that Spectrum Policy needs to be promotional in nature with revenue considerations being secondary. Spectrum pricing (which as I have already explained is different from entry fee) is only referred in the fourth guideline of that document. The CAG deviously quoted selective fragments from documents and sought to create confusion about the DoT's decision taken on entry fee to be for spectrum charge and derided me. In response to the CAG's audit memo, DoT responded on 3 May 2010 "When the recommendation of 'No Cap' was made by the TRAI, the entry fee for new applicants was not revised which is well within the recommendatory scope and domain of TRAI. In the absence of any such specific and clear recommendation from the Regulators, one cannot expect that the same might be fixed or revised either by the DoT or by the Minister which will be arbitrary. Ignoring the recommendation of TRAI and procedures followed thereon, any suggestions as 'enhanced Revenue' to the Government in this regard by any quarter will be 'hypothetical arithmetic' exercise and not a plausible audit derivation. "Even after the Telecom Ministry pointed out that Spectrum Pricing is not Entry Fee in its detailed explanations to the draft report of the CAG, Rai continued with his prejudicial stance and did not even bother to seek further clarification from the Ministry or from the Planning Commission. Even in the verdict given on 2 February 2012, the Supreme Court Bench of Justices Singhvi and Ganguly observed, "The DoT did not get in touch with the Ministry of Finance to discuss and finalise the spectrum pricing formula ... in terms of Cabinet decision 2003 ... in terms of the decision taken by the Council of Ministers in 2003 to approve recommendations of the GoM, the DoT and Ministry of Finance were required to discuss and finalise the spectrum pricing formula." The stand taken by CVC, CBI, CAG and even the Supreme Court regarding Entry fee and Spectrum Charges were entirely contradictory to the decision of Cabinet - 2003.

Here is another piece of fiction in the CAG report, "This is further corroborated by the fact that the date of the meeting of Telecom Commission which was scheduled to discuss the issue relating to issue of pending applications for license and pricing of spectrum was postponed from 09.01.2008 to 15.01.2008 without Telecom Commission getting an opportunity to discuss the matter, 121 LoIs were issued on 10.01.2008." **This is a blatant lie!** I have already detailed my discussion with the PM and the FM regarding opportunity to enhance government revenue through spectrum charges. I had sent a note to the Telecom Secretary and then Telecom Commission Chairman Siddharth Behura. Having pointed out in my note that the spectrum usage charges were disproportionately low, I had advised him to convene the Telecom Commission to discuss spectrum charges for existing telecom providers, in terms of Adjusted Gross Revenue (AGR). This can be verified even with a cursory reading of the Telecom Commission Memo that was prepared as a consequence of my note to Behura. It is very clear that the official 6-page Telecom Commission Memo dated 9 January 2008 on Spectrum Pricing referred only to the Spectrum usage charges and the License Fee from the existing Telecom Providers **(Annexure-VII)**. Entry Fee and the handling of pending (new) applications were not at all on the agenda. The memo clearly spells out, "The MOCIT had desired that a decision needs to be taken on the spectrum charges. He had directed that the issue of spectrum charges in terms of AGR be placed before the Telecom Commission for in-depth deliberations.... A Committee was constituted by Secretary (DoT) to examine the issue of spectrum valuation/pricing has submitted its report on 07.01.2008. The committee has reportedly taken into account Hon'ble PM's observations regarding the need for maximizing revenue from the Telecom sector without creating entry barriers and compromising on growth." Additionally, on 31 August 2010, in the explanatory note written to the CAG by Telecom Secretary Thomas, it was clearly pointed out, "There was no agenda for consideration of full Telecom Commission on 09-01-2008 relating to issue of pending application for allocation of 2G Spectrum." Prior to that on 27 July 2010 also, in the paragraph-wise response to CAG's queries the DoT had asserted, "There was no agenda for consideration of full Telecom Commission on 09-01-2008 relating to the issue of pending applications for license and pricing spectrum. Therefore, the statement that the date of the meeting of full Telecom Commission which was scheduled to discuss the issue of pending application for license and pricing of spectrum was postponed from 09-01-2008 to 15-01-2008 is not correct." In spite of this background and exhaustive explanations supported by relevant documents and the transparency around the procedural due-diligence, Rai clung to his made-up accusations. I am reminded with the letters of French Sculptor Camille Claudel "I am in no mood to be deceived any longer by the crafty devil and false character whose greatest pleasure is to take advantage of everyone." However, in their judgment of 2 February 2012 Justices Singhvi and Ganguly concluded that "the meeting of the full Telecom Commission which are scheduled to be held on 09.01.2008 to consider issues relating to grant of license and pricing spectrum was deliberately postponed on 07.01.2008 so that the Secretary Finance and Secretaries of three other departments may not be able to raise any objection." That judgment which relied entirely on the CAG report appeared hasty and ill-formed and gave me quite a few sleepless nights as I pondered over our country's judicial system. Justice hurried is justice buried! I recall Justice V. R. Krishna Iyer's words, "That is myopic jurisprudence of exaggeration!" The words of Warren E. Burger one of the famous judges of the US Supreme Court are just as applicable to our nation, "The Court which is final and unreviewable needs more careful scrutiny than any other. Unreviewable power is the most likely to self-indulge itself and the least likely to engage in dispassionate self-analysis.... In a country like ours no public institution or the people who operate it, can be above debate."

Let's consider what happened in the PMO as well. On 31 December 2007, a file was sent containing my letter of 26 December 2007 to the Prime Minister, the note of EAM sent by Pranab Mukherjee (on the decisions taken during his consultations with me and Vahanvati) and the note sent by the Telecom Ministry. The file was recorded by Pulok Chatterjee of the PMO and the three documents were placed before T.K.A. Nair the Principal Secretary to the Prime Minister. After discussion, Pulok Chatterjee records on the file:

"17. With the above norms in view, the following approach could be thought of:

a. fix a 'threshold' level of spectrum that each operator must have in order to function with a minimum level of efficiency.

b. Existing operators holding spectrum above the threshold level may be allowed a certain amount of time to raise their subscriber levels to reach full utilization of spectrum, failing which the excess spectrum may be withdrawn.

c. New operators may be allotted spectrum only upto the threshold level on payment of the normal fees.

d. The balance spectrum may be then auctioned among all those who hold spectrum upto threshold level."

Then the file was sent to T.K.A. Nair on 6 January 2008 who also approved it the next day. As I had pointed out earlier, the PM was briefed in full about the issuance of licenses when I met him during that time. He had endorsed the Ministry's course of action as detailed in my letter. On 10 January 2008, LoIs for the new licenses were issued. In the file dated 15 January 2008, recorded by Pulok Chatterjee all that had transpired was duly documented. Paragraph 23 of that note reads, "It is true that certain numbers of operators have already been issued LOIs/licenses/wireless licenses. A suggestion regarding what could be done vis-à-vis those who have been issued all three is given in paragraph 17(b). Those who have been issued only LoI so far could be considered for allocation of spectrum up to the threshold level once they fulfil all the LoI conditions. After they have fully utilised the threshold amount of spectrum, they will be eligible to bid for additional spectrum in open auction." All these were brought to the notice of the Prime Minister and were shared with the Telecom Secretary Behura through Mrs Vini Mahajan the Joint Secretary in the PMO. Even this has been recorded in that file as, "Informally shared with the Secretary, DoT. We may keep on file..." There is no evidence to suggest that Rai made any attempt to discover this information. He just continued with his usual shallow 'investigation' based on media reports and gossip. In his book Rai writes, "Letters written by A. Raja were examined in the PMO and it was concluded by the Joint

Secretary, Vini Mahajan that there was a perceptible difference of opinion between the Ministry of Communication and Ministry of Law and Justice. According to the Transaction of Business Rules cases in which differences of opinion arises between two or more Ministries and a Cabinet decision is desired, shall be brought before Cabinet ... but the Prime Minister desired that a deeper examination be made of the action proposed by the DoT. This was on 7 November 2007. Was time being gained?" He then deduces a conclusion on behalf of Chatterji, "Pulok Chatterji, the then Addl. Secretary to PMO, went into the issue in greater depth. In a note to the PM on 06 January 2008 he concluded, ideally in a situation where spectrum is scarce, it should be auctioned."

According to Rai, Prime Minister asked for a deeper examination on 7 November 2007, therefore Pulok Chatterji examined it. But the information to be examined by Chatterji was in the context of a letter written by me on 26 December 2007 (a date in the future). So, Rai is alleging that the Prime Minister dreamt (on 7 November) about my letter (to be penned on 26 December) and then asked Chatterji to examine it. Chatterji's note was initiated only on 31 December 2007. In that lengthy 24 paragraph note, he had referred to service providers operating in foreign countries and spectrum used per operator, compared that with the Indian Telecom Sector and clearly highlighted the decisions to be taken. In paragraph 14, we find those lines that Rai latched-on to, "14. Ideally, in a situation where the spectrum is scarce, it should be auctioned. However, uncontrolled auction can lead to inflated bids, unacceptably high prices for consumer and threaten the financial sustainability of the industry." Rai conveniently does not bother with the "however" aspect of Chatterji's analysis, thus blatantly misrepresenting the information. In fact, paragraph 15 of the note continues this thought process, "15. At present there are licensed operators who have excess spectrum while at the same time there are many pending applications awaiting allocation of spectrum. It is not practically possible to cancel the spectrum already allotted to operators." But for Rai only that one sentence from the whole file was of relevance.

Rai moralises on his subsequent meeting with the Prime Minister, "The final report was presented to Parliament on 16 November 2010. That day, coincidentally, marked 150 years of the CAG's existence. We had scheduled a major event at Vigyan Bhavan. The President of India and the PM were to participate. The PM arrived at the function at Vigyan Bhavan. He expressed to me his disagreements regarding our conclusion in the report. I mumbled my usual defence. He was visibly upset. Silence from my side was called for." That was the time when the conclusions of the CAG Report were being examined by the PMO and the Telecom Ministry. I had a suspicion about the motive of the CAG audit and had shared my perspective with both the Prime Minister and Pranab Mukherjee on a few occasions. The Ministry officials had been telling me that CAG was not adopting an objective and well-intentioned approach. They expressed their apprehension that both their written replies and oral explanations were proving in vain. After going through the files on 2G in the PMO, no one can say that either the Prime Minister was misled or that I had ignored his advice. Rai has chosen to remain oblivious to the contents of these critical documents. What does he mean when he says, "I mumbled my usual defence"? It only means 'I am not going to change my mind, no matter what the evidence presented or by whom.' There was no inclination shown by him, to actually listen to the 'other side of the story'. There is a proverb in Tamil, "Even an intelligent man's lie cannot last for more than eight days" (kettikkaran pulugu ettu nalaikku). The proverbial eight days for Rai's lies will surely run out soon enough!

On 12 April 2012 a Presidential Reference was filed before the larger Bench of Supreme Court as against the judgement of Justices Singhvi and Ganguly which had adjudged that natural resources like spectrum should be auctioned. Needless to say this judgement was based on the observations of the CAG report. In the Presidential Reference it was stated "Whereas after introduction of UASL in 2003 and until March 2007, 51 licenses were issued based on policy of First Come First Served on payment of the same entry fee as was paid for the 2001 Cellular Licenses (the "2003-2007 Licenses") and the spectrum was also allocated based on FCFS under a separate wireless operating license on case by case basis and subject to availability. Licensees had to pay annual spectrum usage charges as a percentage of AGR, there being a no upfront charge for allocation of spectrum." The larger Bench of Supreme Court in its verdict observed "Therefore auction, an economic choice of disposal of the natural resources, is not a constitutional mandate (para 146).... But categorically decided as ... Finally, market price, its economics, is an index value that a market prescribes to a good. However, this valuation is a function of several dynamic variables; it is science and not a law. Auction is just one of the several price discovery mechanism.... Since multiple variables are involved in such valuation, auction or any other form of competitive bidding, cannot constitute even an economic mandate much less a constitutional mandate (para 147)." Even after two years, in his book (2014) slings mud at Kapil Sibal, the then Telecom Minister for his official Press Conference held on 7.1.2011 where he quoted the NTP-99 for non-auction of 2G spectrum "The row (in) famous conference, propounding the equally (in) famous "Zero Loss" hypothesis was a precise attempt at doing just this – preclaiming that there was no malfeasance and that the CAG had erred. Save a few committed journalists and fellow travellers – who could be counted on the fingers of one hand – none bought the myth. This is the story that reflects a lack of probity. This is a story of the total bankruptcy of any pretense of morality...." Dr B.R. Ambedkar's warning comes to my memory, "Education is a sword and being a double-edged weapon, it can be dangerous to the wield. An educated Man without character and humility is more dangerous than a beast, if his education is detrimental to the society."

II. Presumptive Loss to Exchequer

Most atrocious was the CAG's determination of ₹ 1.76 lakh crore as **presumptive** revenue loss showing three different categories of losses (computed based on 3G auction prices):

1. New Licenses	1,02,498 crore
2. Dual Technology licenses	37,154 crore
3. Issuance of spectrum beyond 6.2 MHz	36,993 crore
Total	**1,76,645 crore**

CAG's "presumed loss figure" was subsequently ignored in both the charge sheet of the CBI as well as in the charges framed by the trial court. Yet, that figure has become engraved in public memory. Item 1 is a complete flight of CAG's fantasy; it is a direct consequence of the 'auction vs entry fee from 2001' debate which I have already covered. Additionally, it is also important to note that 3G is regarded as a premium service and generally priced 5-10 times that of 2G around the world. Would anybody bid or pay the same price for 2G as they would be willing to for 3G? The failed 2G auction in 2012 certainly proved this point. Item 2 is really just 'new licenses' for operators wanting dual technology, so my argument about faulty formula remains the same. Item 3 shows a loss account of ₹ 36,993 crores for spectrum allocation beyond 6.2 MHz. All of this additional spectrum was for allocation prior to my tenure. I have already highlighted the initiative that I took to record that free (bundled with license) spectrum should not be allocated beyond 6.2 MHz and that for any incremental allocation of additional spectrum usage fees must be levied in consultation with the Finance Ministry. Why is the BJP not being held accountable for this (real and not presumptive) loss figure of ₹ 36,993 crores as it was BJP's Ministers Arun Shourie and Pramod Mahajan who had given away this additional spectrum for free?

CAG arrived at ₹ 1.76 lakh crore based primarily on the auction price for 3G. The CBI in its charge-sheet then ignored this and computed its own figure of ₹ 30,000 crore which could have been earned by the Government for spectrum utilization as a percentage of the Adjusted Gross Revenue (AGR). However, the CBI had erroneously applied that calculation to the 'bundled' 4.4 MHz spectrum that companies had to be given with their new licenses. Even after my arrest on 25 March 2011 an Office Memorandum prepared by the Department of Economic Affairs in the Finance

Ministry, was sent to the PMO. In paragraph 16 it has been stated, "It is therefore, clear that there were consultations between MoF and DoT in the first half of 2008, on the formula of changing 2G spectrum based on indexation to the PLR of the SBI which related only to the allocations beyond 6.2 MHz. In the matter presently under consideration (i.e. allotment of 2G licenses in 2007-08) spectrum allocation were not made beyond 6.2 MHz, on pricing which DoT and MoF were in agreement. On the other hand the new licenses have only got 4.4 MHz of spectrum each." CBI's credibility becomes questionable in the face of this faux pas. On the subject of revenue loss, CBI took one stand in its FIR and an entirely different stand in its charge-sheet. CBI further stated, "The number of licenses issued in 4-5 years during 2003-2007 were minuscule as compared to the number of licenses proposed to be issued in 2008." It is ridiculous that CBI refers as minuscule the count of 51 licenses issued prior to my tenure.

The BJP which was now in the Opposition maintained a 'holier than thou' attitude and did not miss any opportunity to fan the flames of public ire. However, their memory was failing or their judgment was very impaired – really an ironic case of spitting into the oncoming wind. The CAG report given on 28 October 1999 had pointed out a loss (real not presumptive) of ₹ 1,153 crores to the exchequer when the Basic and Cellular Telephone Service Providers were migrated on 22 July 1999 (during the BJP's reign) to NTP-99's revenue regime. The BJP, these very 'guardians of the nation' who deterred this CAG report of 1999 from being submitted to the Public Accounts Committee (PAC) for follow-up, then in 2010 stalled the Parliament for months insisting on a Joint Parliamentary Committee investigation into the sensationalized '2G scam'. The policy decision (used from 2003-2007) to continue with entry fee from 2001 was also made during BJP's regime. BJP was in power at the Centre when Arun Shourie in 2003 first formalized the procedure of issuing Licenses and Spectrum on FCFS basis for new licenses. Why was Arun Shourie not condemned for having violated and changed the rules then? Why only the 122 licenses issued under my ministership and not the 51 before me? Why only in 2010 is A. Raja being blamed for huge losses to the exchequer while all his actions are based on administrative decisions taken up to 2007 and have clear precedents? CPI (M), CPI which ought to have discerned this, let themselves get suckered into joining BJP's ruckus.

Here are a couple of more examples of this hypocrisy and volte-face of political convenience. On 26 October 2009 in relation to CBI's raid on the Telecom Ministry, Arun Jaitley quoted, "Raja should quit; It is now for the Government to say who is guilty" (reported in The Hindu the next day). When reporters asked me for my view on Mr. Jaitley's comment, I said, "Jaitley made some allegation that there is a big scandal. I want to go into the tenure of the NDA and ask if the present assessment, according to Jaitley, is a scandal, then the biggest scandal will be in the NDA Government ... the same Jaitley appeared before the High Court for one of the telecom operators, who got license during this regime and ultimately succeeded.... Now there is an in fight within Arun Jaitley. His legal brain is fighting the political brain" (Pioneer-31 October 2009). Similarly, Murali Manohar Joshi who submitted (on 5 August 2011) the PAC Report insisting on the auctioning of spectrum, had written a letter to the Prime Minister on 2 December 2007, "I would, therefore, request you to protect the interests of our PSU's and the interests of the genuine players. Perhaps this can be achieved by ensuring a level playing field through a licensing policy which earns revenue to the Government, unearth the excess spectrum being used without meeting social obligations, protect the interests of the PSUs, allow new players and permit the allocation under a technology-neutral license." Citing this letter on 3 November 2011, The Mail Today published "Senior BJP leader Murali Manohar Joshi had in the letter to PM aired his disfavour for auction of spectrum." Rai cites another validation for his revenue loss hypothesis: a letter written to the PM in November 2007 by telecom company S.Tel volunteering to pay ₹ 6,000 crore for 6.2 MHz in the 900 MHz band. In the related court case filed by S.Tel, the Government's averments in its Affidavit were, "The petitioner (S.Tel) has offered voluntarily to pay additional revenue share to the extent of ₹ 6000 crore.... However, the petitioner has stated that this amount shall become payable after the allotment of 6.2 MHz spectrum in 900 MHz band for all 22 circles and allowing sharing of active network and infrastructure.... It is respectfully submitted that no spectrum is available in GSM 900 MHz band in the country. Therefore, the offer of the petitioner ... does not appear to have any merit for consideration." Need I say more?

In his book, Rai analysed two of my letters sent to the Prime Minister on 15 and 26 December 2007. From the letter of the 15th he refers to, "I agree that telecom tariffs in the country is one of the lowest in the world; However, these may be seen in conjunction with lower inputs costs and per capita income of the country" and again refers to the letter dated 26th ... "It is needless to say that the tariff in India is not as cheap as claimed in terms of purchasing power parity and standard of living of the people of the country since there is no tariff fixation." As is his nature, Rai picks on select words and pieces them together in support of his slander, "What do we believe? Telecom tariff the 'lowest in the world' or 'tariff' in India is not as cheap? Contradicting statements in successive months!" I do not see the contradiction. The context in which each of the letters was written was entirely different but they reflect the same view. When we compare telephone tariff, India would be among the countries with the lowest tariffs. However, that is in absolute terms. The first letter clearly states that it must be viewed in relative terms against the per capita income of our country. In the second letter of the 26th when I said that tariff in India is not so cheap it takes into account purchasing power and the standard of living. In India, we can employ a driver for around ₹10,000; domestic help can be hired for under ₹5,000. Is this possible in USA and Australia? Where is the contradiction here? Additionally, who is the CAG to adjudge or decree that the telephone tariff cannot be lowered?

Rai makes another childish argument: in the NTP the target fixed for 2010 was 15% of telephone connections; since we achieved this in 2007 itself we should have given priority only to revenue earnings. Here we have Rai attempting to guide Government policy even though that is expressly outside the ambit of the CAG! The purpose of fixing targets is to keep raising the bar and to check complacency. The year 2010 was just an intermediate milestone. After NTP-99, the Government fixed a new target to provide 60 crore of telephone connections by 2012. Oblivious of this, Rai does not move past 2010. On 22 February 2010, the President of India mentioned in his address to the joint sitting of both the Houses, "As against the target of 60 crore telephone connections by 2012, the achievement already exceeds 57 crores with an unprecedented addition of nearly 2 crore connections in the month of December 2009 itself." I need hardly state the obvious fact that the Cabinet is intimately involved in formulating the contents of the President's Address. So, if Rai's contention that the Cabinet was not aware of this is true then I (Raja) must have miraculously managed to get these lines inserted in the President's Address– what an utter gossip!

Another point that the CAG kept harping on was the sale of equity by Swan and Unitech. Once licenses are issued to companies and allocation of spectrum is completed, the shedding of shares by them must occur in conformity with the Foreign Direct Investment (FDI) regulations of the Finance Ministry. The telecom department has nothing to do with FDI. Additionally, I was the one who had issued orders to institute a 'lock-in period' so that companies would not abuse the FDI regulation to sell-off Telecom licenses. On 4 November 2008, when the Finance Minister and I met the Prime Minister he asked us about the Swan, Unitech situation. Chidambaram clarified that only the shedding of shares had taken place in order to attract foreign investments under the ambit of the FDI policy, CCEA and FIPB. "Without understanding this, journalists come out with false news giving incorrect information. So, meet the press to explain this" was the advice of the PM. I convened the Telecom Commission on 5 November 2008, with the following note, "Since some misleading articles ... are written in the media about the issuance of new licenses and spectrum allocation more specifically in case of M/s. SWAN TELECOM and M/s. UNITECH TELECOM as these companies allegedly got unlawful enrichment, the matter was discussed with Hon'ble Prime Minister and Hon'ble Finance Minister.... In the meeting Hon'ble Finance Minister clarified that dilution of shares to attract foreign investment for business expansion did not amount to sale of license and as such these companies did their share dilution as per the corporate laws.... Nevertheless, I suggest that in order to remove suspicious clouds in the minds of media and people, Telecom Commission may deliberate this issue to restrict outright sale of licenses and selling of stakes by promoters to 2nd party for money." The meeting established that Swan and Unitech had not privately sold-off their shares and also imposed a lock-in period of 5 years. I then met the press on 7 November 2008 and explained this to them. An official press note was also issued on that day a copy of which was sent to the Prime Minister by me. In it I had pointed out that under the National Telecom Policy (NTP-99), revenue regime was ushered in and the Government was getting revenue through three different categories: Entry Fee, License Fee and Spectrum Usage Charge. Due to inadequate technical and legal understanding about Entry Fee, License Fee and Spectrum Charge the CAG and then even the Supreme Court had started an unnecessary witch-hunt. The Government earned a revenue of more than ₹ 60,000 crore on the basis of the policy till 2006-2007. Thereafter in 2007 and 2008 alone ₹ 12,000 crore were earned by the Government from license fees on the basis of new licenses issued. I also added that going forward the recurring revenue to the Government would increase according to the increase in the number of subscribers. The TRAI recommendation of 2005 calls it a win-win situation for both the Government and the telecom companies while also furthering social progress. In spite of these clarifications that my decisions and approvals recorded in the files were entirely based on the policy, and were legally valid and appropriate I had to face the charge of abuse of power. When it comes to Government policy, a profit and loss account is not maintained. Public Distribution System (PDS) was introduced to ensure a 'hunger free' India and not to improve the Government's balance sheet. Establishing schools is for enriching the human mind and not for immediate economic gains.

III. ELIGIBILITY OF APPLICANTS

The next arrow from Rai's bow was that ineligible companies were issued licenses and enabled to get spectrum. His report quotes,

"Process followed by the DoT for verification of application for UAS licences for confirming their eligibility lacked due diligence, fairness and transparency leading to grant of licences to applicants who were not eligible. Eighty five out of the 122 licenses issued in 2008 were found to be issued to Companies which did not satisfy the basic eligibility conditions set by the DoT and had suppressed facts, disclosed incomplete information and submitted fictitious documents for getting UAS licenses and thereby access to spectrum (para 4.7.1)." It was alleged that Swan Telecom was ineligible because of the cross-holding restriction in clause 8 of the UASL Guidelines. Unitech Group was deemed ineligible because the objects clause of their Memorandum of Association had not been amended. It is not necessary for me to deal with the merits of this allegation at all, except to clarify that the Law Ministry and the Ministry of Corporate Affairs had taken the position that there was no violation of the eligibility criteria. At the field and implementation level, I had never interfered with the examination by any relevant party of any file of any licensee to determine their eligibility. The examination was conducted by a Committee of DoT officers constituted by the Sectory (T). I approved the decision of the officers – whether it was to grant LOI or reject the application – in each and every case. **There isn't a single case where I even attempted to change their decision**. In fact, after the draft CAG report raised some questions on eligibility of companies, I referred the matter to the Legal Advisor (T), who gave a detailed note on the eligibility of the companies on 11 November 2010 with approval of the Law Ministry. No officer took the view that any eligibility norms had been compromised. Although it was not my responsibility to evaluate the eligibility of companies, I need to state certain facts in this regard. The accusation made by both the CAG and the CVC was that some companies which had applied for licenses were ineligible on the date of application and that it was an irregularity on my part to have issued them the licenses. On 7 January 2008, Nitin Jain, Director (AS-I) noted in the policy file, "It is once again mentioned that as per the existing methodology, the eligibility of the applicant company has been considered till the last correspondence received from Licensee Company before issue of LOI for signing the license agreement. In some cases, the applicant company has also been permitted additional time to fulfil the requirement of LOI conditions ... in past the eligibility of applicant has been considered even after the date of application also. This is being brought to the notice for kind consideration whether in the present case for processing the application received up to 25.9.2007, the eligibility on the date of application shall be taken into account, or it may be subsequent date also." This file was reviewed by Srivastava (DDG-AS-I) who observed, "Probably this has already been considered by the Hon'ble MOCIT while taking a decision that eligibility on the date of application is to be considered for examining the cases. Therefore, we may check eligibility on the date of application for grant of LOIs and subsequent eligibility may not be considered." This clearly debunks the cooked-up charge that I was involved in a 'conspiracy' with companies that were ineligible on the date of application. If that was true, then (as pointed out by Nitin Jain) would it not have been better for me to have continued with the previous practice of taking the 'date of issuing LoI' to determine eligibility instead of taking the 'date of application' to ensure eligibility. That alone would have been the safer approach for me, why would I deviate from the earlier practice and 'dig my own grave'? During the tenure of my predecessors, eligibility requirement was not enforced on the date of application even though this was against the established rules. It was I who had pointed out that this earlier precedent was incorrect.

The CAG also flags that these companies did not possess 'previous experience' and were hence not qualified for wireless licenses. Clause 8 of UASL guidelines states, "No single company / legal person, either directly or through its associates shall have substantial equity holding in more than one Licensee company in the same service area for access service. 'Substantial equity' here in will mean 'an equity of 10% or more'." Clause 1 states, "The applicant must be an Indian Company, registered under the Indian Companies Act 1956." Hence, existing telecom companies (like Airtel, Aircel,

Idea) operating with 'previous experience' cannot have more than 10% share in new companies applying for license and these new companies must be Indian companies. So, if previous experience is mandated then only the existing players can continue and their monopoly would grow. It was therefore that in 2005 the 'previous experience' criterion was dropped from the policy. It is not present in either the UASL guidelines or in the TRAI recommendations. Additionally, this is why the companies in question were partnering with experienced international telecom players like Etisalat or Telenor and this is precisely why the mandatory FDI clause had been introduced in the National Telecom Policy.

The CAG in his report raised eligibility concerns about Unitech, Allianz, Loop, Datacom, Swan whereas, the CBI maintained that only Unitech and Swan were ineligible. When complaints about the eligibility of Swan Telecom came to our department, I referred the matter to the Solicitor General Vahanvati for his legal opinion. Vahanvati sent his clarification on 24 March 2009 to the DoT, "The file shows that there has been a full consideration of all materials and conclusion that the applicant fulfilled all the necessary condition cannot really be faulted." The Law Ministry maintained that eligibility existed whereas the CAG claimed otherwise and the CBI filed a case based merely on that opinion. When the CBI arrested me in this case and even when the charge-sheet was filed, no official had given any statement to the CBI nor did any of the files have on record either stating that Swan or Unitech were ineligible or that I had conspired to force their eligibility. The CBI which deposed before the court that they had not based their investigation on the CAG report, concluded 'suo moto' that those companies were not eligible without providing any explanation for how they arrived at that conclusion. In spite of these contradictions, the Supreme Court concluded, "All the applicants including those who were not eligible for UASL license collected their LOIs on 10.1.2008"and cancelled the licenses. When such an august body as the Supreme Court was swayed by this 'smoke and mirrors' then how could the common man not be affected? Justice V.R. Krishna Iyer defines "The Institution of justice has a commanding height matchless, not because it has the power of the purse or the sword but because of the aura of divinity associated with the allegiance the people owe to that supreme value we mundanely call Justice."

IV. CUT-OFF DATE

I have already elaborated on the sequence of events related to cut-off date in the preceding chapter and clarified in detail the rationale for the introduction of cut-off date and the corresponding procedural due-diligence. I had not rigged or forced the cut-off date, nor had I unilaterally passed the verdict that the Law Minister's (personal) comments were 'out-of-context'. This had come about as a collective departmental decision within the ministry which can be easily verified from the files in question. The cut-off date (25th September 2007) was first proposed by the Director (AS) Nitin Jain on 24 October 2007 in the file (for statement of case to Law Ministry) which was signed by the DDG (AS) Srivastava and Member (Tech) Sridhara and later signed by the Secretary (T) on 7 November 2007 in the policy file. On 12 November 2007 also, in all individual company files processed for issuance of Letter of Intent, Srivastava DDG-AS recorded, "as per discussions with Secretary (T) and Hon'ble MOCIT, LOIs are to be issued simultaneously... applications up to 25 September 2007" which was also signed by the Secretary (T). By this note two things are clear that 'decision on the cut-off date' and the 'simultaneous issuance of LoI' was arrived only after the discussions in the Department. This was again reiterated on 3 May 2010 to the CAG by the DoT as "this decision was not taken single handedly but after due process of consultations and incompliance of existing policy and recommendations of TRAI with legal opinion."

Mathur recorded an observation in a note sent to the PMO from the Telecom Department on the issue of cut-off date. When that document from the PMO was submitted before the court, he could not deny any longer his involvement in this matter although when he had deposed before CBI he did not recall this and testified that he was in no way connected with the fixing of cut-off date. In the PMO Note

(PMO/25.10.2007/969566/OD) it has been recorded that, "The DoT has received more than 570 applications for new licenses in various circles. The MCIT was advised that the applications for new licenses should be taken up seriation according to the chronology in which they were received and the number of fresh licenses in any circle should be determined according to availability of spectrum. The Telecom Commission had detailed discussions with the MCIT on the issue. The MCIT was of the opinion that all applications for new licenses should be issued LoI and therefore, all those who deposit the license fee should be issued licenses. They shall also be eligible for spectrum. Since the spectrum is very limited even in the next several years all these licenses would never be able to get the spectrum. This would also be contrary to the Telecom Policy that had been specifically stated that new licenses would be given subject to availability of spectrum." This was sent with a noting 'please speak with me' by the PM's Principal Private Secretary to the Joint Secretary (Telecom) Vinni Mahajan in the PMO. This note clearly indicates that I was not in favour of any cut-off date. It was D.S. Mathur, Secretary (T) who had insisted on the cut-off date concept based on the availability of spectrum. It was one of the most ugly turn of events that even during the course of witness interrogation Mathur gave a statement under section 161 Cr.PC to the CBI on 16 December 2010, "on being asked the reason for recording the provision for NTP-99 in my note dated 25 October 2007 I state that Minister had expressed his desire verbally to grant licenses to all 575 applicants." In spite of these statements I was charged by the Supreme Court and CAG, for rigging the cut-off date. Galileo, the famous Italian Polymath said "all truths are easy to understand ones they are discovered; the point is to discover them."

Among the statutory and the constitutional institutions involved in 2G issues, some failed to understand, and some failed to discover the facts. The most atrocious is Rai who did not want to understand even the truth that was discovered by him!. Even three years later, when CAG started its audit, DoT responded on 27 July 2010. "In the absence of a possibility of issuing licence and spectrum to all the applicants, the issue of number of applicants to be granted LOI in the first phase was deliberated and it was most appropriate to grant LOI to the applicants, who had applied upto 25 September 2007, the date on which press release dated 24 September 2007 appeared in the newspapers as it is the only date which divides all the applicants into two homogeneous groups. Any other date for the grant of LOI in the first phase would have been arbitrary."

Further on 6 October 2010 Srivastava of his own volition wrote a letter to the CAG around the time of their audit, "The then Secretary, DoT observed on 25 October 2007 in the file that opinion of Solicitor General may be obtained as per the draft approved by MCIT. However, the attention of MCIT may be drawn to NTP-99, paragraph 3.1.1 (which inter alia states that availability of adequate frequency spectrum is essential not only for providing additional bandwidth to every operator but also for entry of additional operators.) The policy has stipulated that availability of adequate frequency spectrum is essential for entry of additional operators. Hence, the options to issue LOIs / licenses to all 575 applicants do not stand in the light of this provision. NTP-99 was approved by the Union Cabinet and only the Cabinet can effect a change in the Policy. Therefore, the existing policy of grant of UAS licenses on FCFS basis was to be followed keeping in view the likely availability of spectrum. Accordingly, an internal exercise was done by WPC wing of DoT on likely availability of spectrum. After taking into consideration the likely availability, it was decided that LOIs may be issued to all those applicants who applied up to 25.09.2007. Accordingly, 232 applications received up to and including 25.09.2007 were taken up for consideration. The remaining 343 applications received between 26.09.2007 and the cut off date of receiving applications i.e. 01.10.2007 are still pending consideration by the department and have not been processed till date."

Vinod Rai however, did not care to comprehend these facts and jumped to the conclusion, "Ignoring the advice of law ministry and the Hon'ble PM, MOCIT therefore decided to go ahead with arbitrarily deciding that the cut-off date for issue of LOI would be advanced to 25/9/2007." The Supreme Court bench of Justices Singhvi and Ganguly who did not seek to verify Rai's allegations, adjudged, "While approving the note, the Minister of C&IT on his own recorded the following – 'LoIs may be issued to the applicants received upto 25 September 2007'.... The Minister C&IT introduced cut-off date as 25.9.2007 for consideration of applications received for grant of license (vi)." M/s Sistema had applied last on 25 September 2007, but was left out while M/s Unitech who had applied on a prior date was included. The case against me alleges that it was my 'criminal conspiracy' to determine a date to ensure benefit to Unitech. CBI then claimed that there was no 'criminal conspiracy' on behalf of M/s Sistema thus highlighting once again the shameful contradictions in this investigation. Why is it that one must believe in illegality in the Unitech context but not in the context of Sistema? Voltaire quoted during the French Revolution, "Prejudice is opinion without judgment!" In the same century, the famous Irish playwright Kene O'Hara stated, "When the judgment is weak the prejudice is strong." Article 142 was hijacked by Article 149 - almost as if the rise in serial number raised its intrinsic value!

Another tragi-comical observations made by CAG is leakage of information to select applicants. It is quite evident from the news reports around that time that popular newspapers were publishing all the details of the decisions and actions related to the issuance of LoI's as early as in November 2007 and yet CAG in his Report depicted as if all those proceedings were kept a secret, "... leaking the information about date of issuing LOIs to select applicants, thereby enabling them to keep Demand Draft.... Even this date seems to have been known to a select thirteen applicants in advance of the issuance of press release ... certain applicants appeared with demand draft of thousands crore of rupees having been issued even before the date of press release." PTI in its News Report on 13 November 2007 made it very clear saying, "The Government is also considering making 25 September, the date on which it had announced October 1 as the deadline for filling application for new licences, as the cut off date for issuing LOIs in the first phase.... The procedure for remaining applicants would be decided at a later date, if any spectrum was left after processing the applications received upto 25 September...." After that on 13 December 2007, PTI in a News Report said, "The Government may start issuing from next week letters of intend to 22 companies, which had applied for telecom licenses as of 25 September, as most of them have submitted necessary clarification today." When the date of issuance of LoIs has been publicly broadcast in newspapers and upon knowing that their applications have been accepted, is it not natural that the applicants would have arranged for the entry fee demand drafts in advance? Can anyone arrange such a huge sum (1650 crores) overnight? Even in the Telecom Department's response of 27 August 2010 to the CAG draft report it was made very clear that, "All the eligible applicants who applied till 25 September 2007 knew that their applications were being processed by the Department for grant of license as clarifications on their applications were sought by the Department on 10 December 2007. This could perhaps be the reason that all these applicants were keeping necessary papers and Demand Draft ready for depositing in the Department as soon as they were granted LOIs." On 3 May 2010 itself the DoT in its reply to CAG audit provided a tabular column of news papers report on the cut-off date **(Annexure-VIII)**. Yet, Rai behaved like a cat that shuts its eyes and then declares the universe is dark!

V. First Come First Served and Simultaneous Processing

Another much-emphasized accusation against me was that I wilfully twisted the 'First Come First Served' process to favour some corporations. Let us understand the genesis of the FCFS method and its implementation in this situation. FCFS in the allotment of spectrum was not in place either as a statute or as 'Prescribed Rules' as defined for example in the Mining Acts. The issuance of licenses and the allotment of spectrum are made under the aegis of two separate Acts: licenses under Indian Telegraphy Act-1985; spectrum under Indian Wireless Telegraphy Act-1993. Although Telecom services are offered via three different kinds of technologies GSM, CDMA, and landline services, when it comes to licensing, all three services are governed since 2003 under one umbrella viz., integrated UASL. For the issuance of license and allocation of spectrum, FCFS is applicable. This policy of FCFS was incorporated only in 2001 when the BTS Guidelines were framed. Section 26 of the guidelines read, "For wireless access system in local area, not more than 5.5 MHz in 824-844 MHz paired with 869-889 MHz band shall be allocated to any Basic Service Operator including the existing ones on First Come First Served basis." This guideline for spectrum allocation had the roll-out obligation as a pre-requisite. When UASL was introduced in 2003, the question 'how to issue licenses' was raised. On 21 November 2003, the Director of Licenses branch officially noted, "It is also presumed that such new licenses in the category of UASL would be on a First Come First Served basis on the basis of the application." Another Director (LF) noted, "As regard the point raised about grant of new licenses on FCFS basis, the announced guidelines have made it open for new licenses to be issued on continuous basis at any time. However, the spectrum is to be allocated subject to availability. This in effect would imply that an applicant who comes first will be granted spectrum first so it will result in grant of licenses on First Come First Served basis." The then Telecom Minister Mr. Arun Shourie gave his approval on this file on 24 November 2003. Thereafter the FCFS method was officially adopted: applications for license were to be processed on FCFS basis; after receiving the license, licensees were required to submit separate applications to Wireless Planning Section specifying the kind of spectrum they desired; those applications for spectrum allocation were also to be processed on FCFS basis. A Licensee could even opt for land line service without asking for spectrum whereas those who wanted spectrum could choose between GSM or CDMA technology. In the matter of spectrum allotment, only the date of application for spectrum to WPC would decide the priority and not the earlier priority ascertained as per the date of application for license. This was the method used for issuing 51 licenses during 2003 – 2007.

In the context of dealing with 575 applications received all at once another key decision that the ministry had to take was to process applications simultaneously instead of sequentially. In the file that included the detailed brief sent to the Law Ministry, the Director Licenses Issuing Branch Nitin Jain noted, "The procedure followed hereto for grant of LOIs/licenses in respect of pending UASL applications has been to process them Sequentially in the order of receipt (Date wise) and taking up the next applicant after the earliest applicant has been given LOI.... In the present scenario, the number of applications is very large and therefore such sequential processing will lead to inordinate delays depriving the General Public of the benefits which more competition will bring." This clearly illustrates that in addition to adopting FCFS the decision was to not process each application serially by first issuing the LoI, then waiting for the applicant to fulfil the required conditions, then issuing the License and only then proceeding to the next application. This was the unanimous stand of the officers of the Telecom Ministry and there was no contrary view among the officials from 24 October 2007, the day when the above proposal was initiated till 10 January 2008, the day when LoI's were issued. I believed then as I do even now that this decision was fair and justified.

When the officers discussed this with me and recorded their observations in the files, they ascribed two reasons for advocating this approach. First was that any applicant might ask for an extension of time to fulfil all the conditions (including depositing of the entry fee) in the LOIs. Such extensions of fifteen days each had been granted by the ministry in the past – even though there was no documented legal provision for it. If extensions are requested by and granted to a majority of applicants, then loss of transparency would ensue. After obtaining the LOIs and getting extension of time for fulfilment of conditions, the LoI itself may be used by the applicant for trading with other companies to make a profit. Thus, the processing priority of an applicant might itself become a (dubious) tradable commodity. The second reason was related to the fact that there were only a small number of existing telecom operators who had acquired their license under the (old) sequential process who had developed a certain degree of joint commercial understanding amongst each other. Therefore, there were no objections in earlier situations when extensions had been provided to an operator. But when so many new applications from telecom providers were processed all at once, if multiple applicants started asking for extensions the consequent cascade of delays could be further compounded if applicants lower in the queue filed formal complaints about the adverse effect on their rights and business interests.

Another query surfaced: whether an application could be kept in abeyance even after having fulfilled the pre-conditions just because another applicant higher in the seniority list had not yet fulfilled their pre-conditions. There is no documented procedure for this even in the UASL guidelines. Had such a situation not been faced earlier? CVC responded to that question in its letter to CBI on 12 October 2007, "However, it is seen from the list of new UAS licenses issued since 2003 that certain applications received later were processed first and granted LOI, disregarding the applications which were received earlier." CVC also listed out similar precedents. Even after CBI had filed the case against me, the Telecom Department in its clarification to JPC on 24 May 2011 stated, "On two applications of different date in UP (West) Service area, LOIs were issued simultaneously but the UAS license was signed with the later applicant as detailed below." Yet the CAG in his report insists that, "It was first time in the History of the DoT that the date of compliance of LoI was considered as criteria for the issuance of UAS License." As pointed out earlier, when I met Pranab Mukherjee and Vahanvati (Solicitor General), to discuss about the issuance of new licenses, the SG provided his legal advice in writing, "Thus Government is obliged to scrutinise the pending applications and if the applicants are found eligible to issue licenses on a FCFS basis. Once an applicant becomes licensee after complying with the condition, the applicant then becomes eligible for spectrum as per the WPC guidelines." Let me also point out that while everyone has been harping on the flaws in relation to simultaneous issuance of licenses instead of sequential (one after the other) issuance during my tenure, such concurrent processing had occurred even when 51 licenses were issued prior to 2007. Here is a tabulation of the 51 licenses along with details of service area, operator (applicant) and related dates:

S.No	Service Area	Operator	Date of Application	Date of Issue of LoI	Date of Compliance of LoI	Date of Signing of Licence
49	Andhra Pradesh	Aircel	03.03.06	20.11.06	04.12.06	05.12.06
20	Assam	Dishnet Wireless	05.03.04	06.04.04	20.04.04	12.05.04
28	Assam	Bharti Airtel	15.04.04	24.06.04	13.09.04	17.09.04
32	Assam	Vodafone Essar Spacetel	14.12.04	20.11.06	22.11.06	05.12.06
1	Bihar	Tata Teleservices	12.11.03	24.11.03	30.01.04	30.01.04
9	Bihar	Bharti Airtel	17.11.03	24.11.03	10.02.04	10.04.04
21	Bihar	Dishnet Wireless	05.03.04	06.04.04	20.04.04	12.05.04
33	Bihar	Vodafone Essar Spacetel	14.12.04	20.11.06	22.11.06	05.12.06
48	Bihar	Aditya Birla Telecom	25.01.06	21.11.06	30.11.06	06.12.06
50	Delhi	Aircel	03.03.06	20.11.06	04.12.06	05.12.06
51	Gujarat	Aircel	03.03.06	20.11.06	04.12.06	05.12.06
15	Haryana	Tata Teleservices	29.11.03	17.12.03	30.01.04	30.01.04
39	Haryana	Dishnet Wireless	01.03.05	29.11.06	11.12.06	18.12.06
2	Himachal Pradesh	Tata Teleservices	12.11.03	24.11.03	30.01.04	30.01.04
22	Himachal Pradesh	Dishnet Wireless	05.03.04	06.04.04	20.04.04	12.05.04
34	Himachal Pradesh	Vodafone Essar Spacetel	14.12.04	20.11.06	22.11.06	05.12.06
10	Jammu & Kashmir	Bharti Airtel	17.11.03	24.11.03	10.02.04	10.02.04
23	Jammu & Kashmir	Dishnet Wireless	05.03.04	06.04.04	20.04.04	12.05.04
31	Jammu & Kashmir	Reliance Infocomm	24.06.04	23.08.04	02.09.04	21.09.04
35	Jammu & Kashmir	Vodafone Essar Spacetel	14.12.04	20.11.06	22.11.06	05.12.06
44	Karnataka	Aircel	12.01.06	20.11.06	04.12.06	05.12.06
16	Kerala	Tata Teleservices	29.11.03	17.12.03	30.01.04	30.01.04
40	Kerala	Dishnet Wireless	01.03.05	29.11.06	11.12.06	18.12.06
8	Kolkata	Tata Teleservices	14.11.03	24.11.03	30.01.04	30.01.04
41	Kolkata	Dishnet Wireless	01.03.05	29.11.06	11.12.06	18.12.06
7	Madhya Pradesh	Tata Teleservices	12.11.03	24.11.03	30.01.04	30.04.04
27	Madhya Pradesh	Dishnet Wireless	05.03.04	29.11.06	11.12.06	18.12.06
38	Madhya Pradesh	Vodafone Essar South	14.12.04	05.03.07	19.03.07	19.12.07
45	Maharashtra	Aircel	12.01.06	20.11.06	04.12.06	05.12.06
43	Mumbai	Idea Cellular	26.08.05	20.11.06	30.11.06	06.12.06
47	Mumbai	Aircel	12.01.06	21.11.06	04.12.06	08.12.06
24	North East	Dishnet Wireless	05.03.04	06.04.04	20.04.04	12.05.04
36	North East	Vodafone Essar Spacetel	14.12.04	20.11.06	22.11.06	05-12.06

3	Orissa	Tata Teleservices	12.11.03	24.11.03	30.01.04	30.01.04
11	Orissa	Bharti Airtel	17.11.03	24.11.03	10.02.04	10.02.04
25	Orissa	Dishnet Wireless	05.03.04	06.04.04	20.04.04	12.05.04
37	Orissa	Vodafone Essar Spacetel	14.12.04	20.11.06	22.11.06	05.12.06
17	Punjab	Tata Teleservices	29.11.03	17.12.03	30.01.04	30.01.04
42	Punjab	Dishnet Wireless	01.03.05	29.11.06	11.12.06	18.12.06
4	Rajasthan	Tata Teleservices	12.11.03	24.11.03	30.01.04	30.01.04
46	Rajasthan	Aircel	12.01.06	20.11.06	04.12.06	05.12.06
5	Uttar Pradesh (East)	Tata Teleservices	12.11.03	24.11.03	30.01.04	30.01.04
12	Uttar Pradesh (East)	Bharti Airtel	17.11.03	24.11.03	10.02.04	10.02.04
29	Uttar Pradesh (East)	Dishnet Wireless	21.04.04	29.11.06	11.12.06	18.12.06
14	Uttar Pradesh (West)	Vodafone Essar South	28.11.03	17.12.03	13.02.04	13.02.04
18	Uttar Pradesh (West)	Tata Teleservices	29.11.03	17.12.03	30.01.04	30.01.04
30	Uttar Pradesh (West)	Dishnet Wireless	21.04.04	29.11.06	11.12.06	18.12.06
6	West Bengal Tata	Teleservices	12.11.03	26.12.03	30.01.04	30.01.04
13	West Bengal	Bharti Airtel	17.11.03	26.12.03	11.02.04	11.02.04
19	West Bengal	Vodafone Essar South	13.02.04	09.03.04	09.03.04	23.03.04
26	West Bengal	Dishnet Wireless	05.03.04	06.04.04	20.04.04	12.05.04

As can be clearly seen there are 5 service areas (highlighted above) in which licenses were simultaneously issued to multiple service providers on the same date. Why were my predecessors in the Telecom Ministry not questioned about this? Why such hue and cry over simultaneous processing during my tenure?

There was also the topic (discussed in detail earlier) of the unauthorized insertion in the press note of January 2008 by Behura of a new stipulation that had never been reviewed in the Ministry or the GoM and which I had stricken-off. Rai described this as "DoT proposed" and then alleged that "DoT's own FCFS policy was not followed." On 27 July 2010 DoT responded to the CAG for its audit memo "since the draft press release was contrary to the policy of the Department of FCFS and the communication to the Hon'ble PM, it was changed by the Hon'ble MoCIT. Therefore, it is not correct to conclude the Hon'ble MoCIT deviated from the declared FCFS." In spite of the explanation Rai quotes, "The frequent changes in FCFS criteria, simultaneous issue of LOIs to all applicants on the same day and large number of applicants complying with detailed requirements of LOI (for which 15 days are allowed as per procedure) within hours: all reflect a deliberate and unhealthy haste on par of the DoT in going ahead with the issue of licences which tended to favour applicants who could proactively anticipate such procedural changes well in time. This unusual haste, in spite of repeated concerns expressed by different agencies and by the senior officers within the Ministry raises doubts regarding the intention of the Hon'ble MOCIT in going ahead with issue of licences in an arbitrary manner without letting the matter be debated or discussed and considered at appropriate levels" What is the basis of these falsehoods? I have already elaborated on the actions and notings in relevant files/documents by concerned officers. A Minister is neither a subordinate to the officers; nor their regal master. All members of the ministry are expected to discharge their duties as per the prescribed rules and in adherence to administrative precedents. A Minister as the head of the ministry has the right to correct the views of officers in case they deviate from this. Similarly, officials are also expected to record in the files or bring to the notice of the Cabinet Secretary in case the Minister is in error. I have clearly demonstrated that this was never the case and yet CAG kept foisting the blame solely upon my shoulders. I must now discuss the statement given by Vahanvati to the CBI that the correction in the press note was not present when the file was sent to him based on which charges were framed against me under IPC 468 and 471 for forging and tampering records. Vahanvati is no more and I have moved past my initial anguish and anger to a feeling of pity for him now. I can only quote Edmund Burke's words in this context, "No passion so effectually robs the mind of all its powers of acting and reasoning as fear." Even a dead man is vested with three rights under the Anglo-Saxon legal system: 1) Right to execute the will; 2) Right to a decent burial; 3) Right to uphold one's reputation. I would like to examine, late Vahanvati's stand keeping in mind this third right mentioned above. In his statement to CBI Vahanvati had said that no meeting took place between us and Pranab Mukherjee, the Chairman GoM which I had also referenced in my letter to the PM. The CBI's charge-sheet of 2 April 2011 says that no meeting took place between Pranab Mukherjee, Vahanvati and me; whereas on 25 March 2011, on behalf of Pranab Mukherjee his Personal Secretary Manoj Pant wrote a letter to D.R. Mohanty, Deputy Secretary, Lok Sabha Secretariat (in the PAC proceedings) stating that "In November, Hon'ble PM had asked Shri Pranab Mukherjee, the External Affairs Minister to apprise himself of the issues raised by the COAI and some GSM operators challenging the criteria for allocation of addl. GSM spectrum with Shri A. Raja the then MOCIT and Shri G.E. Vahanvati, the then SG in the context of proceedings pending in the TDSAT. In this context, Shri Pranab Mukherjee held a meeting with MOCIT and the SG in the first week of December 2007." Mukherjee had officially documented the decisions taken in that meeting and sent a copy to the Prime Minister on 26 December 2007 itself.

When Vahanvati gave testimony contrary to my statements then wasn't it the CBI's responsibility to verify this with Mukherjee as well? CBI relied only on the statement of Vahanvati and mentioned in the charge-sheet that no such meeting had taken place and alleged that my letter to the PM was written in order to mislead him. Now, the question is whether the sentence I had struck off, "However, if more than one applicant complies with LOI conditions on the same date, the inter se seniority would be decided by the date of application" was found anywhere in the file, in my letter to the PM or in the note Vahanvati himself had given to Pranab Mukherjee. Is it not true that there was no such reference? Since I had written the corresponding observation in the file using a different pen, CBI made a mountain out of this molehill and alleged 'forgery' and sent the document to the forensic lab! Vahanvati who was representing the Telecom Department in the case, quoted in his affidavit while filing the counter on behalf of the Government, "Accordingly a press release was issued in this respect on 10 January 2008. In the Press Release it was also informed that 'DoT has been implementing a policy of First-Come-First Served for grant of UAS licenses under which initially an application which is received first will be processed first and thereafter if found eligible will be granted LOI and then whosoever complies with the conditions of LOI first will be granted UAS license.' The press release dated 10 January 2008 was to only clarify the continuous stand of DoT regarding the award of UAS Licenses and no new policy of first come first served basis was formed which was actually continuing since November 2003." It is simply unbelievable that the SG would have defended the Press Release if he had not been convinced of its legality. Furthermore, if the Press Release as issued was different from the version seen by him, then these were the perfect occasions to speak out! Vahanvati came to the witness Box of the Special CBI court on 27 February 2013 and just prior to the lunch break he asked the special judge, "Can I speak to the former Minister? He is well known to me. I want to enquire about his health." The judge Honourable O.P. Saini said, "Yes. Yes. You can talk with him. He was former Minister. You were then SG. No problem." Vahanvati should not have come to me and I regret that I vented the bitterness in my heart then. He came near me and asked, "Are you aggrieved with me?" I said, "There is nothing to feel sad. But your behaviour did not befit your stature." He clasped my hands and said, "Please understand my position. Media goes on with whatever they like. I do not have enough of support from the Government too. What can I do?" He felt sorry. I did not want to continue with the conversation, but recalled a poem that was taught to me in my school days. I quoted in Tamil from 'Nalvazhi' and translated it for him. The poem alluded that the house of one who gives false testimony would be doomed. I have regretted and been aggrieved by that emotional utterance ever since Vahanvati's sudden demise soon after that conversation.

There is another atrocious aspect to this which also unfortunately relates to someone who is no more. I hesitate to speak ill of the departed but I must also document the truth. Palsania, DIG, CBI is the man in question. He too did not investigate the matter thoroughly and gave false testimony before the JPC on 24 July 2012. In the JPC meeting Tiruchi Siva, MP raised a question about the discussion held in the office of Pranab Mukherjee. Palsania responded, "The meeting exclusively dealt with vacation of spectrum.... It did not deal with what manner the licenses are to be allocated.... That is reflected in the charge sheet." How could Palsania make such a blatantly false claim given that Pranab Mukherjee himself had documented what was discussed in the meeting and had sent it to the PMO? Yet, his investigation and the CBI's charge-sheet were deemed veritable and treated as key evidence by the Supreme Court Bench. On 16 August 2011, while I was in judicial custody, Palsania and Vivek Priyadarshi (I.O, CBI) came to interrogate me regarding another 2G Case (Essar – Loop). Palsania told me, "Had the licenses been given one after another instead of issuing simultaneously this case would not have come about." I could sense a disturbed look on his face which he perhaps could not suppress. I explained to him even then the reasoning behind simultaneous issuance. He moralized, "Such testing times come in the life of all; facing them is part of life; we simply did our duty." I responded, "The manner in which the charge-sheet has been filed hurriedly without knowing the facts, without considering documents to meet the 'need' of satisfying the courts, political parties and the media would not do any good either to the country or to the CBI." When he died pre-maturely due to sudden illness I felt very troubled. I recalled various instances of sharing my views and arguing with him when I was in CBI custody for 14 days. Rai claims that some companies were adversely affected by the seniority issue in spectrum allocation. He points accusingly at the difference between seniority on the basis of date/time of application and seniority on the basis of date/time of completion of compliance. Was that really such a glaring flaw and am I to be held criminally responsible even for that? I allege that the CAG did not take any steps to even ascertain whether any company was actually adversely affected. On 15 February 2008, Madan Chaurasia, the Section Officer wrote, "As per the date of application in respect of applications received before 25 September 2007, the order of companies for issuance of LOIs/responses of DoT simultaneously on FCFS basis were as follows.... Then, it is pertinent to mention that most of the compliances were received on 10 January 2008 itself and difference in receipt of compliances are of the order of few minutes." When this file came to Behura on 18 February 2008, he raised the following queries in the file,

1. What is the status of availability of spectrum vis-a-vis the LOI holders?

2. If we attempt to allocate spectrum to maximum people at one go, what is the extent to which we can cover?

The Wireless Advisor who gave his reply in the same file wrote, "Spectrum availability is being worked out and will be put up separately." I gave my approval on 26 February 2008. Clearly the Telecom Ministry's intention was to issue LoI's simultaneously and then issue licenses while attempting as far as possible to allocate spectrum along with it, also simultaneously. The PTI news agency in a press report on 26 February 2008 reported, "In fact, officials said, Raja has a vision to bring local tariffs of mobile phones down to 25 paise per minute and STD calls to 50 paise. This will be possible only by increasing the competition. Asked by when the players would be allocated spectrum to start services, the officials did not give any time frame but said DoT was considering allocating the radio frequency simultaneously depending upon the quantum of air waves available." The PTI news report may not have reached CAG, but the reply sent by DoT to the draft report of CAG on 3 May 2010 clearly indicates "However the date and time of compliance of LoI's and date of signing license agreements did not in any manner prejudice their right as allocation of spectrum to all of them in most of the service areas were made on the same day. A tabular statement showing date of UASL application, date of LoI, date of signing of License agreement, effective date of license and date of allocation of spectrum service area wise is enclosed...." Here is a tabulation of all the LoI's issued on 10 January 2008 for reference:

Details of new UAS licences where LOIs were issued on 10.01.2008 and Spectrum Allocation

S.No	Service Area	Name of the Operator	Date of Application	Date of Issue of LoI	Date of Signing Licence	Date of Allocation of spectrum
1	Andhra Pradesh	Spice Communications Ltd.	31.08.06	10.01.08	29.02.08	Licence terminated
2	Andhra Pradesh	Etisalat DB Telecom Pvt. Ltd.	02.03.07	10.01.08	03.03.08	27.05.08
3	Andhra Pradesh	Videcon Telecommunications Ltd.	28.08.07	10.01.08	27.02.08	27.05.08
4	Andhra Pradesh	Loop Telecom Ltd.	06.09.07	10.01.08	04.03.08	27.05.08
5	Andhra Pradesh	Unitech Wireless (South) Pvt. Ltd.	24.09.07	10.01.08	28.02.08	27.05.08
6	Andhra Pradesh	Sistema Shyam Tele Services Ltd.	25.09.07	10.01.08	05.03.08	11.04.08
7	Assam	Tata Teleservices Ltd.	21.06.06	10.01.08	03.03.08	03.04.08
8	Assam	Idea Cellular Ltd.	26.06.07	10.01.08	28.02.08	22.12.08
9	Assam	S Tel Pvt. Ltd.	07.07.07	10.01.08	04.03.08	22.12.08

10	Assam	Videcon Telecommunications Ltd.	28.08.07	10.01.08	27.02.08	22.12.08
11	Assam	Loop Telecom Ltd.	06.09.07	10.01.08	05.03.08	22.12.08
12	Assam	Unitech Wireless (East) Pvt. Ltd.	24.09.07	10.01.08	29.02.08	22.12.08
13	Assam	Sistema Shyam TeleSercies Ltd.	25.09.07	10.01.08	07.03.08	03.04.08
14	Bihar	S Tel Pvt. Ltd.	07.07.07	10.01.08	29.02.08	03.10.08
15	Bihar	Videocon Telecommunications Ltd.	28.08.07	10.01.08	27.02.08	03.10.08
16	Bihar	Loop Telecom Ltd.	06.09.07	10.01.08	03.03.08	03.10.08
17	Bihar	Unitech Wireless (East) Pvt. Ltd.	24.09.07	10.01.08	28.02.08	03.10.08
18	Bihar	Sistema Shyam Tele Services Ltd.	25.09.07	10.01.08	04.03.08	11.04.08
19	Delhi	Spice Communications Ltd.	31.08.06	10.01.08	03.03.08	Licence terminated
20	Delhi	Etisalat DB Telecom Pvt. Ltd.	02.03.07	10.01.08	27.02.08	28.08.08
21	Delhi	Videocon Telecommunications Ltd.	28.08.07	10.01.08	28.02.08	Not yet allotted
22	Delhi	Loop Telecom Ltd.	06.09.07	10.01.08	04.03.08	Not yet allotted
23	Delhi	Unitech Wireless (Delhi) Pvt. Ltd.	24.09.07	10.01.08	29.02.08	Not yet allotted
24	Delhi	Sistema Shyam TeleServices Ltd.	25.09.07	10.01.08	05.03.08	28.08.08
25	Gujarat	Etisala DB Telecom Pvt. Ltd.	02.03.07	10.01.08	03.03.08	25.09.08
26	Gujarat	Videcon Telecommunications Ltd.	28.08.07	10.01.08	27.02.08	25.09.08
27	Gujarat	Loop Telecom Ltd.	06.09.07	10.01.08	03.03.08	09.03.09
28	Gujarat	Unitech Wireless (West) Pvt. Ltd.	24.09.07	10.01.08	28.02.08	25.09.08
29	Gujarat	Sistema Shyam TeleServices	25.09.07	10.01.08	04.03.08	29.05.08
30	Haryana	Spice Communications Ltd.	31.08.06	10.01.08	29.02.08	Licence terminated
31	Haryana	Estisalat DB Telecom Pvt. Ltd.	02.03.07	10.01.08	03.03.08	04.12.08
32	Haryana	Videocon Telecommunications Ltd.	28.08.07	10.01.08	27.02.08	04.12.08
33	Haryana	Loop Telecom Ltd.	06.09.07	10.01.08	04.03.08	04.12.08
34	Haryana	Unitech Wireless (North) Pvt. Ltd.	24.09.07	10.01.08	28.02.08	04.12.08
35	Haryana	Sistema Shyam TeleServices Ltd.	25.09.07	10.01.08	05.03.08	11.04.08
36	Himachal Pradesh	S Tel Pvt. Ltd.	07.07.07	10.01.08	29.02.08	04.12.08
37	Himachal Pradesh	Videocon Telecommunications Ltd.	28.08.07	10.01.08	27.02.08	04.12.08
38	Himachal Pradesh	Loop Telecom Ltd.	06.09.07	10.01.08	03.03.08	04.12.08
39	Himachal Pradesh	Unitech Wireless (North) Pvt. Ltd.	24.09.07	10.01.08	28.02.08	04.12.08
40	Himachal Pradesh	Sistema Shyam TEleServices Ltd.	25.09.07	10.01.08	04.03.08	11.04.08
41	Jammu & Kashmir	Tata Teleservices Ltd.	21.06.06	10.01.08	03.03.08	03.04.08
42	Jammu & Kashmir	Idea Cellular Ltd.	26.06.06	10.01.08	28.02.08	24.12.08
43	Jammu & Kashmir	S Tel Pvt. Ltd.	07.07.07	10.01.08	04.03.08	24.12.08
44	Jammu & Kashmir	Videcon Telecommunications Ltd.	28.08.07	10.01.08	27.02.08	24.12.08
45	Jammu & Kashmir	Loop Telecom Ltd.	06.09.07	10.01.08	05.03.08	24.12.08
46	Jammu & Kashmir	Unitech Wireless (North) Pvt. Ltd.	24.09.07	10.01.08	29.02.08	24.12.08

47	Jammu & Kashmir	Sistema Shyam TEleServices Ltd.	25.09.07	10.01.08	07.03.08	03.04.08
48	Karnataka	Idea Cellular Ltd.	26.06.06	10.01.08	28.02.08	Licence terminated
49	Karnataka	Estisalat DB Telecom Pvt. Ltd.	02.03.07	10.01.08	03.03.08	30.05.08
50	Karnataka	Videcon Telecommunications Ltd.	28.08.07	10.01.08	27.02.08	30.05.08
51	Karnataka	Loop Telecom Ltd.	06.09.07	10.01.08	04.03.08	30.05.08
52	Karnataka	Unitech Wireless (South) Pvt. Ltd.	24.09.07	10.01.08	29.02.08	30.05.08
53	Karnataka	Sistema Shyam TeleServcies Ltd.	25.09.07	10.01.08	05.03.08	29.05.08
54	Kerala	Estisalat DB Telecom Pvt. Ltd.	02.03.07	10.01.08	03.03.08	15.05.08
55	Kerala	Videcon Telecommunications Ltd.	28.08.07	10.01.08	27.02.08	15.05.08
56	Kerala	Loop Telecom Ltd.	06.09.07	10.01.08	03.03.08	15.05.08
57	Kerala	Unitech Wireless (South) Pvt. Ltd.	24.09.07	10.01.08	28.02.08	15.05.08
58	Kerala	Sistema Shyam TeleServices Ltd.	25.09.07	10.01.08	04.03.08	14.05.08
59	Kolkata	Idea Cellular Ltd.	26.06.06	10.01.08	28.02.08	09.01.09
60	Kolkata	Videcom Telecommunication Ltd.	28.08.07	10.01.08	27.02.08	09.01.09
61	Kolkata	Loop Telecom Ltd.	06.09.07	10.01.08	03.03.08	09.01.09
62	Kolkata	Unitech Wireless (Kolkata) Pvt. Ltd.	24.09.07	10.01.08	29.02.08	09.01.09
63	Kolkata	Sistema TeleServices Ltd.	25.09.07	10.01.08	04.03.08	29.05.08
64	Madhya Pradesh	Videocon Telecommunications Ltd.	28.08.07	10.01.08	27.02.08	28.08.08
65	Madhya Pradesh	Loop Telecom Ltd.	06.09.07	10.01.08	29.02.08	28.08.08
66	Madhya Pradesh	Unitech Wireless (West) Pvt. Ltd.	24.09.07	10.01.08	28.02.08	28.08.08
67	Madhya Pradesh	Sistema Shyam TeleServices Ltd.	25.09.07	10.01.08	03.03.08	11.04.08
68	Maharashtra	Spice Communications Ltd.	31.08.06	10.01.08	29.02.08	Licence terminated
69	Maharashtra	Etisalat DB Telecom Pvt. Ltd.	02.03.07	10.01.08	03.03.08	10.09.08
70	Maharashtra	Videocon Telecommunications Ltd.	28.08.07	10.01.08	27.02.08	10.09.08
71	Maharashtra	Loop Telecom Ltd.	06.09.07	10.01.08	04.03.08	14.11.08
72	Maharashtra	Unitech Wireless (West) Pvt. Ltd.	24.09.07	10.01.08	28.02.08	10.09.08
73	Maharashtra	Sistema Shyam TEleServices Ltd.	25.09.07	10.01.08	05.03.08	14.05.08
74	Mumbai	Etisalat DB Telecom Pvt. Ltd.	02.03.07	10.01.08	27.02.08	09.09.08
75	Mumbai	Videocon Telecommunications Ltd.	28.08.07	10.01.08	28.02.08	09.09.08
76	Mumbai	Unitech Wireless (Mumbai) Pvt. Ltd.	24.09.07	10.01.08	29.02.08	09.09.08
77	Mumbai	Sistema Shyam TEleServices Ltd.	25.09.07	10.01.08	03.03.08	28.08.08
78	North East	Tata Teleservices Ltd.	21.06.06	10.01.08	03.03.08	03.04.08
79	North East	Idea Cellular Ltd.	26.06.06	10.01.08	28.02.08	23.12.08
80	North East	S Tel Pvt. Ltd.	07.07.07	10.01.08	04.03.08	23.12.08
81	North East	Videocon Telecommunications Ltd.	28.08.07	10.01.08	27.02.08	23.12.08
82	North East	Loop Telecom Ltd.	06.09.07	10.01.08	05.03.08	23.12.08
83	North East	Unitech Wireless (East) Pvt. Ltd.	24.09.07	10.01.08	29.02.08	23.12.08
84	North East	Sistema Shyam TeleServices Ltd.	25.09.07	10.01.08	07.03.08	03.04.08
85	Orissa	Idea Cellular Ltd.	26.06.06	10.01.08	28.02.08	24.04.08

86	Orissa	S Tel Pvt. Ltd.	07.07.07	10.01.08	03.03.08	24.04.08
87	Orissa	Videcon Telecommunications ltd.	28.08.07	10.01.08	27.02.08	24.04.08
88	Orissa	Loop Telecom Ltd.	06.09.07	10.01.08	04.03.08	24.04.08
89	Orissa	Unitech wireless (East) Pvt. Ltd.	24.09.07	10.01.08	29.02.08	24.04.08
90	Orissa	Sistema Shyam Teleservices Ltd.	25.09.07	10.01.08	05.03.08	29.05.08
91	Punjab	Idea Cellular Ltd.	26.06.06	10.01.08	27.02.08	Licence terminated
92	Punjab	Etisalat DB Telecom Pvt. Ltd.	02.03.07	10.01.08	03.03.08	10.09.08
93	Punjab	Loop Telecom Ltd.	06.09.07	10.01.08	03.03.08	09.03.09
94	Punjab	Unitech Wireless (North) Pvt. Ltd.	24.09.07	10.01.08	28.02.08	10.09.08
95	Punjab	Sistema Shyam TeleServices Ltd.	25.09.07	10.01.08	04.03.08	25.07.08
96	Rajasthan	Etisalat DB Telecom Pvt. Ltd.	02.03.07	10.01.08	03.03.08	23.12.08
97	Rajasthan	Videcom Telecommunications Ltd.	28.08.07	10.01.08	27.02.08	23.12.08
98	Rajasthan	Loop Telecom Ltd.	06.09.07	10.01.08	03.03.08	23.12.08
99	Rajasthan	Unitech Wireless (North) Pvt. Ltd.	24.09.07	10.01.08	28.02.08	23.12.08
100	Tamilnadu (incl: Chennai)	Idea Cellular Ltd.	26.06.06	10.01.08	28.02.08	22.04.08
101	Tamilnadu (incl: Chennai)	Etisalat DB Telecom Pvt. Ltd.	02.08.07	10.01.08	03.03.08	22.04.08
102	Tamilnadu (incl: Chennai)	Videcom Telecommunications Ltd.	28.08.07	10.01.08	27.02.08	22.04.08
103	Tamilnadu (incl: Chennai)	LoopTelecom Ltd.	06.09.07	10.01.08	04.03.08	22.04.08
104	Tamilnadu (incl: Chennai)	Unitech Wireless (Tamil Nadu) Pvt. Ltd.	24.09.07	10.01.08	29.02.08	22.04.08
105	Tamilnadu (incl: Chennai)	Sistema Shyam TeleServices Ltd.	25.09.07	10.01.08	05.03.08	11.04.08
106	Uttar Pradesh (East)	Etisalat DB Telecom pvt. Ltd.	02.03.07	10.01.08	03.03.08	10.09.08
107	Uttar Pradesh (East)	Videcon Telecommunications Ltd.	28.08.07	10.01.08	27.02.08	10.09.08
108	Uttar Pradesh (East)	Loop Telecom Ltd.	06.09.07	10.01.08	03.03.08	21.01.09
109	Uttar Pradesh (East)	Unitech Wireless (North) Pvt. Ltd.	24.09.07	10.01.08	28.02.08	10.09.08
110	Uttar Pradesh (East)	Sistema Shyam TeleServices Ltd.	25.09.07	10.01.08	04.03.08	11.04.08
111	Uttar Pradesh (West)	Etisalat DB Telecom pvt. Ltd.	02.03.07	10.01.08	03.03.08	25.09.08
112	Uttar Pradesh (West)	Videcom Telecommunications Ltd.	28.08.07	10.01.08	27.02.08	25.09.08

113	Uttar Pradesh (West)	Loop Telecom Ltd.	06.09.07	10.01.08	03.03.08	26.12.08
114	Uttar Pradesh (West)	Unitech Wireless (East) Pvt. Ltd.	24.09.07	10.01.08	28.02.08	25.09.08
115	Uttar Pradesh (West)	Sistema Shyam TeleServices Ltd.	25.09.07	10.01.08	04.03.08	11.04.08
116	West Bengal	Idea Cellular Ltd.	26.06.06	10.01.08	28.02.08	09.01.09
117	West Bengal	Videcon Telecommunication Ltd.	28.08.07	10.01.08	27.02.08	09.01.09
118	West Bengal	Loop Telecom Ltd.	06.09.07	10.01.08	03.03.08	09.01.09
119	West Bengal	Unitech Wirless (East) Pvt. Ltd.	24.09.07	10.01.08	29.02.08	09.01.09
120	West Bengal	Sistema Shyam TeleServices Ltd.	25.09.07	10.01.08	04.03.08	11.04.08

* Tata Teleservices Ltd and Sistema Shyam Teleservices Ltd were alloted CDMA Spectrum

Of the total 22 Telecom Circles in the country spectrum was allocated on a single day in more than 10 circles and within a few months in the remaining circles. Is it not true that in the past some companies had to wait for almost 2 years to get spectrum allocation? Did the CAG or the Supreme Court pay heed to this? Is there any Telecom Company that got the benefit of its specific seniority in any circle? Is there anything to show that any particular company was deliberately prevented from obtaining spectrum? No company lodged any complaints with the Telecom Department that some company was favoured over another in terms of processing priority or seniority. Clearly the seniority issue was cooked up and did not manifest itself in reality due to the simple method of allotting spectrum to all applicants on the same day. Wherever spectrum fell short in a few districts, consent of the concerned applicants was taken for district-wise allocation of spectrum. Thus, LoI's were given simultaneously and spectrum was also allotted simultaneously. This ensured that seniority would not become a cause for grievance to any UASL applicant. In spite of all this Rai's fabricated allegations as in the introduction (foreword) of his report that, "The issuance of licence for 2G spectrum allotment underscored procedural irregularities that were intentionally committed. Even though alarm bells were ringing loud and clear within and outside the Government. No one had courage to stop the entire process from being hijacked. Goal posts were shifted and every protesting department of the Government was told to stay out with their advice being labelled as "out of context." Admittedly Rai's 'goal post' in the 2G game is allotment of spectrum. When the goal post was designed to be static (simultaneous allotment), where and how the 'shift' is possible?. Elbert Hubbard warns "Genius may have limitations; but stupidity is not thus handicapped." Without weighing the fact the Supreme Court Bench consisting of Justices Ganguly and Singhvi in their verdict observed, "The first come first served policy which was being followed since 2003 was changed by him on 7 January 2008 and was incorporated in press release dated 10 January 2008." A judicial order has to be based on two counts namely 'assessment of facts' and 'interpretation of law'. The lofty as Everest Indian Judicature has to decide whether these two factors have been met!

Chapter 6

The Resignation

The CVC had listed possible irregularities in its letter to the CBI. This ought to have been investigated by the CBI which was aiding the CAG in its audit. Hence, it is a logical conclusion that the CBI must have finalized its stand-point before CAG delivered his report in November 2010. Even the Supreme Court in its judgment order on 16 December 2010 had stated, "CBI shall conduct thorough investigation into various issues highlighted in the report of CVC, which was forwarded to the Director, CBI vide letter dated 12-10-2009 and the report of CAG, who has prima facie found serious irregularities in the grant of licenses." So, the charge-sheet filed against me as ordered by the Supreme Court could have been prepared on the basis of investigations in line with the CAG report also. I have established how absurd and faulty Rai's report is. On that basis, I believe that Vinod Rai must be called as a witness in the criminal case filed against me so that my defence has the opportunity to cross-examine and legally challenge him. I have stated this in my interview given to 'The Week' (3 August 2012), "To my knowledge, it was for the first time that a CAG report was accepted as a basis for a criminal investigation. A CAG report is usually meant for Parliament. Having taken the CAG's report as prima facie evidence, I do hope that I will be permitted to call the CAG to the trial court as witness, to ensure a fair trial and to uphold the majesty of law." The CBI stated before the Trial Court (on 18 November 2013) that they did not take the CAG report as the basis of their investigation. Whatever it is, they cannot cover up the fact that the CBI charge sheet contains only the 'irregularities' pointed out by the CAG in its report. Clearly, Rai whose statements would not have stood the test of cross-examination in the court was being protected by the CBI from being called in as a witness. Individual egos were being protected at the cost of institutional values! The 3C's claimed that there were procedural irregularities in the implementation process of issuing licenses and allotment of spectrum, apart from loss to the exchequer due to the non-auction of spectrum and the non-revision of entry fee. They also severely criticised both me and the Ministry for the cut-off date and FCFS process. I have already referred to the disparaging comments made against me in the open court by the Supreme Court Bench and also about the contradictions in their judgement.

The conviction and zeal shown by the Government in denying the charges of loss to the exchequer was missing in the context of accusations related to irregularities in the implementation process. I could not understand whether this was due to some sort of apprehension or lack of understanding or whether it was in order to find a scapegoat – a fall guy – given the storm of criticism and public ire that UPA-II was weathering regarding several purported 'scams'. Kapil Sibal who succeeded me as the Minister of Telecommunication convened an official Press Meet on 7 January 2011 to establish that there was ZERO LOSS. To substantiate his stand, he explained in detail the Government's policies and the successive recommendations of TRAI that had been adhered to strictly. But he said, "However the CAG's findings regarding procedural irregularities in the implementation of FCFS policy are in a different category and must be taken very seriously. In this case the nature of the lapses and the criminal investigations are underway. The Government is totally committed to take stringent action against any person found guilty of corruption and misconduct." On 24 February 2011, the Prime Minister Dr Manmohan Singh stated in Parliament, "While the policy was sound, the way it was implemented gave rise to problems. Those problems will now be looked into by the JPC and if there are any criminal aspects, they are looked into by the CBI." The intention of the Government became quite clear when the 2G case was divided into two parts making one as their shield and the other as a sword for the CBI to wield against me. To quote George Orwell, "In a time of universal deceit; telling the truth is a revolutionary act." I continue searching in vain for such revolutionaries in the 2G scenario.

All those who had unsuccessfully attempted to prevent the issuance of licenses started stirring up a ruckus through the media about irregularities in the implementation process. There were newspapers which splashed on the front page in bold type sarcastic queries about the number of zeros in ₹ 1.76 lakh crore. However, the question of why the CBI did not mention that amount in its charge-sheet remains unasked and unanswered by the media. At airports, railway stations and all other public places where I passed by, I could hear the whisperings of my having scammed ₹ 1.76 lakh crore. All this even after the CBI, Income Tax Department and the Enforcement Directorate had jointly conducted investigations at the instance of the Supreme Court and concluded that I did not have any disproportionate assets. Even in Parliament, questions on this subject were raised incessantly. I too provided my responses equally tirelessly. Even though perceptive individuals knew that there was no violation, they did not tone down their criticism out of political prudence. Thus, there was a continuous barrage aimed at me as well as at the Government. The Spectrum issue was raised first in Tamil Nadu on a massive scale by both TV and print media. While some used this mud-slinging with the aim that I should be chastised or removed from the Telecom Ministry, others used this excuse to sully the image of DMK.

It hence became necessary to hold a Press Meet on 11 October 2008. I was questioned about the rumours that I had shares in the companies which were issued Telecom licenses. As observed by Joseph Pulitzer "An able, disinterested, public-spirited press, with trained intelligence to know the right and courage to do it, can preserve the public virtue without which popular government is shame and a mockery. A cynical, mercenary, demagogic press will produce in time a people as base as itself. The power to mould the future of the Republic will be in the hands of the journalism of future generations." I too look forward to such a generation. Justice V.R.Krishna Iyer has also observed, "An enslaved press with biased bosses is doubly fatal to the people's interests." I tried my best to keep responding appropriately to the onslaught of speculative and hypothesized allegations in relation to the 2G case. An AIADMK MP mocked at me using the honorific 'Spectrum King'. I replied, "Yes, I am proud to be called spectrum king." After the issuance of licenses when the allocation of spectrum was going on, my interview to the 'The Hindu' was published on 8 September 2008 titled, 'I called the bluff on the spectrum story.' In that interview, I had referred to the earlier obfuscation of available spectrum and the plans to auction 3G spectrum shortly. I had said, "The various policy issued in terms of the recommendations of TRAI and otherwise are considered the representative of the Finance Ministry ... whatever we have done so far is in line with the decision of the Cabinet relating to spectrum pricing that was laid down in 2003.... I think we are not far away from the day we will have a phone call at 30 paise!" My expectation did not prove wrong. Around 2010, telephone tariffs were close to that number.

The National Telecom Policy established in 1999 was entirely different from the one of 1994. Those who got licenses through auction in 1994 asked the Government to change the policy as they could not operate profitably and this led to the creation of NTP-99, based on which UASL Regime of 2003 was instituted. The left-wing parties were strongly criticizing the Government over NTP-99 and UASL regime. In his book 'Big Egos small men', Ram Jethmalani has referred to the campaign by the leftists and their publication titled, "The greatest Telecom Robbery and other Murky dealings of the Vajpayee Government." The legal opinion tendered by the then Attorney General Soli Sorabjee which formed the basis for an estimated loss of ₹ 4,000 crore to the exchequer was severely criticized. Jethmalani who was part of the Union Cabinet made several critiques both inside and outside Cabinet. The CAG Report 6/2000 also concluded that the decisions were inappropriate. It was alleged that the Government was acting in favour of the telecom operators at the expense of the exchequer. Jethmalani writes, "But the operators were determined to have their way. The Government had caved in. Many have reasonably conjectured that this volte face was induced by massive corruption." At that point of time too there were charges that the Finance Ministry's advice had been ignored. Conveniently forgetting this background of NTP-99/UASL and the policy that was continuously followed till 2007 before I took charge as Telecom Minister, BJP – and following in their footsteps CPI and CPI (M) also – joined in the uproar of purported losses of ₹ 1.76 lakh crore when I issued licenses based on the same policy precedents. It is my humble submission that it is a shameful failure on the part of the Leftists who got so caught up in the rhetoric of 'corrupt government' that they lost sight of the monopoly in the telecom sector. Even the most astute capitalists would agree that the breaking of a cartel, freeing up so much obscured spectrum for public utility and dramatically reducing tariffs was a significant socialistic achievement. Yet the judgement of our nation's left-wing proved miserably off-target. In an interview given to 'The Hindu' on 1 November 2008 I had said, "If the spectrum were shared with the existing operators, there would have been no controversy. I am the first Minister who has tried to break the cartel ... I am not against any one. The existing operators do not want competition. There are four or five operators in all circles. I added another four or five. This will only mean more people will benefit. The new operators will go to the rural and semi-urban areas.... I am presiding over a silent revolution in the Telecom sector." Given the influence of the affected telecom companies which were resolute to bring me down, the people who wanted to smear DMK's image and the opposition parties who were seeking ammunition against the Government there was no majority with the drive to ascertain the truth of my assertions. As discussed earlier in November 2008, I met the Prime Minister along with the Finance Minister, to discuss the upfront charges and 2G Spectrum pricing – including the method for calculating charge per MHz – for those providers who had allocation beyond 6.2 MHz, as well as the introduction of 3G spectrum. Towards the conclusion of that meeting, the Prime Minister steered the conversation to the allegations of theoretical loss in the allocation of 2G spectrum. He referred to the press campaign as "mischievous" and felt that someone malicious could be "influencing it."

On 6 November 2008, the Politburo of the CPI (M) issued a press statement titled, "Big scam in spectrum allocation; Hold Enquiry." DMK President Kalaignar Karunanidhi reacted to this and shared his perspective in a news release which 'The Hindu' published in their Chennai Edition on 8 November 2008 under the title 'Karunanidhi defends Raja – 2G spectrum sale had PM's approval.' Kalaignar referenced the points raised by Nambudiri, a Trade Union leader of CPI (M), "It has come to our notice that reports have been published in certain newspapers in Tamil Nadu on behalf of some functionaries of BSNL Unions expressing doubts about the 2G spectrum policy of the Government. We do not find any deviation in the prevailing policy of the Government and endorse the decision of the Government in this regard. In fact we congratulate and thank the Hon'ble Communication Minister for taking the courageous decision to allot 3G Spectrum to BSNL in advance without any auction, which is in the best interest of BSNL and its workers."Even after all those clarifications made both in the Press and Parliament the vested interests including the opposition parties continued their assault. Prakash Javadkar of BJP and some of the AIADMK MPs wanted to raise this matter in Parliament.

Subsequent to my press meet of 7 November 2008, the press carried extensive reports the next day. 'The Hindu' printed an article titled, 'Ready to resign if proved wrong in spectrum allocation' stating, "readdressing a press conference here Raja said, 'The decision of issuing new license to the new operators was based on the Cabinet approved NTP 99 and supported by the recommendations of TRAI,"' 'Times of India' in its article, "Raja ready to quit over spectrum allocation row," stated, "Interestingly 2003 Cabinet decision endorses auction. In section 7.39, TRAI writes, '... if the Government ensures additional spectrum, they may introduce addl. players through multi-stage bidding process as was followed for the fourth cellular operator." The correspondent Shalini Singh who filed that story held the view that spectrum must be auctioned and also stated that I had ignored the question on this topic. However, no one was heeding the fact that as much as para 7.39 states that licenses could be auctioned as in the past (CMTS) this was only meant as a stop-gap for licenses to be issued ahead of migration to the UASL Revenue Sharing model. That point became redundant because the UASL regime was implemented in just a couple of days following the recommendation. Nirpendra Mishra who officiated in the TRAI recommendations of 2007 gave an interview to PTI on 14 December 2008 which was reported as, "Telecom Regulator (TRAI) today endorsed Communication Minister's view that for existing 2G service (spectrum) cannot be auctioned saying that the Telecom policy does not permit this." On 30 December 2008, 'Business Line' (Hindu) published, "Despite the controversy over spectrum allocation and slowing economy, the telecom sector continued to grow at a scoring pace this year. The number of telephone users in the country grew from 233 million in December 2007 to nearly 380 million at the end of December 2008.... There were lots of controversies too. The decision to allocate spectrum on a 'First Come First Served' basis to new players, including Unitech, Videocon, Swan, Loop and S.Tel has brought communication Ministry under the scanner of the Central Vigilance Commission, the Parliamentary Standing Committee on IT and the High Court." It is hence quite clear that even towards the end of 2008 the reporters of leading newspapers, Members of Parliament and Public institutions were unfamiliar with or deliberately glossing over the Telecom Policy and TRAI recommendations. They had either not understood the documents or they had formed an influenced and partisan perspective!

It was Subramanian Swamy who initiated the legal battle to give direction to the parliamentary debates, media outcry and political witch-hunt. I often feel that Swamy continually vents the frustration over his limited success in achieving ministerial positions by being vindictive and frivolously litigious. All his petitions were based on press reports and not the relevant policy documents. In his letter written to the Prime Minister on 29 November 2008, he stated that ineligible companies like 'Swan' and 'Unitech' were issued license and allocated spectrum vide the First Come First Served method resulting in huge profits for them. Additionally, he sought permission to file a case against me under the Prevention of Corruption Act. After their review, the PMO forwarded that letter to the Telecom Ministry seeking suitable explanation and details of actions taken. On 13 February 2009, appropriate replies were sent by the Telecom Ministry officials with the approval of the Telecom Secretary. In particular, the Finance wing had provided suitable responses about the dilution of shares in the case of Unitech and Swan. They had pointed out clearly, "Finance Ministry has also concurred that it is a case of dilution of equity and not sale of equity of promoters. It is a normal practice in the corporate world to bring investment into the company for rolling out an expansion of business.... To cite one example, one of the original license holders in one metro circle later on inducted the Essar Group. The subsequent entity has from time to time inducted Swiss Con, Hutchison and Vodafone which are international companies, as its strategic partner." The contents of the memo were formally reviewed in the PMO until 17 June 2009, by the PM's Principal Secretary and the Joint Secretary (Telecom) in consultation with the DDG-AS Srivastava. A copy of Swamy's letter was also forwarded to me by the PMO, directing me to provide a suitable explanation to the Prime Minister. I sent my reply on 18 June 2009 with suitable responses to all the questions raised in the letter. Normally during a prosecution, the defence argument would be that the crime did occur but the accused (in this case I) did not commit it. It has been my stand from day one that I have been charged for a 'murder' but the alleged 'murder victim' is still alive! My plea is hence rooted in righteousness and truth and not the usual defence of 'benefit of doubt'.

On 14 January 2008 – 4 days after the commencement of issuance of licenses – the telecom company S.Tel filed a case before Delhi High Court seeking nullification of the press release issued by the Government on 10 January 2008. Their contention was not that the Government's policy was incorrect or loss-making, but that after the issuance of LoIs to applications received till 25 September 2007 (the cut-off date announced) the remaining applicants should also be issued licenses. S.Tel did not question either the entry fee fixed by the Government or FCFS. S.Tel argued that the advancement of cut-off date from 1 October to 25 September 2007 was arbitrary. That change of date was nullified by the Delhi High Court with the opinion, how could there be a cut-off date when TRAI had said 'no cap' in the issuance of licenses. The Government did not follow-up adequately to establish before the court the need that arose for a cut-off date due to the potential lack of available spectrum given the very large number of applications. Subramanian Swamy in his complaint letter to the Prime Minister referred to that order obtained by S.Tel from the Delhi High Court and gave an interview too claiming that the High Court itself had affirmed that the 'actions of Raja were wrong'. This opinion obviously resonated in Parliament as well. The Court's order had only meant that remaining applications (received after 25 September 2007) like S.Tel's must also be considered for issuances of licenses; it made no mention of wrong-doing or procedural impropriety. However, to avoid any possible confusion that might arise due to that order, the Government decided to appeal before the Supreme Court. Upon learning about the non-availability of spectrum and understanding that their application had not been disqualified or rejected, S.Tel withdrew their petition on 11 March 2010. During the Supreme Court proceedings, Subramanian Swamy even without locus-standi appealed to the Apex Court not to intervene in the findings of the High Court regarding the change in cut-off date. The Supreme Court adjudged, "This appeal is disposed of as requiring no further adjudication.... Findings recorded by the High Court in this regard to the cut-off date is not interfered with and disturbed by this Court in the present case." This order is strange and somewhat confusing. When the petitioner himself had withdrawn the case, this follow-up action instigated by Subramanian Swamy was clearly politically motivated. When this file was sent to the Law Ministry, it gave its clarification on 13 August 2010, "Important fact of this case is the statement made by M/s. S.Tel on the affidavit stating the decision of the Government for giving UASL licenses to those who applied up to 25 September 2007 was not arbitrary but based on likely availability of spectrum and the administrative decision thereon. If the observation of Supreme Court and the statement made by M/s. S.Tel are read together it may be concluded that there is no substance in Dr Subramanian Swamy's allegation that 2G allotment was arbitrary or grossly unfair."

Around the same time, a PIL was filed by one Arvind Gupta in the Delhi High Court against the issuance of licenses and allocation of spectrum. COAI was also simultaneously fighting with the Government by appealing to TDSAT. Gupta's petition alleged improprieties in spectrum auction, cut-off date, FCFS and dilution of shares by Swan and Unitech. Here too instead of actual policy documents, media reports were cited as evidence. Vahanvati once again vetted the Counter Affidavit and appeared before the High Court on behalf of the Government. In para 22 of his Affidavit it was pointed out that, "A perusal of the petition would show that the petitioner's sole arguments are based wholly on the facts derived from news paper reports which have no authenticity.... It has been held by the apex court in a number of judgments that the news paper reports are merely hearsay and not proof of the facts stated therein." Additionally, an organisation called 'Social Action Forum for Manav Adhikar' filed a case in the Supreme Court alleging that the issuance of license and allocation of spectrum was unlawful and arbitrary, "(d) direct an independent and impartial enquiry by the CBI / CVC to inquire into the scam by which substantial loss has been caused to national exchequer by gifting / squandering a valuable resource." On the basis of the Counter Affidavit filed on 28 April 2008 by the Government that case was dismissed. TDSAT in its judgment highlighted with documentary evidence how COAI was opposing the Government decision to auction spectrum, "From the foregoing it would prima-facie appear that the petitioners have themselves opposed allocation of spectrum auction. The challenge to the allocation effected on such ground and the prayer for the relief thereon would therefore be untenable." This information was also included in the counter affidavit filed against Arvind Gupta's petition. With reference to Swan/Unitech, the affidavit stated, "Both these companies have categorically mentioned that the investment brought in by their strategic foreign partners would be used for rolling out the services and this could enhance their capital base keeping the absolute shareholding of the promoters intact. Finance Ministry has also concurred that it is a case of dilution of equity and not sale of equity of promoters. It is a normal practice in the corporate world to bring investment into the company for rolling out or expansion of business." The stand of the Government legally vetted by Vahanvati in that affidavit filed on 8 December 2008 was never changed at any point.

On 23 and 30 October 2009, around the time when the CBI had filed their initial FIR, Subramanian Swamy again wrote to the Prime Minister. His letters were sent to the Law Ministry for legal opinion who responded that further action could be taken only after conclusion of ongoing investigations and pointed out what Swamy had quoted in his letter, "Substance of the allegation made by me in the above cited letters are already under investigation." However, on 8 March 2010, Swamy filed a petition seeking permission to prosecute me. Apart from his earlier claims, he alleged that a sum of ₹150 crore was deposited in the account of Green House Promoters Pvt Ltd – in which my wife Parameswari was a Director (Legal) – at the T. Nagar Branch of Canara Bank from some Middle Eastern source. He also cited that Equas Estate Ltd in which my relatives are Directors had accumulated ₹755 crore in its accounts within just a year of its inception and complained that the Prime Minister's Office had not been informed of this. He claimed that all this information had been gleaned through investigations by 'The Pioneer'. 'The Pioneer' – which is well known to be BJP's mouthpiece – had started personally targeting me through its investigative reporter J Gopikrishna, from December 2008. On 11 December, it published 'How to become a crorepati overnight, ask A. Raja', 'His wife ran business from official residence'. On 15 December, they published my picture and my wife's in the front page with the caption 'Zero to 755 crore in one year'. The charge-sheet filed by the CBI and the

Enforcement Directorate did not accept any of the allegations published by 'The Pioneer', but still J Gopikrishna was honoured on 23 December 2010 by CNN-IBN with the citation, "Being the journalist who first brought the telecom scandal to light several years ago ... much before the rest of the media picked it up." Ironically it was Pranab Mukherjee who presented the awards at that event even though his notes in the official records had been filed in the courts as key evidence for the defence. How ironic that such a senior minister and later President of the nation, publicly rewarded a 'hired press-parrot' for reports contradicting his own prior official actions!

I decided to send a lawyer's notice to 'The Pioneer' in May 2010 demanding an apology for their speculative and defamatory reporting. Mahendra Nahata from the Telecom Sector wanted me and 'Pioneer' editor Chandan Mitra to meet. At this meeting, I highlighted to Chandan Mitra the vested interests behind the news reports and how his reporter had been used. Conveying his regrets, he said that if I gave him my version of the facts then he would print it. Accordingly, on 17 Aug 2010, 'The Pioneer' published,"In the interest of fair play and ethical journalism, we are reproducing his response in full." The arguments I had presented then remain unchanged to this day. Yet no action was taken against J Gopikrishna's ugly journalism and his star continues to shine at 'The Pioneer'. Even though there had been no evidence of disproportionate assets either in my name or in the name of any of my family members, 'Times of India' published a frontpage article stating that ₹ 3,000 crore were parked in foreign countries in my wife's name. They have never come back to apologise for this false and slanderous report. In 2008, some newspapers stooped to the level of even printing a photograph of my eleven-year old daughter. Lord Dennings quoted, "The freedom of the press is extolled as one of the great bulwarks of liberty. It is entrenched in the constitution of the world. But it is often misunderstood. It does not mean that the press is free to ruin a reputation or to break a confidence or to pollute the course of Justice or to do anything that is unlawful." Ram Jethmalani has also stated, "Media trial is anti-thesis of the Rule of Law and results in miscarriage of Justice. Pre-trial publicity prejudicially pervades and saturates the community and renders virtually impossible the possibility of fair trial."

The Tamil press added another perverse dimension to the media attacks already underway in the national capital. The 2G case became the media scapegoat for deflecting attention from the Jayalalitha's disproportionate assets case. This was perhaps an excuse for projecting the accumulated political antipathy towards the DMK as well as me personally. 'Dhinamani' Tamil Daily even published caricatures with captions like, "If the punishment for 66 crores can be 4 years (for Jayalalitha) then the punishment for 176,000 crores would be 10,828 years." This is in spite of knowing that in my case, it has been proven that I have no assets either in India or outside apart from my salary while in office, the one-fourth inheritance of my parents' property and the savings from my years as an advocate. A Tamil weekly 'Junior Vikatan' published a noxious article based on the Delhi 'Pioneer' report, with a photograph of my wife and my minor daughter on the cover page. They trumped up the baseless allegations regarding channelling of profits from the 2G scam into Green House Promoters and Equas Ltd. Justice A.M. Ahmadi once wrote, "The foremost danger is that since the press is a potent instrument of mass communication, newspapers are sought to be used by powerful parties and individuals having vested interests to further their private interests to the detriment of public.... One of the biggest sources of the abuse of the modern press is the fact that, while originated as an instrument of free discussion in a democracy, the press has largely become a hand maid commercial propaganda. Impelled by such a commercial motive, most newspapers have to indulge in stunts, such as blackmailing, 'yellow journalism' intrusion into privacy, veiled pornography and the like, which have little value from the stand point of democratic interests upon which rests the claim for freedom of the press." I filed a defamation case in Madras High Court claiming ₹ 1 crore as compensation. I asserted that no such transfer of funds had occurred and also pleaded for an interim legal stay on such baseless defamatory news reporting. Yet, Justice K. Chandru not only rejected my petition but also fined me ₹ 10,000. It will be more relevant to remind the Anglo-Saxon maxim, "High and extraordinary Justice is injustice!." I therefore appealed before the Division Bench comprising Justices Chockalingam and Subbiah which on 1 October 2009 nullified the earlier order and also condemned Justice Chandru's action as 'thoroughly unwarranted and unjustified'. I highlight this because the very same points were being distorted by Subramanian Swamy as well as the Centre for Public Interest Litigation who had filed cases in the Delhi High Court and were demanding a CBI enquiry. Whenever I notice such dishonourable reporting I am always reminded of this couplet from the Thirukkural, "it is no more than an act akin to embracing an anonymous corpse in the dark."

When the CAG Report on spectrum allocation was being discussed, 'The Hindu' published my exclusive interviews on three different occasions. I have to make specific note of the fact that Ram of 'The Hindu' remained an objective and neutral person with a constructive outlook and informed perspective on wireless spectrum and its utility. The Hindu too could be influenced by the rest of the media's malicious reports, and I also do not expect Ram to think that I am beyond suspicion. Although I differ with the same publication for its editorials and news articles at the time of my arrest, I perceive such reports as healthy criticism. I respect Ram and his personal and professional integrity as he did not hesitate to publish the fair claims of the other (my) side in that context also.

I wrote to the Prime Minister on 21 April 2010 in the context of Subramanian Swamy's petition, "The allegations made by him are all taken out of the news published in the magazine called 'Pioneer', which is the party magazine of BJP. Dr Subramanian Swamy has chosen to call the articles published in the said magazine as 'investigative reports'. The term investigative reports attributed to the said magazine, particularly in respect of the news items in question are absolutely motivated and malafide exhibiting a deliberate attempt to malign me. This malicious exercise had been started by this magazine against me since the year 2008. Dr Subramanian Swamy had deliberately chosen to place reliance on these reports because his intention in filing the above said Writ Petition before the Delhi High Court is not in any way different from the motive or intention behind the said reports published in the said magazine.... Since the matter is coming before the High Court of Delhi on 18 May 2010 for hearing, I am placing on record the aforesaid facts for necessary further course of action with relevant copies of documents referred." The Solicitor General, Gopal Subramanian appeared on behalf of the Government. That case was rejected in the admission stage itself. On 21 May 2010 another interview of mine appeared in 'The Hindu'. Since the CBI had already filed an FIR on 21 October 2009, that interview assumed further importance. I was asked, "BJP and the CPI (M) want you out of office because your policies on 2G spectrum led to serious loss to the exchequer. They are basing this on the 3G auction prices." I replied, "Let me explain chronologically. The National Telecom Policy 1999 was framed by the NDA Government. It laid down that the 2G spectrum has to be allotted on revenue share basis, since the 1994 policy (of auctioning) failed miserably. The operators who bought the spectrum and the licenses at that time, went to court on the grounds that they were unable to pay, and sought a direction to government to bail them out. The court directed the government to consider. In 1999, the government devised a policy that favoured the revenue route over that of the auction route. Policy-wise, 2G is connected to the common man because it is a basic service meant for public health purposes, education and valuable tool for improvement of rural economy. 3G is for the business community and for entertainment." The next question, "The CBI, the CVC and even the CAG are investigating the 2G spectrum allocation. You say you followed existing policy. Then why is every investigating agency at your door step?" I responded, "No minister is beyond scrutiny. Simply because your blood has been offered to a lab, voluntarily or involuntarily, no one can conclude that you have a chronic disease. The amount of Rs.1650 crore was determined by TRAI as license fee in 2001 and new licenses were issued at the same price even 40 days prior to my taking charge of this Ministry. This was because TRAI did not give any new recommendations after 2001. But it continued to enhance the share in the adjusted gross revenue every year. Due to this, annual revenue of about Rs.15000 crore was accruing to the government. The second criticism is about our following the 'first-come-first served' policy. In 1999, the Cabinet decided not to auction spectrum bandwidth and preferred revenue-sharing method. Since then, right through the tenure of Pramod Mahajan, Arun Shourie, till the tenure of Dayanidhi Maran, this policy continued. There is no other option when there is no scope for auction. Hence, the same method was adopted during my tenure also. I've recorded this in Parliament in the presence of Arun Shourie. No one has denied this and no one can dispute it. The third criticism is about non-auctioning of spectrum bandwidth. In 2007, the Telecom Commission accepted the recommendations of TRAI, which stated that it is not fair to go for auctioning to maintain a level playing field as we have allocated spectrum without auction to the existing operators from 1999. The government too accepted and implemented it. The fourth criticism is about the disposal of shares by the new firms that got the allotment. After scrutiny of both Swan and Unitech at the hands of the Finance Ministry, the Cabinet Committee has approved its finding that these firms have not sold their shares but only diluted the shares to get FDI to raise towers and other infrastructure, well within the legal framework for promoting their business. Neither my Department nor I have any role in it. When this issue was raised for the first time, I discussed this with the Prime Minister and the then Finance Minister, P. Chidambaram. The Finance Ministry is also of the firm view that shares have not been sold."

When the cases of both the CPIL and Subramanian Swamy were rejected by the Delhi High Court on 25 May 2010, they appealed to the Supreme Court in September 2010. I was included as 5th Respondent. At that stage also, a press release was issued by the Telecom Ministry on 27 September 2010 titled 'DoT clarifies that UASL license issued as per the Government Policy.' **In October**

2010, CAG's draft report was 'leaked' even before the DoT could review and respond holistically. On 13 October 2010, 'The Economic Times' printed an article, 'CAG asked to show proof of foul play in license allocation' and 'Financial Express' published an article, 'CAG loops Raja again' on 14 October 2010. The media accorded so much importance to the queries of CAG but did not bother to pay even a fraction of that attention to the elaborate responses furnished by the Telecom Ministry. A news despatch was sent out by PTI on 3 November 2010 titled, 'DoT dismissed CAG charges; Spectrum decisions based on policy,' stating, "In conformity with the established procedures and rules as well as provision enshrined in UASL guidelines and NTP 99, the policies were only implemented by the present Minister of Communication and IT which resulted in the tangible, exponential and unprecedented growth in the sector with high tele-density and lower tariff." At the time of CAG's 'leaked' report Parliament was in session and pandemonium broke out in both Houses. There were rumblings of this being the biggest scam ever in our country. I had no reason to be afraid but started to feel disheartened with the reaction of the Gatekeepers of Justice. On 30 October 2010, 'Times of India' published an article quoting the oral observations of Justice Ganguly of the Supreme Court Bench, "The nature of the complaint is serious, but the same minister (A.Raja) continues.... Is that way the Government function? How long will it take to complete the probe, 10 years?" My counsel T.R. Andhyarujina cautioned the Court, "CBI registered an FIR on October 21 last year and on the very next day raided the Department of Telecom Office and took away 150 files. Then it raided the office of the Telecom Service Providers. Let the CBI give its report. No one should jump the gun." Even so, the CAG report was treated almost like a judicial finding and the due process of law was not adhered to by the Supreme Court Bench. I was unable to express my views in Parliament as proceedings were stalled due to the uproar. I wanted to express my views in public, but my legal counsel advised against it to avoid any negative bearing on the court proceedings. I felt helpless but remained steadfast in the belief that truth and justice would eventually prevail.

I finally spoke my piece in an elaborate interview to the 'The Hindu' on 13 November 2010 which was published the next day with the caption, "It is an institutional aberration; that needs intervention." I stated, "What we have here is a difference of opinion between one constitutional functionary the CAG and other constitutional functionaries, the union Cabinet and the Parliament. The CAG appears to disagree with the Cabinet, Parliament and Telecom Regulating Authority of India (TRAI), a statutory body as well as the Planning Commission. In my opinion, these institutional aberrations must be resolved either by the Judiciary or by the parliamentary mechanism." The irony is that instead of resolving the said aberrations, I was being hounded for punishment by Parliament and the Supreme Court. I came to Delhi from Chennai on the evening of the 14th of November. That morning when I was with our party leader Dr Karunanidhi in the Secretariat, Pranab Mukherjee spoke to him about the pandemonium in the Houses of Parliament. I could sense that our leader felt it would be better for the nation to break the logjam in Parliament, so I offered to resign. When I landed in Delhi around 9.00 pm, T.R. Baalu informed me that I could resign as per the advice of our party leader. While on the way to my official residence 2A, Motilal Nehru Marg I sought an appointment with the PM. I called in my PA, prepared my resignation letter and then went to the PM's residence. The Prime Minister appeared to be gloomy and perturbed. He offered me tea and I handed him my resignation letter. He spoke dejectedly about the whole situation, the oral observations of the Supreme Court and about his name having been unduly dragged down. I carefully listened to him and then with all humility I clearly told him, "The procedure I followed in the allocation of spectrum was all legally valid and correct. Your principal secretary discussed with me once or twice in this regard (The Prime Minister was not aware of this). You came to know only later that an annexure sent along with your letter dated 2 November 2007 which spoke about spectrum auction, was against the NTP-99, the Cabinet decision and the TRAI Recommendation. But, who was responsible for that annexure to be sent along with your letter from the PMO?

How did your senior officials including the Principal Secretary permit that to happen? Had that letter not been sent from your end, you would not be in a mess. CAG too would not have made the absurd comment that I had ignored the advice of the Prime Minister. Without informing you, an unsigned annexure containing the write-up of COAI, contrary to NTP-99, UASL guidelines and TRAI recommendation 2007 was sent to me even without the knowledge of the Joint Secretary (Telecom) in the PMO. I am prepared for any kind of enquiry. Even at this stage I am fully satisfied with my performance in the Telecom Ministry and I am prepared for a debate in the Parliament if need be." I thanked him for the faith he had shown in me as well as his concern and regard for me. The Prime Minister touched upon the introduction of 3G service to the nation and agreed with the impropriety of the CAG's views. While I was clear and firm as I spoke to him, I was unable to make out anything from the vexed-look of the Prime Minister. Was it due to the condemning remarks from the Supreme Court or due to his assuming that there were irregularities in the files in a big way? I was not sure and could not guess. Bertrand Russell once said, "The whole problem with the world is that fools and fanatics are always so certain of themselves, but wiser people so full of doubts." In fact, he had no need to be worried on either front. He came up to the door and fondly saw me off.

After submitting my resignation, I told the press, "I enabled a revolution in the telecom sector. When I took over there were only 300 million connections in the country. Due to my efforts today's teledensity is 729 million. The rate per call for mobile telephone users has also fallen dramatically from ₹ 1.60 to just 40 paise. My conscience is very clear that I have done nothing wrong and I put in my papers based on the advice from my party leader." When I returned to my residence Dr. Kalaignar Karunanidhi's statement was on my table. No sooner had I completed perusing the statement, I received a telephone call from Chennai saying that my leader wanted to speak to me. I told him, "If your heart and pen can greet me like this, I can relinquish office even ten more times." Kalaignar's note had started with the greeting, "My beloved brother Raja, the DMK

Headquarters Propaganda Secretary, the one who has been following steadfast the path of the self-respect movement, the one who has been ceaselessly following the way shown by the reformist leaders like Thanthai Periyar EVR, Perarignar Anna, Dr Ambedkar, the one who continues to be one among my heart-winning young ones as the revolutionary zealot blooming from the parched rustic area in Perambalur of the erstwhile Tiruchirappalli District." Thereafter the statement read, "Refusing to accept any of the explanations that brother Raja merely followed the same procedure followed by the Telecom Ministry in allocating 2G spectrum right from 1999 and stubbornly insisting only on his resignation, a stalemate is on stalling the proceedings of both the Houses of Parliament. All of us have a duty to ensure a flourishing condition to retain the values and neutrality of our Indian Parliamentary Democracy. In order to uphold our part of that duty, it has been decided to withdraw A.Raja from the office of the Union Ministry and it has also been conveyed to A. Raja who is both a Member of Parliament and a Union Minister." The words of Thiruvalluvar rang in my mind,

The death that elicits tears of the Leader
Is worth seeking even by begging - (Tirukkural 780)

The Prime Minister in his acceptance letter written the next day (15 November 2010) remarked, "I would like to take this opportunity to thank you for your contribution to work of our Government." I was content with that and went back to Chennai that week. Thousands of DMK workers were there at the airport to welcome me and console me. On behalf of Dravidar Kazhagam which has groomed me, its leader K. Veeramani was present with a big group of black shirt volunteers. He embraced me to console and to encourage me. That night I met Kalaignar and provided my explanations to allay any lingering doubts, "All my decisions in the 2G issue were not only conforming to the rules; but also the exponential assertion of the Dravidian principle to stand against hegemony and the dominance of monopolists. Unlike the imaginations of many I have not done any wrong. Constitutional bodies themselves have thoroughly misunderstood things and still there is no need to feel fear. I can face the case. My only worry is about the attempts to tarnish our party's image." Once Abraham Lincoln quoted, "There is something significant in politics; Stand with him when he is right. Part with him when he goes wrong." But unfortunately, those who did not stand with me when I was right and those who parted with me even when I did no wrong were greater in number.

On 11 November 2010, the mediatory peace talks initiated by the Hon'ble Speaker of the Lok Sabha Mrs Meira Kumar to end the thirteen-day impasse of the Parliament ended in failure. The opposition was seeking a Joint Parliamentary Committee. For reasons unclear to me, the Government kept shying away from it. The same day, PTI reported a remark made by Gurudas Gupta, CPI, "Why the Government is refusing to accept JPC is bewildering. Government feels many skeletons will come out of its cupboard." I never ever skirted any discussion in Parliament even after the CAG Report was 'leaked'. After my resignation too, when I was speaking to Kalaignar I repeatedly affirmed that the CAG Report was fundamentally and procedurally flawed. "The demand for Joint Parliamentary Committee can be accepted" was my humble submission. Kalaignar also issued a statement that we were prepared for a Joint Parliamentary Committee. Following that, when T.R. Baalu, the leader of the DMK Parliamentary Party conveyed the views of our party leader in the All-Party Meeting, it was P. Chidambaram who openly opposed it and stated that Congress would prefer facing an election rather than a JPC. P. Chidambaram's stand on the 2G case is still a puzzle to me. He is an administrator of strong acumen, an able lawyer and a seasoned Parliamentarian. Yet, I was surprised to see him shying away from discussing the 2G situation with me and even avoiding speaking to me when we happened to pass each other in the airport. The only grouse that I have is that he did not support the idea of the JPC and as a result the Supreme Court Bench had – what I can best describe as – an emotional outburst against me and the government. He need not have done anything to protect or support me, but he could certainly have helped a good Government from being subjected to ignominy and its image being tarnished. I have heard from his Congress party cabinet colleagues that he was of the view that there might be a big scam and hence my arrest was temporarily essential to steer the wrath of the Supreme Court and to avoid criticism against the Prime Minister. This is hearsay and is possibly untrue gossip. However, Chidambaram's silence and his avoiding me put me on caution about what might be coming down the road. I sensed that a decision to put me behind the bars had been taken to salvage the Government's image. I was preparing myself both mentally and physically for jail life – I became vegetarian and started exercising twice daily.

The Government's fitful demeanour due to the negative public opinion and the impasse in Parliament was cleverly exploited by Subramanian Swamy and Prashant Bhushan. Article 32 and 226 respectively enabled the Supreme Court and the High Court to admit PIL cases. The Supreme Court Bench had observed on many occasions "The figure is mind-boggling" referring to CAG's fantastical presumptive loss figure of ₹1.76 lakh crore. The questions raised, the opinions expressed by the Supreme Court Bench on both days (1 and 2 December 2010), made it clear that the Bench was not prepared to raise its head from out of the CAG Report. I watched PTI's exclusive report on TV, dumbfounded by the comments from the bench expressed in open court. Let me recall a quote by Justice V.D. Tulzapurkar, "If the Judiciary is regarded as the heart of a Republic then the Indian republic is at present suffering from serious heart ailment. In fact, the higher Judiciary of the country has, of late, been under constant onslaughts, external as well as internal." On 1 December 2010, PTI published a news report titled, "SC grills Government on spectrum allocation." The report mentioned, "It is noted that only 45 minutes were given to prospective licensees for submitting documents including demand draft and completing formalities. The bench, in a sarcastic manner wondered whether government acted through Telepathy to convey them about the impending allocation within a fraction of 45 minutes." This was the Supreme Court's demeanour in spite of the Counter Affidavit having already clarified, "The Department on 10 December 2007 sought clarification from all the applicants who applied till 25 September 2007 on their UASL applications. It is therefore clear that all the applicants who applied for UASL till 1 October 2007 and particularly those who applied till 25 September 2007 knew by 10 December 2007 about the status of processing of their applications. On 10 January 2008, in the 2nd Press Release, the applicant companies who have submitted applications to DOT for grant of UAS licenses in various service areas on or before 25 September 2007 were requested to depute their Authorized signatory/Company Secretary/ authorized representative with authority letter to collect response(s) of DOT. All were requested to assemble at 3:30 pm on 10 January 2008 at Committee Room, 2nd Floor, Sanchar Bhawan, New Delhi. It was also mentioned that the companies which fail to report before 4:30 P.M. on 10 January 2008, the responses of DOT will be despatched by post. All eligible LOI holders for UASL were to submit compliance to DoT to the terms of LOIs within the prescribed period (15 days from the date of issue of LoI) during the office hours i.e. 9.00 A.M. to 5.30 P.M. on working days. It has been wrongly contended by the Petitioners that 10 January 2008 was the deadline to deposit the entry fee of Rs. 1650 crore within one hour. It is submitted that there was no such deadline."

PTI also reported, "The PM has made his reservations clear which was not treated with respect. There are requirements of collective responsibility. Its action has to be reasonable and in public interests.... In the context of sequence of events bypassing the PM was not at all proper the bench said.... The bench of Justice G.S. Singhvi and A.K. Ganguly took strong exception to the tone and the tenor of Raja's letter to the PM wherein words, 'unfair, discriminatory, capricious and arbitrary' were used.... Look at the command of his (Raja's) language. When you address a letter to the highest Executive, the tenor of the language should be temperate. Here, it is a question of attitude' the bench said, also faulting Raja's attitude." I must reference here Dr Ambedkar's view on collective responsibility, "In my judgment collective responsibility is enforced by the enforcement of two principles, one principle is that no person shall be nominated to the Cabinet except on the advice of the PM. Secondly, no person shall be retained as a minister of the Council, if the PM says that he shall be dismissed. It is only when the member of the Cabinet both in the matter of appointment as well as in the matter of their dismissal are placed under the PM; that it would be possible to realize our ideal of collective responsibility. I do not see any other means or way of giving effect to the principle." Admittedly the PM is the head of the Council of ministers and both are under the constitutional obligation of collective responsibility to the Parliament. Speaking in the Constituent Assembly, Pandit Nehru had quoted "No Supreme Court and No Judiciary can stand in judgment over the sovereign will of the Parliament representing the will of the entire community. If we go wrong here and there, it can point out; but in ultimate analysis where the future of the community is concerned, no judiciary can come in the way.... It is obvious that no court, no system of judiciary can function in the nature of a Third House." The Prime Minister had never expressed chagrin over 'the tone' of any of my letters to him but the Supreme Court was feeling miffed on his behalf. Is it the Supreme Court's place to make sound on grammar and emotional tenor instead of focusing on the legal substance of the matter? Even so, when I knew that my actions were legal and correct why should I refrain from being emphatic? Why should I have diluted the pitch of my voice or the intensity of my words?

According to PTI, the justices of the Supreme Court continued, "The letter of law ministry for taking opinion of AG was ignored; the PM's letter was ignored. Is this the way for Government functioning?" But the Government's Counter Affidavit had already affirmed, "The Petitioners have contended that the advice of the Ministry of Law and Justice has been disregarded. It is submitted that the Ministry of Law and Justice has not given any advice regarding the policy in force on grant of UAS licenses or the first-come first-served issue. The sole question referred to the Ministry was regarding possible options to deal with the large number of applications in a fair manner, i.e., a purely procedural issue. The Ministry of Law and Justice had suggested that the matter be referred to an Empowered

Group of Ministers. However, it was felt that it was not necessary to constitute a Group of Ministers on such a procedural issue since no policy issue was to be examined. In any event, it is submitted that within different branches of Government, sometimes different views are expressed and eventually a particular course of action is adopted. This is part of the normal functioning of Government and no action is questionable simply because it was not as per the suggestion of a particular department." This counter affidavit was prepared entirely by the Telecom Ministry officials with the approval of Telecom Secretary Chandrasekhar. No official including Srivastava, DDG (AS) – a prime witness on the prosecution side – had said on any occasion that the affidavit was faulty or prepared at my instance. The Supreme Court Bench of 2 February 2012 right from the outset observed that whatever happened in the allocation of 2G Spectrum was illegal, unfair and arbitrary just on the basis of CAG's report without giving due accord to the defence's Counter Affidavit and supporting evidence. This must have been the first time in India's judicial history that a Supreme Court Bench had so flippantly ignored the statements made under oath by the Government.

The Presidential Reference filed on 12 April 2012 did not approve of the oral observations of the Supreme Court Bench except for certain observations in their final verdict. Ergo, the judgment was neither accepted by the Cabinet nor was it approved by the larger Constitutional Bench. On the subject of judicial activism S.P. Sathe, opines, "Having become absolutely helpless against growing corruption and misuse of power by persons holding positions of power, the people saw a ray of hope in Judicial Intervention. The courts went up in public esteem because the public saw in it an institution that could protect them from such pollution of democracy." We must also heed the advice of Justice A.S. Anand, "Care has to be taken to see that PIL essentially remains public interest litigation and does not become either political interest litigation or personal interest litigation or publicity interest litigation or used for prosecution." Time will tell which category the 2G litigation falls into. In the second week of November 2010 T.R. Andhyarujina who appeared on my behalf in the Supreme Court called me and spoke openheartedly. "Going by the noise made by the press and media and the happenings in the Parliament, chances are less for the court to proceed as per our expectation; CBI would come to you for enquiry. Prepare yourself mentally and gather documents appropriately. This is my intuition in my long experience." How true was his apprehension about the dominance of emotions over the legal proceedings in the 2G issue! Exactly as he had foretold, the CBI officers surrounded my official residence in 2A, Motilal Nehru Marg, in the cold wintry morning of 8 December 2010 at 7.00 a.m. At first, I thought they had only come for an inquiry. When they told me that they would search my house, I extended total co-operation to the CBI team led by Investigation Officer Vivek Priyadarshi who took my permission to search every single room in my house. Until 9:30 pm they thoroughly checked my residence, camp office, car shed, servants' quarters and all around. Vivek Priyadarshi engaged in conversation with me. I asked him whether the CBI had a legal wing or persons qualified enough to understand the legal/departmental procedures and to consider the appropriate documents including the Telecom policy, its implementation guidelines and the TRAI recommendations. He replied, "Yes, they are there." I pointed out to him that CVC's Assessment Report, CBI's First Information Report and CAG's Audit Report were faulty in the light of the underlying policy documents and also tended to contradict each other. He patiently listened to my elaboration on the monopolies in the telecom sector, the concealing of spectrum availability, the vested interests and about the discussions I had with the Prime Minister. He did not share any of his views. His team had come in strongly believing that they might uncover documents proving hundreds of crores were in my possession. My wholehearted support and pleasant demeanour surprised them. They thanked me as they left my residence. The houses of R.K. Chandolia my Private Secretary, Behura Secretary (Telecom), Srivastava DDG (AS) and Sridhara Additional Secretary and Member (Technology) DoT were also raided because they were suspected to be guilty in the 2G case. Later on, both Sridhara and Srivastava were called as witnesses for the prosecution. Sridhara never wavered from the truth. He and his wife were both suffering from cancer. I was really moved when he said, "The length of my life is known, why should it end with lies? Death is more universal than life; every one dies but not everyone lives" (I recall the works of Alan Sachs). At that same time, the office of my friend Sadiq Batcha, the owner of Green House Promoters Pvt. Ltd was also raided. He was taken into custody for an enquiry and was freed later in the night after day-long grilling. I received many phone calls to inquire after my wellbeing during the course of that day: Kamaraj the journalist and a native of my district; Akilan Ramanathan my former Additional Private Secretary; Dr Krishnamoorthy my friend and family physician. In the following week, their residences and those of many of my relatives were also raided by CBI. Their only fault had been to be related to me or to have called to wish me well. I can never repay my near and dear ones for the persecution that they had to face because of me. Need I even mention what my wife and young daughter had to suffer? After the completion of my tenure as Member of Parliament, when I was required to vacate my official residence in Delhi, no one was willing to even rent a house to me. Some were apprehensive that CBI or Income Tax Department may question them, others were apprehensive due to a foregone conclusion that I was guilty of misappropriating ₹ 1.76 lakh crore.

CHAPTER 7

Unjustified Arrest and Unwarranted Exile

It was disappointing to realize that the Supreme Court's case became not only against the policies of the Government but also against my personal conduct. Our country's media for the most part continued to remain irresponsible and sensationalise uncorroborated information. On 9 December 2010, 'Times of India' under the caption "Raids throw up more dirt on Raja" reported, "searches conducted so far at around 14 places have yielded recovery of incriminating documents' said Vineeta Thakur, DIG of CBI, who was officiating as agency spokesperson." After the CBI raids, when in Chennai I went to a hospital for treatment of my chronic health issues of severe ulcer and irritable bowel syndrome, CBI through its summons on 18 December 2010, asked me to appear for an inquiry in the CBI Headquarters in Delhi on 20 December 2010. When I sought time to complete my medical treatment, CBI granted me an extension until 23 December 2010. Some TV channels stooped to the level of reporting, "Raja tries to escape by getting admitted in hospital."

When I appeared before the CBI at 10.30 a.m. on the appointed day, I found the print media and visual media had already gathered there to 'welcome me'. Around 10.45 am, Vivek Priyadarshi Addl. Superintendent of Police and Rajesh Chegal, Inspector began their enquiry. They started with the question of 'cut-off date'. They had no other files with them except the policy file related to issuance of license. Even from that they were only asking about certain specific notings that had been recorded. Since spectrum availability is inter-alia connected with the fixing of the cut-off date, they asked me about that also. I politely requested them to go through the other related files also to get more explanations and the reasons for the notings in the policy file. Similarly, I requested them to ask for files from the Prime Minister's office and go through the records of the discussions that I had with the PM. But they did not deem that necessary. The first day's inquiry ended in an unsatisfactory state for me as well as for them but the proceedings went on with mutual respect even if the media tried to play things up. On the second day, I was asked about entry fee and auctioning of spectrum.

The second day's inquiry also ended without any turbulence. In between the inquiry on both the days I was also asked about my family genealogy, our family members, their occupation and their property details. They asked me about my friend Sadiq Batcha's Green House Promoters Ltd including the details of my wife's role as Director (Legal) in that company. I started to sense that my name might now be included in the FIR registered against 'unknown officers' earlier in October 2009. After returning home in the night from the inquiry, I was trying to recall the records in the various files and documents. It was not possible for me to leverage my personal secretary or other ministry officials to dig up the information because all of them had also been separately summoned for inquiry. All of them were fearful. In particular, Srivastava (DDG) was hesitant even to talk to me at CBI Headquarters or in court. I still vividly recall my brief encounter with Srivastava after he had completed his final deposition in court. His eyes voiced his heart's muted disquiet as I said, "I am happy that you and your family were not put to any hardship. Have a peaceful retirement life." Srivastava, D.S. Mathur, Sridhara and other officers including Nitin Jain were summoned by CBI for inquiry. CBI must presumably have wanted to cross-check my explanations with the other officials. I was asked to appear for further inquiry only on 31 January 2011. CBI had confirmed by then from the documents seized during their searches that I did not have the evidence they thought of finding. Till that date no DoT official had deposed before the CBI that irregularities had taken place or that "the Minister had taken all the decisions and coerced the department."

CBI began its inquiry from a new angle that TATA Telecom was adversely affected by my actions – which was contrary not only to their earlier perspective but also to the public perception that I had in fact been unduly favourable to TATA in collusion with Nira Radia. I will first deal with the allegation that I had caused significant delay in clearing TATA's file. TATA's application for dual technology was received on 22 October 2007. The letter of in-principle approval was issued to them on 10 January 2008 alongside the LOIs for the new UASL applicants. TATA also deposited the crossover fee on the same day, like all the other applicants. TATA had also applied for new UASLs in three circles, and LOI for these were also issued on the same day. Thus, two files of TATA were being processed together – one file for grant of UASL and one file for amending the existing UASL to permit dual technology. TATA did not produce the 'No Dues Certificate' from the WPC – which is a mandatory pre-condition as per DoT policy and TRAI recommendations – for a considerable period of time and it is only on 27 February 2008 that there came a note by the Secretary (T) that this Certificate has been issued and the license may be signed. I approved the papers on the same day and also cleared the file for amendment of TATA's existing UASL to enable dual technology. Though there is no discussion in this file regarding No Dues Certificate, the fact is that both files were considered together by me and the moment TATA furnished the No Dues Certificate, I cleared both files. Thus, there is no substance in the allegation that I delayed the clearing of the TATA file. In spite of all this, on 31 January 2011, the CBI officers showed me only the file (F.No. 1021/2004/BS- II) related to TATA Telecom's application for Dual Technology and tried to make out that there was criminal intent in such an inordinate delay for processing the application. Through that they wanted to establish that Swan Telecom was unjustifiably enabled to get GSM spectrum ahead of TATA and accordingly 200 crores had been paid off to Kalaignar TV. A superficial look might give the impression that this suspicion was justified because the file did not have any reference to the pending dues that TATA owed to the Government. Only the file that did not contain reference to 'No Dues

Certificate' was shown to me by the CBI while the other related file was not produced. I could not remember all the details then. I just said that the valid reason must be in some other file. The CBI started to view this as a chink in my 'armour'. That day's interrogation ended with CBI asking me to appear again on 2 February 2011. I could not sleep all night as I kept trying to recollect the details of the TATA application. Next day i.e. on 1 February 2011, I recalled the actual reason for keeping the TATA Telecom file on hold from 23 January 2008 to 27 February 2008. In fact, TATA Telecom themselves did not want their file to be turned down for pending dues with consequent action on it and hence the delay was based on a fair request made on behalf of TATA themselves. That too had been noted in another file as 'Taking a view whether signing of the UASL agreements is to be done after fresh no dues certificate from WPC'. I verified this thoroughly and then I contacted and explained this to T.R. Baalu and requested him to get an appointment with Kapil Sibal – my successor as Telecom Minister – the same night. Baalu got me an appointment for 8.00 PM at Sibal's residence. I told Sibal, "I have not come to seek any favour from you. I want to give certain clarifications to the Government. CBI's argument is that there was a wilful delay on my part in signing TATA's application for dual technology. As you are also an able lawyer in addition to being the Telecom Minister, you may please go through the file notings yourself to understand that I was only waiting for the 'No Dues Certificate' from WPC to provide my signature. Had I signed without this certificate it is only then that it could have been termed as abuse of power." He was of the opinion that my point was justified. I asked him whether he could consider issuing a statement on behalf of the Telecom Ministry about the stand taken by the CBI. Sibal explained, "Even my press meet has been criticized by the Supreme Court. When the bench has conveyed that even such press meets are to be avoided, how can I or the officials of the Department meet and express views or give clarifications even if they are justified as it would be construed to be wrong?" He also suggested that I should explain this to the CBI the next day. I said, "It occurs to me that CBI is not in a mind set to listen to this," to which he responded, "In fact, some in the Cabinet would like the Government to distance itself from explaining things in 2G case. Not only that but some of them are also against you." I had to finally accept the fact that no one would come forward to speak on my behalf in this case due to the media attention, political imbroglio and the direct monitoring by the Supreme Court.

On 2 February 2011 at 10 am I went to the office of the CBI and found a big crowd of newsmen with cameras. My friend N. Rajendran an advocate and Perambalur Town Secretary of DMK, and my brother-in-law Dr Gowthaman a physician had accompanied me that day. They remained in the lower floor of the CBI office while I went to the office of Rajesh Chegal the DSP. I tried to give my explanation to the questions that had been raised by the CBI on 31 January 2011. It appeared that only Rajesh Chegal had some understanding of the file notings and policy decisions but it was also evident that he was not in a position to persuade his higher-ups to see reason. He was looking at me sympathetically when I explained about TATA's Dual Technology license, spectrum allocation and 'No Due Certificate' issue. I requested him to record my statement. He asked me to wait for a while and went out of the room. I could discern that he was talking to his DIG and SP. At the same time, on the ground floor clamour and tension was visibly building up. I also heard the rumblings, "Former Minister has been arrested." At around 12.30 p.m. Chegal, returned. I was not really surprised by the hesitant look in his eyes when he told me that I was under arrest. The CBI officers had called my friends Rajendran and Dr Gowthaman to inform them of my arrest. I was surprised to see Rajendran entering the room weeping so openly. I had never seen him cry before. With tears in his eyes, Dr Gowthaman tested my blood pressure using the equipment he had brought along with him. My reading was 120/80. The DSP requested him to test his BP as well. It was 160/110. I joked, "Who has been found culprit? Me or CBI?" He not only laughed but also shared it over the phone with his DIG and SP. I said, "I have nothing to hide and I have nothing to fear."

There was no further inquiry that day. The next day around noon,

I was produced before Hon'ble O.P. Saini, Judge of the Special court. Former Telecom Secretary Behura and my Private Secretary Chandolia were also arrested and produced before that court. When I was boarding the police vehicle, a lot of reporters were trying to question me and capture me on their cameras. I raised my hands and said, "I will face the case." When I was presented before the special court, the CBI sought permission for police custody which was granted. I was remanded to police custody till 17 February 2011. The court permitted my family members to meet me for about an hour every day. The statements of the prosecution witnesses Sridhara, Srivastava and Aggarwal were obtained in my presence. I was shown their statements and was asked to confront them. They had referred to several contexts and file notings which were all favourable to me. In fact, when the CBI arrested me they did not have adequate evidence even after obtaining statements from many parties. The senior officers gave fair statements that would enable anyone to conclude that the entire case itself was half-baked. The DSP, CBI who knew in detail the file notings and statements of the witnesses faced embarrassment in several legal situations. It could be seen that he was often going into the rooms of the DIG and SP. It was only after my arrest that CBI initiated full scrutiny into all the relevant files. Till then only raids and preliminary enquiries had been conducted. Most of the statements obtained prior to my arrest hardly bolstered their case against me.

Palsania, the DIG wanted to see me and called me to his room once. The SP and DSP were also present. He was young and earnest. His interest in knowing what actually happened even after my arrest, made two things clear to me: (1) The CBI's information to that point was inadequate; (2) I was arrested due to the pressure from external influences. Palsania candidly accepted one thing, "It has to be appreciated that you broke the 'cartel' which was manipulatively protected in the telecom sector. But the haste you had shown to break it gave rise to many doubts." His open acceptance was a consolation for me. As he was aware of my health issues and the related treatment, he suggested that I could try to apply for medical privileges while in police custody. I said that I had been a minister for ten years and was not a coward to find excuses to avoid imprisonment. I stated categorically that I would not ask for bail until all those who had been arrested with me were released on bail. Their expressions clearly revealed their surprise over my reply. Palsania told me then that they were not in agreement with the view that there was a loss to the exchequer. He also told me that the CBI would not accept the yardstick used by the CAG to arrive at a loss figure. But later on, the CBI applied a new yardstick to compute revenue loss to the Government in order to play along with the Supreme Court and placate the media. I asked, "If that illusion is not there, where is the need for the arrest? All details are in the files. Even if I had made wealth as suspected by you, will it be possible to hide those property documents?" He replied, "You may know this yourself. This is a political decision considered to be a needed measure."

On 16 February 2011, a day before I was to be handed over to judicial custody, I was sent to meet Y.P. Singh Joint Director, CBI. He started the conversation in a normal manner and showed interest in my perspective about the monopoly in the Telecom sector. He was of the view that there were many violations of rules in the 2G case. He asked, "Just because there was an injustice going on, you had acted ignoring the law. Are you a Robin Hood?" I raised my voice and asked in response, "If you would agree with me that there was injustice prompting me to act like a Robin Hood, can my agreeing to that role be a corruption / a scam?" Then I simmered down, "I say this just for arguments' sake." Mark Twain appropriately warned us all, "The History of our race and each individual's experience, are shown thick with evidence that a truth is not hard to kill and that a lie told is immortal." Those who lie need to remember things, which is why as I have demonstrated the ministry files, official documents and the earlier actions of the parties concerned contradicted these lies. It is inherent in the nature of motivated persons to show passion and to be expeditious in action especially in the face of resistance. I am no exception to this. It is perhaps also natural to think in hindsight that the emotions and drive could have been mellowed and I am willing to accept such criticism. However, I can sincerely reaffirm that there was no self-interest, violation of law or subterfuge on my part.

On 17 February 2011, I was sent to judicial custody in Tihar Jail. I was admitted to ward No.9 of jail No.1. Behura and Chandolia were already in custody there. Some ex-policemen from Delhi were also there serving life sentences for their involvement in a fake encounter. An IPS Officer Ravi Kant Sharma was also imprisoned there. Shahid Balwa who was arrested the next day was put in the adjacent ward. I became friendly with the fellow prisoners and jail staff that night itself. Most of them had some role in the jail's administration. They diverted my restless mind through their show of concern and co-operation. After many days, I had a good night's sleep. After breakfast the next morning, I started reading books that I had brought with me. I spent some time discussing the court case with Behura and Chandolia. Sahid Balwa and Asif Balwa who were in the next ward would also join us during the daytime. Neeraj Kumar Director General of the prison and R.N. Sharma DIG who came for an inspection met us individually and enquired after our health. It occurred to me that right from the superintendent to the jailers all were trained in how to deal with first-time prisoners. In a week or two, many prisoners came to me seeking legal assistance. I felt sad that there were many prisoners in custody who were neither being tried in court nor granted bail. Shahid Balwa who was imprisoned along with me was keen to find legal remedy for this injustice. We filed a PIL through his lawyer Vijay Aggarwal in Delhi High Court based on which many under-trials were freed.

Around the same time a discussion occurred in Parliament regarding setting up of a Joint Parliamentary Committee to deliberate on the 2G case. As a Member of Parliament as also an affected party, I was eager to participate in the proceedings of the JPC. I expressed my desire by sending a message to T.R. Baalu. I was saddened to note that the Government did not like my action. On 2 April 2011, the first charge-sheet was filed which in addition to me included Siddharth Behura, Chandolia, Shahid Balwa and Vinod Goenka of Swan Telecom, Sanjay Chandra of Unitech, Gowtham Doshi, Surender

Pipara and Hari Nair of Reliance. The companies Swan, Unitech and Reliance were also named. The charge-sheet that was filed with five subheadings: cut-off date, first come first served, dual technology, eligibility and non-revision of entry fee also highlighted "DB group companies paid Rs.200 crores to M/s. Kalaignar TV Pvt Ltd between December 2008 and August 2009 following a circuitous route through Kusegon Fruits Pvt Ltd and Cineyug Film Pvt Ltd." Asif Balwa and Rajiv Aggarwal were already under arrest because of this. The charge-sheet also mentioned, "However chain of this and another suspected quid pro quo related to Green House Promoters Pvt Ltd needs to be consolidated and further evidence needs to be collected to prove the allegation." The second charge-sheet filed on 25 April 2011 did not state that I had any association with the Income, Expense or Equity (shares) of Green House Promoters Pvt Ltd nor did it mention any commercial irregularities or offences by the company. There was no charge except for the mention that some of my relatives including my wife were associated with that company. However, with reference to money transfers pertaining to Kalaignar TV, Mrs Kanimozhi, MP who was a Director in the company for a brief period was named as an accused in the charge-sheet. The case was on the question of whether the money transfer was a legal loan or a quid pro quo for my alleged favours to Swan Telecom. As the case is pending before the court, going into it now would be construed as interfering in the court proceedings. The Patiala House Special Court rejected the bail application of Vinod Goenka, Sanjay Chandra, Gowtham Doshi, Surender Pipara and Hari Nair on 20 April 2011. They were sent to prison that very evening. Similarly, the bail applications filed by Mrs Kanimozhi and Sharad Kumar who were included in the second charge-sheet were rejected by the Patiala House Special Court on 20 May 2011 and they were also sent to prison. An exclusive van was provided for us the '2G accused'. Every day after the trial, permission was given to interact with family members and lawyers for an hour. I was motivated to complete the case proceedings even quicker than the fast pace that the Supreme Court had prescribed. Even when I fell sick with diarrhoea and fever on 17 April 2012, I suffered through the night and was being treated by the jail doctors till 4 am but I proceeded to the trial court at 11 am once I was sure that the diarrhoea had stopped. I explained to the court when asked to explain my delay that I was unwell and had yet come ignoring the doctor's advice with the continued intention to expedite the trial proceedings. Life in prison gave me more time to read books. Kalaignar's 'Nenjukku Neethi' (Justice to Heart) is the book that bolstered my spirit with each page that I read. Passages like, "more than the pleasure derived in sharing joy, the real pleasure is in sharing suffering.... It is easy to criticize; wagging tongues may also get wide applause; but doesn't the critic's heart also, require peace." The needless imprisonment of 15 months was a loss of personal liberty, but I consider it a small price for bringing mobile phones to the hands of India's rural masses. Adhering to the thoughts of the great American writer Henry David Thoreau, "Be not simply good; Be good for some cause," I never backed away from facing the consequences of my well-intentioned actions. In a Convocation Address at Annamalai University, Arignar Anna said,

"Fight against Caste which cannot co-exist with Democracy
Fight against superstition which cannot co-exist with Science
Fight against tyranny which cannot co-exist with Liberty, Equality and Fraternity"

Those lines have not only impressed me but have been guideposts for me. Periyar EVR has also quoted "Human life devoid of yeomen service is an animal life." Life without a cause is meaningless; fighting for a cause always involves struggle. Taking the beaten path and steering clear of struggles is like the existence of a domesticated animal, which is not acceptable to me.

While in prison, I was disheartened and distressed on three occasions. One was the sad demise of Sadiq Batcha, my good friend and the Managing Director of Green House Promoters Pvt Ltd. I heard the news on TV while conversing with T.R. Baalu in the jail visitors' room. Baalu tried his best to console me but I broke down grief-stricken. It was agonising to see the kind of end that he had – he was found hanging at his home in Chennai. He had left Delhi affirming that there was no financial irregularity in his company. Yet he took his own life because he felt shamed and persecuted. Based on newspaper reports the CBI's scanner was on Green House Promoters right from 2009 and raids were conducted in their Chennai offices in January 2010. The second incident was the untimely death of my brother-in-law Deepak. He had met me in jail just a few days before his sudden death due to a heart-attack suffered while exercising. The third was on 2 February 2012 when the Supreme Court Bench cancelled all 122 telecom licenses issued during my tenure. Even though, I was not a party named in that case, several inappropriate accusations were directed at me. I feel deeply hurt at the manner in which this was conducted. For instance, that judgment states, "the scarce natural resource spared by the Army has been grabbed by those who enjoy money power and who have been able to manipulate the system." In reality, not even one Mega Hertz of Spectrum was received from Defence Department (Army). I have already explained how I was the one who had dug up 'hidden spectrum'. I still don't know what evidence was used to confirm that spectrum had been obtained from Defence. Whereas the DoT's response dated 27 July 2010 to the CAG was submitted as evidence where it has been clearly stated on page 23, "The WPC Wing of DOT was directed by the Hon'ble MoC&IT to coordinate utilised spectrum from various agencies. As a result, about 30-40 MHz of unutilised spectrum was found in each of the telecom circle." Similarly, the judgment points out, "to say the least the entire approach adopted by TRAI was lopsided and contrary to the decision taken by the Council of Ministers and its recommendations became a handle of the then MOCIT and the officers of the DoT who virtually gifted away the important natural asset at throw away prices." As pointed out earlier, the Presidential Reference presented to the Constitutional Bench on behalf of the Government put forth a diametrically opposite version and the Bench had accepted it. I was sad not only due to the abuse spewed at me but also because of the socio-economic and political fall-out from the cancellation of 122 licenses. The view of the larger Constitutional Bench that the spectrum need not be auctioned should clearly nullify a primary reason cited by the Supreme Court Bench, for the cancellation of licenses.

It is the norm for justices to steer of Media appearances and more specifically to avoid commenting on their own judgements. Lord Kilmuir (AG of England) concluded, "as a general rule it is undesirable for the members of the Judiciary to appear on television by suggesting so long as a judge keeps silence his reputation for wisdom and impartiality remains unassailable; but every utterance which he makes in public, except in the course of actual performance of his Judicial duties, must necessarily bring him within the focus of criticism." However, A few days after his retirement as Supreme Court Judge, Ganguly gave an interview to CNN-IBN TV channel on 19 February 2012. The interviewer was Karan Thapar. A portion of the interview runs this way:

Karan Thapar: But you are absolutely convinced that in this instance the principle of collective responsibility does not apply?

Jutice Ganguly: Possibly ... that is not followed.

Karan Thapar: It was not followed. Raja acted unilaterally which is why his colleagues in Cabinet don't share any blame?

Justice Ganguly: Possibly ...Yes.

Are conclusions that are prefaced with 'possibly' acceptable in Jurisprudence? Can they be used to punish not only an individual (me) but the entire nation? It would mean that his judgment is 'presumption of possibility' rather than being a judgment based on either 'presumption of law' or 'presumption of fact'. I recall US Justice Robert Jackson's perspective on the ideal for the Supreme Court, "We are not final because we are infallible. We are infallible because we are final." Justice Ganguly also said, "Every judgment is open to criticism. I don't say that no judgment is just ... it can be criticized. But you need reasons why.... There is nothing called a senior judge or a junior, He is doing his duty, He is a judge, Every judge is independent of...." But it was he who raised the question whether a Junior Minister (I) can ignore the advice of a Senior Minister (Law Minister) during the court hearings. An editorial related to this interview was published by The Indian Express on

22 February 2012. "Let the verdict speak – 2G case, Justice Ganguly should avoid commenting on the 'meaning' of his judgment. There is a trial on in the trial court and some of the parties affected by cancellation order have said they intend to file review or seek the court clarifications while Justice Ganguly is free to reflect on his own decisions – and such reflection does richly add to public discussion – It would be advisable to refrain from any commenting, while the legal process is on." Another editorial from the Hindu on 23 July 2015 is also worth quoting. "That all these tasks are crucial but tardily undertaken by the Government can scarcely be questioned. But for an unelected and largely unaccountable institution such as the Supreme Court to be at the forefront of matters relating to Governance is equally dangerous. The choice of issues it takes up is arbitrary, their remit is not legal, their results often counter–productive, requiring a degree of technical competence and institutional capacity in ensuring compliance that the court does not possess." How apt are the words of the great Irish political rebel Robert Emmet, "My lords, it may be a part of the system of angry justice to bow a man's mind by humiliation to the purposed ignominy of the scaffold; but worse to me than the purposed shame or the scaffold's terrors would be the shame of such foul and unfounded imputations as have been laid against me in this court."

Even now I cannot believe why the (UPA-II) Government which had a number of accomplished lawyers in its ranks, never bothered to probe deeper and expose the truth? After my release from prison on bail on 15 May 2012, I cautiously but steadfastly continued to follow up. In July 2012, I along with T.R. Baalu met Pranab Mukherjee at his residence. The Telecom Minister Kapil Sibal, Law Minister Salman Khurshid, Minister of State for Personnel and PMO Narayanasamy were also present there. I was direct and emphatic in my message to them, "I thank all of you for the consoling words. But words cannot be a medicine to the pain. The Government's manner of conducting itself in the 2G case was completely unjustified. I wholeheartedly want the CBI to remain an autonomous body. I do not mind the imprisonment for 15 months. I still feel I had brought about a revolution in the telecom sector. That way, it is not new for history to depict a revolution as a crime. But, have you ever read the CBI charge-sheet at least once? The CBI files a charge-sheet accusing 'Investigation reveals that no such meeting took place between accused Raja, External Affairs Minister Pranab Mukherjee and Solicitor General as claimed by Raja in his letter to PM.' The Solicitor General of the Government was telling an unadulterated lie saying that the meeting did not take place at all when the same had really taken place in your office at the instance of the PM. As a consequence, I was charged for 'forgery'. When the situation had gone to that extent why did you and the Government maintain silence and how could it be justified? Even now, I have not come to seek any favour. But, when the CBI was alleging that the PM's advice was ignored and the advice of Finance Minister was ignored, was it not necessary for the Prime Minister and the Finance Minister to tell the CBI their views? Those who said in the Parliament 'policy is correct; implementation may be wrong' could have written to the CBI at least that much. Have you and your people ever sat down calmly to think about the so called 'fault' in the implementation? I was for JPC. Only your ministers were saying no to the setting up of JPC. You were not even having people to watch what was happening in the JPC. I would like to say humbly just one thing. Some of you might have considered that it was politically prudent to think that there was nothing wrong in sending an individual Raja to prison in order to save an institution called the Government. Such thinking is flawed as sacrificing the individual would lead to the institution itself being taken to the sacrificial altar." After that we were together for around 10 minutes more. They enquired about the case's progress in court. They expressed their views and shared their concern about the Supreme Court judgment. Putting his hands on my shoulder, Pranab Mukherjee said "Let bygones be bygones; let all that is to happen be good." I thanked him and the others. We came out with the satisfaction of having vented our anguish. I had shared the same thoughts with Union Minister G.K. Vasan who came to console me at my residence both after my resignation and after my release from prison. My warning of the UPA government's downfall came true in the results of the 2014 General Elections. "Those who ignore history are condemned to repeat it."

The proceedings of the JPC shocked me. Some of the depositions were very guarded and appeared to be motivated by self-preservation. The first place in this regard goes to Vahanvati. I had written both to P.C. Chacko, the Chairman of the JPC and Mrs Meira Kumar, the Lok Sabha Speaker on multiple occasions requesting them to invite me as a witness.

S.No	Date	From	To	Letter Details
1	22-Feb-13	A. Raja	Lok Sabha Speaker	Requesting permission to appear before the JPC as a witness to tender evidence
2	8-Mar-13	Director JPC	A. Raja	Request to furnish replies to a questionnaire on the grounds of paucity of time
3	13-Mar-13	A. Raja	Chairman JPC	Requesting permission to appear before the JPC to tender evidence
4	18-Mar-13	A. Raja	A. Raja	Enclosure containing written response to the queries provided by JPC Secretariat
5	18-Mar-13	Chairman JPC	A. Raja	Acknowledgment of Raja's letter of 18-Mar-13
6	26-Mar-13	A. Raja	Chairman JPC	Claim of appearance before the JPC
7	4-Apr-13	Chairman JPC	A. Raja	Declining request because JPC was in possession of all relevant documents to prepare its report
8	9-Apr-13	A. Raja	Chairman JPC	Expressing disappointment in not being permitted to depose before the JPC
9	16-Apr-13	Chairman JPC	A. Raja	Per Speaker Lok Sabha only secretary of a Minister/Former-Minister can give evidence in JPC
10	22-Apr-13	A. Raja	Chairman JPC	Detailed note on the entire issue of 2G
11	22-Apr-13	Chairman JPC	A. Raja	Since JPC deliberations are concluded, draft report is before the committee for adoption
12	23-Apr-13	A. Raja	Chairman JPC	Reiterating stand that he should be permitted to depose before JPC
13	23-Apr-13	Chairman JPC	A. Raja	Declining permission to appear before JPC based on majority decision of the JPC members

My first letter to Hon'ble Lok Sabha Speaker read, "... It is perhaps unprecedented that an issue has attracted the simultaneous attention of so many agencies. Unfortunately however, the truth of the matter is being suppressed on the basis of the preconceived notions, deliberate bias, faulty investigation and erroneous conclusions, aided by media intent on sensationalism.... While I have fullest respect for the Judiciary, the fact remains that I have been condemned unheard. The Judgment also contains finding that are demonstrably contrary to the facts and documents on record.... I recall the words of Justice V.R. Krishna Iyer who said that 'Parliament is a grand inquest of the nation, the great auditor and ombudsman of the executive, the final arbiter, the policy monitor and destiny decider of the people' ... and therefore, I beg to bring a few shocking facts regarding the observation of the CAG and the consequential order of the Supreme Court before the august Parliament for proper appraisal and resolution." However, I was continually declined invitation to the JPC and given excuses like paucity of time and practical difficulties. On 22 April 2013, I sent a written statement of 103-pages attached with my letter to the JPC as per their request. I said "Even without waiting for my statement, you have prepared a draft report and also leaked it to the media. I would submit that this is not the way the JPC is expected to function.... I trust that it (my statement) will be a part of the report to be given." My statement was a befitting rejoinder to every allegation made by the CBI in its charge-sheet. I gave clarifications on the issuance of license and allocation of spectrum from 1994 to 2008. I stated the sequence of all that had happened in order to reiterate the administrative integrity in all my actions. I stressed, "The controversy was looked into by the Supreme Court, the CAG and by this JPC. None of these bodies have bothered to give me a hearing.... It must be understood that the CBI is the investigative and prosecuting arm of the Central Government. If the Hon'ble PM says in the Parliament that there has been no loss to the exchequer, how can the Government stand by silently while the CBI prosecutes me for alleged loss to the exchequer? It is truly unbelievable and this attitude of the Government can perhaps only be explained as an exercise in blame-shifting or acting on political consideration." I also met P.C. Chacko, the Chairperson of the JPC on two or three occasions. But he had a closed mind and remained firm that he would not invite me before the JPC perhaps because he incorrectly felt that my deposition in JPC would show the PM, FM and the UPA-II government in a bad light on parliamentary record. When I met him along with T.R. Baalu who is also a Member of JPC, he pacified us with an assurance that my 103-pages rejoinder would be attached intact in totality as part of the JPC Report. There was nothing more that I could expect from such a weakling. This deliberate stance led to people like Yashwant Sinha to write to the Prime Minister (on 23 April 2013), asking, "Is it not time Prime Minister that you speak on these issues by appearing before the JPC? Your silence will confirm the worst fear of the people of India that you were fully involved in the 2G scam and if Shri Raja is guilty so are you."He was only mocking us both as if we had orchestrated a big scam but he refused to acknowledge my detailed statement which stressed that there was no irregularity or corruption. P.C. Chacko broke even his last flimsy promise and did not attach my written statement to the JPC Report. More than ten Members of Parliament including Yashwant Sinha, T.R. Baalu and Jaswant Singh wrote to the speaker of Lok Sabha to reject the JPC Report – but to no avail. On 9 November 2013, Yashwant Sinha wrote, "My request to you is to reject the report even at this stage in order to ensure no permanent damage is done to the (institution of JPC) Parliament itself and to the Parliamentary system of democracy in our country." Yet there was some small consolation for me in that the JPC Report established with appropriate documentary evidence that there was no loss to the Government. I was also feeling proud that my 103-page statement was not criticized or denounced. However, the JPC report did still find fault with the implementation of FCFS in order to shift the burden of blame from the government to me as an individual.

When the examination of witnesses was almost over in the 2G case, the Enforcement Directorate initiated its case. The CBI's charge-sheet was filed only after the Supreme Court issued an order on 16 December 2010 directing the Enforcement Directorate, CBI and Income Tax Department to share the information gathered amongst each other. Yet, the Enforcement Directorate filed their case extremely late and that too just a day after the 2014 General Election. Had the Supreme Court's order been followed diligently, the Enforcement Directorate's case ought to have been filed much before. It gave rise to many doubts about the political motivation as the alliance between Congress and DMK had been broken by that point. Strangely, Amritham and Mrs Dayalu Ammal, the Directors of Kalaignar TV who were brought in as witnesses in the CBI case were included as accused in the ED's case. It is not clear how it is logical or just for one government agency to assign some people as prosecution witnesses while another agency treats them as accused in the same matter. Many rumours floated that the ED's case was meant to put political pressure on the DMK. The CBI's investigating officer Vivek Priyadarshi admitted in open court on 13 November 2013 that there were no Disproportionate Assets held by me or my family members. On 18 August 2015, the Chennai wing of the CBI conducted raids on the properties on which the Delhi Head Quarters CBI had already completed their search and inquiry in 2010 itself. They then erroneously calculated all the assets which were already scrutinised by CBI Delhi and declared to be not connected to me as belonging to me and added it up to claim that I had ₹ 27 crores of Disproportionate Assets. This contradiction between the Delhi HQ of CBI and the Chennai branch of CBI has again tarnished the image of the CBI's integrity and credibility. Even though the Supreme Court did not heed my pleas, I came forward to uphold the order of the Judiciary without seeking adjournment or postponement of hearings even on health grounds for even a single day. I had only asked for exemption in certain contexts where my presence was not strictly required. Above all these, I volunteered to step into the witness box to depose evidence for 14 days. Many senior lawyers commented that it was the first time an accused and that also a former Minister had voluntarily opted to be a witness in such a big case. I say this not to pat myself on the back but to highlight my motivation for revealing the Truth. Let me quote again Justice V.R. Krishna Iyer whom I had quoted in an interview published in 'The Hindu', "The Highest is not above the law; the humblest is not beneath the law."

CHAPTER 8

Closing Arguments

I am reminded of the story of the elephant and the four visually challenged men when I think about how the CVC, CBI, CAG and JPC have perceived the 2G situation. In the original anecdote when four visually challenged men encountered an elephant, one of them touched only the ears and concluded that the elephant was like a winnower; another felt just the body of the elephant and deduced that it was like a wall; the third person stroked the elephant's trunk alone and declared that it was like a pillar; the last one held merely the tail of the elephant and proclaimed that it was like a rope. Similarly, the "2G elephant" was handled in isolated pieces and without a holistic vision and perspective by these four august bodies resulting in false conclusions and consequent unjustified accusations against me. Again, the words of Justice V.R. Krishna Iyer can be recalled "Administrative incompetence matched by judicial laze hubris and inadequate appreciation of ground realities-what can be the recipe?." The oral comments passed in the open court and the observations /findings made in the order of cancellation of 122 licences by their Lordships Singhvi and Ganguly were absolute preconception on the basis of the CAG Report. If we trust in Umeshwar Prasad Verma words from his book Law Legislature and Judiciary "When the performance of the Government is far behind the normal expectations of the people, when the individual interests and the social interests clash, when the Government fails to govern, when the civil service instead of being a steel frame of administration turns into a wooden frame, when the parliament and legislature remain merely ventilating chamber and when the game of politics becomes unethical, activism of the judiciary remains the only hope"; then we must also heed the caution of David Pannic QC in his famous book 'Judges', "Unless and until we treat judges as fallible human being whose official conduct is subject to the same official analysis as that of other organs of government, judges will remain members of a priesthood who have great powers over the rest of the community, but who are otherwise isolated from them and misunderstood by them, to their mutual disadvantage." After having examined hundreds of witnesses and reviewed more than ten thousand pages of document exhibits, the real elephant must now be discerned in the Trial Court by his Lordship O.P. Saini. I concluded my defence arguments in a short span of fifteen days whereas the CBI conducted a marathon argument lasting more than a year. Despite these efforts of the CBI it has become quite apparent that the case framed by them is non-est. It is assumed that the object of a trial is to unearth the truth – to find answers. However, this trial against me has brought to the surface more questions than answers.

It is my contention that the sanctity of the CAG was severely compromised by its then head Vinod Rai. Rai clearly had ulterior motives in overreaching the bounds of his constitutional function. He tried to foist his personal (or influenced) agenda by sensationalising information and creating the appearance of procedural lapses and financial misappropriation. His presumptive loss figure of ₹ 1.76 lakh crore has been subsequently debunked but it became engraved in public memory and led to my tribulations. The views and comments of R.P. Singh, a former director general of audit and part of the CAG's team during the 2G audit have been published widely in the news. Singh told the parliamentary panel investigating the 2G spectrum scam that he had been forced to sign on the CAG's report. He disputed the CAG's presumptive loss calculation, dubbing the figure of ₹ 1.76 lakh crore to be 'subjective' and declared that presumptive loss was not part of the accounting code accepted internationally. Responding to cross-examination at the JPC on multiple occasions, Singh said he was only asked to provide inputs for the report, while it was prepared at the CAG headquarters; and that he had deleted the presumptive loss figure from the report, but it was later included by senior officers at the insistence of Rai. The differences between Singh and the CAG first surfaced when he said that field audit team of the national auditor had calculated the loss figure at ₹ 2,645 crore in the draft report and not ₹ 1.76 lakh crore. Singh had also emphasised that as the government had taken a policy decision against auctioning spectrum and TRAI had not recommended it, there was in fact zero loss to the exchequer. He opined that the CAG should not have looked into policy decisions taken by the government and that the loss figure of ₹ 1.76 lakh crore was at best the mathematical speculation of an individual with no evidence to support it. However, the political build-up in the 2G case has been so heavy that even this open rebuttal has left Rai quite unscathed. All attempts to clarify the truth to Rai during the CAG audit and even thereafter have been fruitless.

It is my conviction consequent to the whole experience of the trial that there was political motivation to kill UPA-II and Rai's was the shoulder on which the gun was placed. It is indeed sad that in spite of having so many intelligence agencies and eminent legal minds at its disposal the UPA-II government could not sense this and only tried to use me as a shield but were still unable to escape the bullet. I admired the strongly worded observation of Justice Amitava Ray in his judgement by which Ms J. Jayalalitha's, (the former Chief Minister of Tamil Nadu) conviction was upheld in the Supreme Court "A self-serving conduct in defiance of such solemn undertaking in infringement of the community's confidence reposed in them is therefore a betrayal of the promise of allegiance to the Constitution and a condemnable sacrilege. Not only such a character is an anathema to the preambulor promise of justice, liberty, equality, fraternal dignity, unity and integrity of the country, which expectantly ought to animate the life and spirit of every citizen of this country, but also is an unpardonable onslaught on the constitutional religion that forms the bedrock of our democratic polity." I sincerely hope that I have clearly and factually

demonstrated that Rai in his unscrupulous quest for self-aggrandizment betrayed the community confidence and committed condemnable sacrilege. In the aftermath of the Jalianwala Bagh massacre, Colonel Wedgewood MP said in the British Parliament, "If you are to find anything so damning to the reputation of the British you have to go back centuries... It has not only destroyed that but also destroyed our reputation throughout the world... Even Germany never did anything worse in Belgium." Wedgewood had the fortitude to point out the faults of his own Government and the conviction to confront the moral implications of a travesty of justice. He kept the nation's conscience alive. The UPA government's and even more so Dr Manmohan Singh's palpable silence in relation to defending my wholly justified actions especially when the governing bodies (CVC, CBI, JPC, Supreme Court) were refusing to hear my defence felt to me like a silencing of our nation's collective conscience. It is also interesting to note what Sanjaya Baru says about Dr Singh and the 2G saga in his book 'The Accidental Prime Minister', "Inevitably, we discussed 2G. My advice to him was that he should defend the policy itself and have the charges against Raja investigated. The Comptroller and Auditor General (CAG) of India, it could be credibly argued, was taking an 'accountant's' view on policy. Several analysts had already said so and that was also the editorial line I had taken at Business Standard. The government's policy had enabled it to offer cheaper telecom services and made it possible for millions of Indians to become connected. The economic and social benefits of the policy far outweighed the revenue loss to the exchequer, which the CAG had focused on. However, the government persisted with its ill-advised 'zero loss' argument (that the deal had caused no revenue loss to the exchequer), revealing how little control the prime minister had over the political narrative." I can only wistfully recall the words of the English author Charles Colton and heed their message, "The greatest friend of truth is time, her greatest enemy is prejudice, her constant companion is humility."

Effective policy-making is rarely a one-step process – successful policies generally take a few iterations to mature. This is especially true in the case of telecom where technology and socio-economic factors play such a massive role and are both evolving at such a rapid pace. The whole difference of opinion related to Telecom Policy boils down to the relative prioritization of telecom as an enabler for the masses versus Telecom as a source of revenue for the government. The fairly nascent history of India's telecom sector has continually highlighted this. Initially telecom operators were burdened with such heavy fees that they were unable to invest in infrastructure, grow their service base or become profitable. Consequently, the government implemented a series of industry-friendly initiatives in an attempt to stimulate growth: allowing operators to renegotiate on their license fee obligations or waiving off past dues, giving additional spectrum for free, allowing incoming calls to be chargeable for 4 years beyond the policy stipulation, etc. In the face of weak teledensity and high call charges, it is perhaps natural for the public to have the notion that there is corruption or lack of wherewithal in the government. Consequently, it has remained easy for public ire to be riled in this context by vested interests. N.K. Goyal, president, CMAI Association of India has stated, "The defining moment in the history was when the sector was opened up to private players in the 1990s, and then the entry of new mobile players in 2007-08 which brought down mobile tariffs to the lowest level and industry grew rapidly."

P.J. Thomas, Secretary (T) replied to the audit reference of CAG on 27 July 2010 itself "It is only after May, 2007 when Hon'ble MoC and IT took over as Minister of Communications and IT and particularly after the grant of new UAS licences in 2008, the tele-density in India and particularly in rural areas started increasing at an unprecedented rate. As a result by June, 2010, the rural tele-density has increased to about 26% and all-India tele-density has reached to 57%. It may also be noted that for the last two years, country is adding more than 10 million subscribers per month which has even touched 20 million subscribers in a month and is presently adding 15 million subscribers per month. The number of total telephones in the country has increased to 671.7 million by June 2010. The targets of 11th Plan of 600 million total phones, 200 million rural phones and

25% rural tele-density have already been achieved two years in advance." Later in 2014, Thomas made a courtesy visit to my house and expressed his anguish over the crafty behaviour of Rai in the 2G audit and adjudged that he (Rai) had tarnished the image of the constitutional body CAG.

Perhaps the fact that the actions taken during my tenure had such a significant impact is why the furore could be staged to such unprecedented proportions, even though there hasn't been a shred of actual proof of corruption whereas there has been actual proof of growth in teledensity and dramatic reduction in call charges. There is mixed opinion about the relative success of the 2G auction held after the licenses issued under me were cancelled. However, it is quite evident that the telecom sector in India realised its potential as a result of the honest and diligent implementation of the National Telecom Policy that I had steered as Telecom Minister. 2G is quite ubiquitous and has spread even to the smallest villages in our country now; 3G and even 4G services are available at very affordable rates; there are many service providers competing healthily in the marketplace and there is no monopoly. Reliance Jio came into existence due to the policies implemented during my tenure. Their latest venture to provide voice service for free is a huge milestone of the telecom sector's growth story in India.

My sense of victimisation was compounded by the fact that for the first time in history an individual (I) was thus hounded by various institutions (constitutional bodies) with the full force of their bureaucratic machinery. Even for argument's sake if we agree with the conjecture that the implementation was faulty, was I (and could I be?) running the Telecom Ministry all by myself? Haven't I proved repeatedly that all actions were taken collectively and transparently as per the ministry procedures? Not only did the institutions gloss over most aspects of my defence but even those who knew I was not in the wrong did not step up to publicly voice support for me or denounce the injustice being meted out to me. I am reminded of Dante's quote, "the hottest places in Hell are reserved for those who remained neutral at the time of moral crisis." I have already mentioned how hopeless and utter despondent I felt during the darkest days of my tribulations. I wonder sometimes and feel that perhaps my parents and grandparents might have in fact succumbed and not been able to bounce back from this despondency if they were faced with such a situation. I say this not because I feel I am better or stronger than them, but because of the feeling of empowerment fostered in me by the Dravidian ideology, the steadfast backing of the DMK party leadership and the faith in our constitutional assurance (validated by my education and career in the field of Law) that justice will eventually prevail. I rest my case with this belief and the hope that history will set the record straight and finally by quoting Winston Churchill "The truth is incontrovertible. Malice may attack it; ignorance may deride it; but in the end, there it is."

Annexure - I

D-358

A. RAJA

मंत्री
संचार एवं सूचना प्रौद्योगिकी
भारत सरकार,
इलैक्ट्रानिक्स निकेतन, 6, सी.जी.ओ. कॉम्प्लेक्स,
नई दिल्ली-110 003

MINISTER
COMMUNICATIONS & INFORMATION TECHNOLOGY,
GOVERNMENT OF INDIA,
ELECTRONICS NIKETAN, 6, C.G.O. COMPLEX,
NEW DELHI-110 003

D.O. No.20-100/2007-AS.I
Dated 2nd November 2007.

Respected Sir,

After the announcement of TRAI Recommendations on Review of Licence Terms and Conditions for (Telecom) Access Service Providers on 28th August, 2007, an unprecedented number of applications were being received by the Department due to Recommendation of TRAI recommending " No Cap" on number of Licences in a Service Area.

2. As unprecedented number of applications were being received, a cut-off date of 1st October, 2007 was announced by the Department on 24th September, 2007 and a Press Release was given. In all 575 applications for 22 Service Areas were received.

3. The Department wanted to examine the possibility of any other procedure in addition to the current procedure of allotment of Licences to process the huge number of applications. A few alternative procedures as debated in the Department and also opined by few legal experts were suggested by the Department of Telecom to Ministry of Law & Justice to examine its legal tenability to avoid future legal complications, if any. Ministry of Law and Justice, instead of examining the legal tenability of these alternative procedures, suggested referring the matter to empowered Group of Ministers. Since, generally new major policy decisions of a Department or inter-departmental issues are referred to GOM, and, needless to say that the present issue relates to procedures, the suggestion of Law Ministry is totally out of context.

4. Now, the Department has decided to continue with the existing policy (first-cum-first-served) for processing of applications received up to 25th September 2007, i. e. the date when the news-item on announcement of cut-off date appeared in the newspapers. The procedure for processing the remaining applications will be decided at a later date, if any spectrum is left available after processing the applications received up to 25th September 2007.

4. As the Department is not deviating from the existing procedure, I hope this will satisfy the Industry.

Ack. being put up separately.

Continuation Sheet 1

5. You will appreciate that I am writing this letter to apprise you about the latest developments in the Department.

I take this occasion to extend my warm Diwali Greetings.

With regards,

Yours sincerely,

(A. RAJA)

Dr. Manmohan Singh,
Prime Minister of India,
New Delhi.

Annexure - II

D-359

सत्यमेव जयते

प्रधान मंत्री

Prime Minister

New Delhi
2 November, 2007

Dear Shri Raja,

A number of issues relating to allocation of spectrum have been raised by telecom sector companies as well as in sections of the media. Broadly, the issues relate to enhancement of subscriber linked spectrum allocation criteria, permission to CDMA service providers to also provide services on the GSM standard and be eligible for spectrum in the GSM service band, and the processing of a large number of applications received for fresh licenses against the backdrop of inadequate spectrum to cater to overall demand. Besides those, there are some other issues recommended by TRAI that require early decision. The key issues are summarized in the annexed note.

I would request you to give urgent consideration to the issues being raised with a view to ensuring fairness and transparency and let me know of the position before you take any further action in this regard.

With regards,

Yours sincerely,

(Manmohan Singh)

Shri A. Raja
Minister of Communications and IT
New Delhi

5/11

Dir (AA)

Annexure

1. **Enhancement of subscriber linked spectrum allocation criteria**

In August 2007, the TRAI has recommended interim enhancement of subscriber linked spectrum allocation criteria. Service providers have objected to these recommendations, alleging errors in estimation / assumptions as well as due procedure not having been followed by the TRAI while arriving at the recommendations.

2. **Permission to CDMA service providers to also provide services on the GSM standard and be eligible for spectrum n the GSM service band**

Based on media reports, it is understood that the DoT has allowed 'cross technology' provision of services by CDMA service providers and three such companies have already paid the license fee. With the deposit of the fee, they would be eligible for GSM spectrum, for which old incumbent operators have been waiting since last several years. The Cellular Operators Association of India (COAI), being the association of GSM service providers, has represented against this. It is understood that the COAI has also approached the TDSAT against this.

3. **Processing of a large number of applications received for fresh licenses against the backdrop of inadequate spectrum to cater to overall demand**

The DoT has received a large number of applications for new licenses in various telecom circles. Since spectrum is very limited, even in the next several years all these licensees may never be able to get spectrum. The Telecom Policy that had been approved by the Union Cabinet in 1999 specifically stated that new licenses would be given subject to availability of spectrum.

4. **In order that spectrum use efficiency gets directly linked with correct pricing of spectrum, consider (i) introduction of a transparent methodology of auction, wherever legally and technically feasible, and (ii) revision of entry fee. which is currently benchmarked on old spectrum auction figures**

5. **Early decision on issues like rural telephony, infrastructure sharing, 3G, Broadband, Number Portability and Broadband Wireless Access, on which the TRAI has already given recommendations.**

Annexure - III

अ. இராசா
ए. राजा
A. RAJA

मंत्री
संचार एवं सूचना प्रौद्योगिकी
भारत सरकार,
इलैक्ट्रॉनिक्स निकेतन, 6, सी.जी.ओ. कॉम्प्लेक्स,
नई दिल्ली-110 003
MINISTER
COMMUNICATIONS & INFORMATION TECHNOLOGY,
GOVERNMENT OF INDIA,
ELECTRONICS NIKETAN, 6, C.G.O. COMPLEX,
NEW DELHI-110 003

D.O. No. 20-100/2007-AS.I
2nd November, 2007.

Respected Sir, Vanakkam.

Kindly refer to your letter dated 2.11.2007 regarding various issues related to Telecom sector. In this regard I have already written to you a letter earlier today (copy enclosed) clarifying the position on processing of large number of applications received for fresh licences. Before giving clarifications to the averments contained in the Annexure to your letter, I would like to inform you that there was, and is, no single deviation or departure in the rules and procedures contemplated, in all the decisions taken by my Ministry and as such full transparency is being maintained by my Ministry and I further assure you the same in future also.

Clarifications with respect to other issues are as follows:

1. **Enhancement of subscriber linked spectrum allocation criteria**

TRAI had recommended in August 2007, enhancement in subscriber linked criteria for allotment of additional spectrum to existing operators in order to increase spectrum efficiency which is scarce. Independent to this, Telecom Engineering Centre (TEC), which is the competent body to look into such matter, was asked to examine the spectrum efficiency issues scientifically. TEC submitted its recommendations on 26.10.2007, which was in principle accepted by me. It has been placed on the website of the Ministry and therefore, anybody much less COAI is at liberty to challenge the report of TEC with scientific basis. **However, the fact still remains that no such attempts have been honestly made by them.**

.....2/-

9714/68 18479/Andn 3/11

-2-

2. **Permission to CDMA service providers to also provide services on the GSM standard and be eligible for spectrum in the GSM service band**

This matter was referred to TRAI for its comments on use of dual technology. TRAI, after due deliberations on the issue, recommended use of dual technology, enabling existing Universal Access Service licensees (USAL) to provide services under both (GSM and CDMA) technologies. It was examined in the Ministry and was agreed to as they will be able to rollout the network fast which will ultimately benefit the customers because of increase in teledensity and also resulting lower tariff. **These operators will get spectrum only after the allotment of spectrum to the existing operators according to their eligibility and also licence holders awaiting for initial spectrum.**

3. **Processing of a large number of applications received for fresh licenses against the backdrop of inadequate spectrum to cater to overall demand**

The issue of auction of spectrum was considered by the TRAI and the Telecom Commission and was not recommended as the existing licence holders who are already having spectrum upto 10 MHz per Circle **have got it without any spectrum charge**. It will be unfair, discriminatory, arbitrary and capricious to auction the spectrum to new applicants as it will not give them level playing field.

I would like to bring it to your notice that DoT has earmarked totally 100 MHz in 900 MHz and 1800 MHz bands for 2G mobile services. Out of this, so for a maximum of about 35 to 40 MHz per Circle has been allotted to different operators and being used by them. The remaining 60 to 65 MHz, including spectrum likely to be vacated by Defence Services, is still available for 2G services.

Therefore, there is enough scope for allotment of spectrum to few new operators even after meeting the requirements of existing operators and licensees. An increase in number of operators will certainly bring real competition which will lead to better services

......3/-

-3-

and increased teledensity at lower tariff. **Waiting for spectrum for long after getting licence is not unknown to the Industry and even at present Aircel, Vodafone, Idea and Dishnet are waiting for initial spectrum in some Circles since December 2006.**

I would like to bring to your kind notice that M/s Aircel and M/s Spice Telecom, who were party to the petition to the TDSAT challenging DoT orders on acceptance of TRAI recommendations, have disassociated with the petition after having clarifications from me. These operators have openly admitted that the COAI had misled them, media and the public in general.

Since assuming charge, on more than three occasions I have reviewed all the long pending TRAI recommendations **announced during the tenures of my predecessors** including Number Portability, 3G, Wimax etc. and directed my officers to process them in a transparent manner. As a result we are almost reaching to shape the modalities to auction 3G and Wimax as contemplated by TRAI. I am told that divergence of views on implementation of Number Portability have been expressed by various stakeholders and I am trying to resolve it. The final decision on all these recommendations will be taken soon.

To conclude, I would like to assure you that all my decisions and endeavours are honestly aimed at development of the telecom sector, increasing the teledensity and lowering the tariff for the benefit of the public in general and customers in particular.

With regards,

Yours sincerely,

(A.RAJA)

Dr. Manmohan Singh
Hon'ble Prime Minister of India
7, Race Course Road
New Delhi.

Annexure - IV

Urgent y/c I/C

PM wished this letter to be examined urgently

29.12

Prin Secy

(1)

आ. இராசா
ए. राजा
A. RAJA

मंत्री
संचार एवं सूचना प्रौद्योगिकी
भारत सरकार
इलैक्ट्रानिक्स निकेतन, 6, सी.जी.ओ. कॉम्प्लेक्स,
नई दिल्ली-110 003

MINISTER
COMMUNICATIONS & INFORMATION TECHNOLOGY,
GOVERNMENT OF INDIA,
ELECTRONICS NIKETAN, 6, C.G.O. COMPLEX,
NEW DELHI-110 003

D.O. No. 260/M(C&IT)/VIP/2007

26th December, 2007.

Pl. link with a note from FAM to PM on this & put up urgently. 29/12

JS(VM)

Dir(AA)

Respected Sir, Vanakkam.

Kindly refer to my letters dated 2.11.2007, and subsequent personal discussions with you on various issues related to Telecom sector. As discussed with you I also had several discussions with the External Affairs Minister, who is also heading GOM on vacation of spectrum on these issues. The major issues viz., (i) Subscriber based criteria for additional spectrum to existing operators; (ii) issue of dual technology; and (iii) issue of new licences were discussed with External Affairs Minister at length. Since the cases filed by Cellular Operators Association of India (COAI) on these issues before Telecom Disputes Settlement & Appellate Tribunal (TDSAT) and Delhi High Court are being represented by Solicitor General of India, he was also called for the discussions to explain the legal position.

I must recall that there are three reports available with the DoT with regard to subscriber based criteria for additional spectrum to existing operators viz., Telecom Regulatory Authority of India (TRAI), Telecom Engineering Centre (TEC) and the Report of the Committee which was constituted under the chairmanship of Additional Secretary, DoT with two Professors from IIT, Kanpur and IIT, Chennai who have done their specialisation in Radio Frequency. For one or the other flimsy reason, COAI neither accepted any one of the report nor co-operated with the DOT to arrive at an amicable solution. Similarly, on use of Dual Technology also, they want to challenge the policy decision taken by the Government on the basis of TRAI recommendations.

Since TDSAT refused to grant stay they moved the Delhi High Court for stay on subscriber based criteria, dual technology and in addition to these, the issue of new licences. This clearly shows that the attitude of COAI is to maintain their monopoly in the sector by avoiding healthy competition and level playing field. The only malicious intention of COAI, it appears, is that they want to procrastinate the issues through frivolous and vexacious Court proceedings endlessly.

Original given to CBI

Original given to CBI

........2/-

1000656 28894/PmV/17 29/12

1000656 29/12/07

-2-

(2)

As I have already promised to you, my efforts in this sector are intended to give lower tariff to the consumer and to bring higher tele-density in the country, more specifically in rural areas. It is needless to say that the tariff in India is not as cheap as claimed in terms of purchasing power parity and standard of living of the people of the country since there is no tariff fixation.

In these circumstances, the discussions with the External Affairs Minister and Solicitor General of India have further enlightened me to take a pre-emptive and pro-active decision on these issues as per the guidelines and rules framed there under to avoid any further confusions and delay. The issue wise details and my decisions are given in the enclosed annexure.

This is for your kind information.

With regards,

Yours sincerely,

(A.RAJA)

Dr. Manmohan Singh
Hon'ble Prime Minister of India
New Delhi.

Encl: Annexure

③

Annexure

1. **Subscriber Linked Spectrum Allocation Criterion for CMTS/UAS Licensees**

DOT provides Radio spectrum for providing mobile services to Wireless Operating Licence holders for roll out of GSM / CDMA services. An initial spectrum of 4.4 MHz for GSM and 2.5 MHz for CDMA based technology is provided to operators. Additional spectrum is provided to operators based on the number of subscribers, availability of spectrum, optimal use of spectrum, competition and other interest of public. To ensure optimal utilization of spectrum, TRAI while giving recommendation on other issues as requested by the DOT, also recommended that **"there is a need to tighten the subscriber criteria for all the service areas so as to make it more efficient from the usage and pricing point of view. In order to frame new spectrum allocation criteria, a multi-disciplinary committee may be constituted. However, it is necessary to enhance the present subscriber norms as an ad-hoc measure so that the task of spectrum allocation is not stalled"**. This recommendation was accepted by the department on 17-10-2007.

However, COAI and existing GSM operators challenged recommendations of TRAI saying it lacks scientific basis. In the meantime, TEC which was simultaneously working on the subscriber based criteria for allocation of additional spectrum submitted its report to the Ministry which was accepted in-principal. Incidentally, TEC norms, which were based on scientific basis, came out to be stricter than TRAI norms. COAI challenged these reports in the TDSAT. To avoid any controversy and to find an amicable solution, as suggested by TRAI a Committee headed by Additional Secretary, DOT, including Representatives of COAI and AUSPI and two Professors from IIT Kanpur and IIT Chennai was setup. However, on 7-12-2007, COAI disassociated itself from the proceedings of the Committee. The committee has submitted its report and has suggested that another Committee as suggested by TRAI may be set up to look into broader issues of allotment of additional spectrum and till then recommended to go with TRAI's interim report for allotment of additional spectrum. This recommendation of the Committee is accepted.

In view of above, DOT is proceeding ahead to implement the recommendation of TRAI on subscriber based criteria as an interim measure and allot additional spectrum to eligible existing operators as per TRAI norm, followed by those who got licence in Dec 2006, dual technology and to new applicants as and when licences are given. An affidavit to this effect will be filled in both TDSAT and Delhi High Court.

2. **Use of Dual Spectrum (Alternate technology) by UAS Licensees**

(h)

DOT sought the recommendations of TRAI on Use of Dual Technology / Alternate Technology under USA License and other issues on 13-4-2007(prior to taking over by the present Minister). The recommendations of TRAI were received by DOT on 29-08-2007 which suggested that **"A licensee using one technology may be permitted on request, usage of alternative technology and thus allocation of dual spectrum. However, such a licensee must pay the same amount of fee which has been paid by existing licensees using the alternative technology or which would be paid by a new licensee going to use that technology"**. This recommendation was accepted by the department on 17-10-2007.

This policy makes existing UAS Licence holders (Reliance, TATA, Airtel, Vodafone, etc.) eligible for allotment of spectrum for alternate technology. COAI challenged Dual technology policy in the TDSAT. TDSAT has adjourned the case to 09-01-2008. Failing obtaining stay from TDSAT, COAI moved to Delhi high court on 20-12-2007. The matter was heard on 24-12-2007 and is posted for 3-1-2008 without granting any stay.

In view of above, DOT is proceeding ahead for allotting initial spectrum under dual technology policy to eligible applicants subject to the court order, if any. Application of TATA Telecommunication will also be processed as per the policy and guidelines. An affidavit to this effect will be filled in both TDSAT and Delhi High Court.

3. **Issue of New Licences**

Although UASL guidelines issued in December 2005 clearly indicates that **"Licences shall be issued without any restriction on the number of entrants for provision of Unified Acess Services in a service Area"**, DOT sought recommendation of TRAI on number of UAS licences to be issued in a Service Area on 13-4-2007(prior to taking over by the present Minister). The recommendations of TRAI were received by DOT on 29-08-2007 which suggested that **"No Cap be placed on the number of access service providers in any Service Area"**. This recommendation was accepted by the department on 17-10-2007 in order to encourage more competition in the Telecom Sector and decided to grant new UAS Licences. This is first time that December 2005 UASL guidelines are being implemented in letter and spirit in view of TRAI recommendation.

Annexure - V

Minutes of the exit conference held on 20th May 2010 with the Officers of the Department of Telecommunications on the performance audit of "Issue of Licenses and allotment of 2G spectrum by the Department of Telecommunications"

The following officers attended the exit conference held on 20th May 2010 in the conference hall of DoT at Sanchar Bhavan, New Delhi for discussing the audit findings in the draft report on the performance audit Issue of Licenses and allotment of 2G spectrum by the Department of Telecommunications"

From the Department of Telecommunications	From the O/o the Director General of Audit (P&T)
1. Shri P.J. Thomas, Secretary, DoT 2. Ms Vijayalakshmi. K Gupta Member(Finance) 3. Ms Sadhana Dikshit, Advisor(Finance) 4. Dr Ashok Chandra, Wireless Advisor 5. Shri. T.K.Varadakrishnan, Joint Wireless Advisor 6. Shri.A.K.Srivastava DDG(AS) 7. Shri.R.K.Gupta, Director(AS-I)	1. Shri.R.P.Singh, DGA (P&T), 2. Shri. Subu R. Director (Report), O/o the DGA (P&T), 3. The Performance audit team of P&T Audit Office Delhi. 4. Senior Audit Officers of Report Group in the O/o DGA (P&T)

2. At the outset the Secretary (DoT) welcomed all the participants.

3. Department of Telecom informed that in a meeting held on 3.3.2010 between officers of P&T Audit and DoT, it was informed by DoT that all the related files are under the custody of CBI and in the absence of related files DoT may not be able to offer any comment on the observations. DoT, based on the information available in the computers or in other documents, had furnished para-wise replies to these Inspection Memos to the audit team.

4. Director, Report made a presentation which apart from the major audit findings explained the scope of audit, its objectives, the methodology adopted and criteria used for drawing the audit findings. Audit observations and the response of DoT to each of them were discussed in detail as given below:

- ***The entry fee fixed in 2001 was not revised by DoT while issuing licenses in 2008 which could have resulted in loss ranging Rs.5000 to 65000 crore.***

  Secretary (T) observed that the audit finding was based on the rates offered by a private operator and hence it can not be concluded that the

Government incurred loss. He expressed the view that Audit should rephrase the audit comment.

DDG (AS) explained that the complete facts and chronology of events establishing continuation of the policies, as approved by the Union Cabinet in the year 2003, had been made available to the Audit team. The existing policies have resulted in unprecedented growth in Telecom sector. Moreover, TRAI did not favour auctioning of 2G spectrum or change in entry fee for grant of UAS License. Therefore, Government did not consider any policy changes. The revolution has taken place as the entry barriers were low and spectrum was given based on availability Most of the new licensees have rolled out their networks and there is fierce competition in the market to the best advantage of general public which has brought the tariff to such a low level which could not have been imagined in the year 2008. So the decisions of the Government has yielded results by way of increased competition, increased volume and enhanced revenue.

Director (Report) responding to the views of the Secretary (T) and the DoT team accepted that Audit has taken the rates offered by the private operators as indicator of the market perception of the value of spectrum. Hence, the word 'loss' *needs to be substituted* and also include the views expressed by DoT in the performance audit report.

- ***Flawed implementation of First-Come-First-Served Policy to benefit M/s. Swan Telecom.***

The audit finding was discussed in detail and DDG (AS) expressed the view that the views of the Department submitted to the audit team does not seem to have been considered while framing the audit observation.

The audit team intimated that in certain cases specific replies were not there. Director (Report) said that the phrase 'flawed' will be substituted.

- ***Loss due to non-processing of applications***

Audit observed that out of 575 applications received till 1st October 2007 for UAS licenses only 232 were processed and LoIs were issued to only 121 applicants. With the cap on the number of players in a service area removed DoT should have considered applicants as per the waiting list maintained by DoT.

It was explained by the DDG (AS-I) that it was not possible to grant UAS License to all the 575 pending applicants in view of various factors including likely availability of GSM Spectrum for Access, Micro-wave Access Spectrum for setting up links between BTS and BSCs and between BSCs and MSCs and Micro-wave Back bone spectrum for connecting MSCs to MSCs. When it was decided that all the pending applications cannot be considered together and based on various factors, applications received up to 25.9.2007 were only considered initially, there is no question of losses to the Government as the existing policy guidelines were followed in true spirit. Later, in view of TDSAT judgement dated 31.03.2009, Government sought the recommendations of TRAI for processing of the pending 343 applications which has recently been received on 11.05.2010.

Director (Report) explained that the response of DoT has been considered while finalising the audit findings.

- ***Issue of license to ineligible operators***

DoT recollecting informed that when the complaint of substantial equity violation was received in respect of Loop Telecom, an administrative decision was taken to obtain comments of Ministry of Corporate Affairs before further processing the case. However, when the complaint of M/s. Swan Telecom was being processed, the matter was already being argued before the Delhi High Court in the Petition of Dr. Arvind Gupta vs. Union of India where Ld. Solicitor General was defending the case on behalf UOI. Therefore, full facts related to equity holdings of Swan Telecom were sent to Ld. Solicitor General before further processing. As per the legal opinion of Ld. SG the matter was not found to be fit for further investigation and therefore there is no case of referring to Ministry of Corporate Affairs.

Director (Report) said that in the light of the explanations given by DoT, Audit will attempt to revisit the observation.

- ***Allotment of Spectrum beyond 6.2 MHz to GSM operators***

Wireless Advisor explained that TRAI, in May 2010 had recommended for charging those operators who have spectrum more that 6.2 MHz and the recommendation is under consideration of the Government.

It was agreed to include the explanation enclosed as **Annexure – I** in the performance audit report.

5. Secretary (DoT) suggested that the performance audit team and the Officers of DoT should hold another sitting to have a better understanding of the different issues involved in the issue of licenses and allotment of spectrum. Such a meeting would facilitate reconciliation of the position of audit queries and their replies.

6. DGA (P&T) agreed to the suggestion of Secretary (DoT).

7. The meeting ended with Director (Report) extending vote of thanks to the Secretary (DoT) and the entire team of Officers from DoT for facilitating the audit team in completion of the performance audit.

Subu R. **Director (Report)**	**R. P. Singh** **DGA (P&T)**	**Vijayalakshmi. K. Gupta** **Member (Finance), DoT**	**P.J. Thomas** **Secretary, DoT**

Annexure - VI

PRADIP BAIJAL
Chairman
TELECOM REGULATORY AUTHORITY OF INDIA

सत्यमेव जयते

November 14, 2003.

My dear Vinod,

Kindly refer our telecon regarding Entry Fee of the new Unified Licensee.

2. In this regard I am reproducing para 7.18, 7.19 and 7.20 of our recommendations :-

7.18 *The 3rd alternative is that the existing entry fee of the fourth Cellular Operator would be the entry fee in the new Unified Access Licensing Regime. BSOs would pay the difference of the fourth CMSP's existing entry fee and the entry fee paid by them. It may be recalled that, even in the past, entry to cellular and basic services has been on fixed fee basis, e.g. for metros in the case of cellular and the second BSO.*

7.19 *It is recommended that the 3rd alternative as mentioned in para 7.18 above may be accepted for fixing the entry fee for migration to Unified Access Licensing regime for Basic Cellular services at the circle level.*

7.20 *In service areas where there is no fourth operator - viz. Bihar, Orissa, W.B. & A.N. and Assam, etc. - no extra entry fee would be charged from the existing operators migrating to the Unified Access Licensing Regime, since in these areas operators did not see a potential mobile market at the time of repeated bidding for the 4th cellular operator.*

It would be clear from the above that the entry fee of the new Unified Licensee would be the entry fee of the 4th cellular operator and in service areas where there is no 4th operator - the entry fee of the existing BSO fixed by the Government (based on TRAI's recommendations). Incidentally, in such States where no 4th cellular operator came in, the entry fee for BSOs was fixed by the Government and as per our recommendations in para 7.20 above, it will be the same for new or existing unified licensee.

With regards,

Yours sincerely,

(Pradip Baijal)

Shri Vinod Vaish,
Secretary,
Department of Telecommunications,
Sanchar Bhavan,
New Delhi-110 001.

ए-2/14 सफदरजंग एन्क्लेव, नई दिल्ली -110 029 दूरभाष : 91-11-2616 1236 फैक्स : 91-11-2616 6026 ई-मेल : pbaijal@trai.gov.in
A-2/14, Safdarjang Enclave, New Delhi-110029 PHONE : 91-11-2616 1236 FAX : 91-11-2616 6026 E-mail : pbaijal@trai.gov.in
Website : www.trai.gov.in

Annexure - VII

ITEM No. 1.2 (469

Confidential

473

Government of India
Ministry of Communications & IT
Department of Communications
(WPC Wing)

No. R-11020/02/2008-PP   Dated the 9th January, 2008

TELECOM COMMISSION MEMO

Subject: Spectrum charging from cellular Service Providers

1. Proposal

This proposal is for bringing the annual AGR-based spectrum charges to realistic levels to reflect the true value of this scarce, vital economic resource – radio spectrum, in respect of commercial telecom service providers using 2G spectrum.

The Hon'ble MOC&IT had desired that a decision needs to be taken on the spectrum charges. He had directed that the issue of spectrum charges in terms of AGR be placed before the Telecom Commission for in depth deliberations.

2. Background

2.1 The WPC Wing charges 'License Fee' and 'Royalty' for grant of wireless licenses. This 'License Fee' is charged as a documentation fee and the 'Royalty' is charged for the Government surrendering its right of providing 'communication' (Section 4 of the Indian Telegraph Act, 1885) to the applicant and this royalty is based on the amount of spectrum, area of network coverage, etc. The 'Royalty' was thus charged from the date the network had been put in use/ operational (licensed).

The 'Royalty' which is equivalent to spectrum charges is dependent on the amount of spectrum, number of wireless stations/ terminals and the area to be covered by the network, as per the formula. It was last general revision was in 1988 and a revision for GSM services was made in 1995. Subsequently, a revision for captive services was made in 2003.

During 1999 – 2000, the spectrum charges/ royalty and the wireless license fee for cellular mobile service providers were changed over to 'Revenue share'. To simplify the calculation of these charges, **a single 'revenue share'** was prescribed in lieu of both the spectrum charges/ royalty as well as [illegible]

2.2 License Provisions Concerning Wireless Charges:

2.2.1 Extracts from Basic Service Agreements Signed in 1997:

"1.7.5.2: License fee and royalty shall have to be paid by LICENSEE to WPC for grant of license which will be subject to revision from time to time."

"5.3: License fee/ royalty as prescribed by WPC from time to time, shall have to be paid by LICENSEE towards grant of license for usage of frequency spectrum. Quantum of License fee/ Royalty shall depend upon number of RF channels, the frequency band, maximum link distance and other related aspects."

2.2.2 Extracts from Basic Service Agreements Signed in 2001:

"5.3 An additional revenue share of 2% (Two percent) of ADJUSTED GROSS REVENUE earned from Wireless Local Loop (WLL) subscribers shall be

-2-

payable as spectrum charge for allocation of up to 5 plus 5 MHz in 824-844 MHz band paired with 869-889 MHz band for wireless subscriber access system. This will include royalty for spectrum of 5+5 MHz as well as the LICENSE Fee for the base station and SUBSCRIBER terminal (handheld or fixed). The same principle shall be followed for spectrum charges in 1880-1990 MHz band for micro-cellular technology based system."

2.2.3 Extracts from Fresh UAS License Agreements (Licenses Signed in 2004)

"18.3.1: The LICENSEE shall pay spectrum charges in addition to the License Fees on revenue share basis as notified separately from time to time by the WPC Wing. However, while calculating 'AGR' for limited purpose of levying spectrum charges based on revenue share, revenue from wireline subscribers shall not be taken into account."

"20.9: The Fee/ Royalty payable towards WPC charges shall be payable at such time(s) and in such manner as the WPC Wing of the DoT may prescribe from time to time."

2.2.4 Extracts from Cellular Service Agreements Signed in 1995:

"19.4 The annual license fee referred to above does not include Royalty fees payable to WPC Wing of Ministry of Communications (WPC) for use of Radio Frequencies which shall be paid separately by the licensee on the rates prescribed by the WPC and as per procedure specified by it."

2.2.5 Extracts from Cellular Service Agreements Signed in 2001:

"19.3 In addition, the cellular licensees shall pay spectrum charges on revenue share basis of 2% of AGR towards WPC Charges covering royalty payment for the use of cellular spectrum up to 4.4 MHz + 4.4 MHz and license fee for Cellular Mobile handsets & Cellular Mobile Base Stations and also for possession of wireless telegraphy equipment as per the details prescribed by Wireless Planning & Coordination Wing (WPC). Any additional bandwidth, if allotted subject to availability and justification shall attract additional License fee as revenue share *(typically 1% additional revenue share if Bandwidth allocated is up to 6.2 MHz + 6.2 MHz in place of 4.4 MHz + 4.4 MHz)."*

"21.9 The Fee/ Royalty payable towards WPC Charges shall be payable at such time(s) and in such manner as the WPC Wing of the Ministry of Communications may prescribe from time to time."

2.2.6 Extracts from CMTS Licences/ agreements, after migration to UASL:

"18.3.1 In addition to the license fee as per clause 18.2, the Licensee shall pay spectrum charges on revenue share basis of 2% of AGR towards WPC Charges covering royalty payment for the use of cellular spectrum up to 4.4 MHz + 4.4 MHz and License fee for Cellular Mobile handsets & Cellular Mobile Base Stations and also for possession of wireless telegraphy equipment as per the details prescribed by Wireless Planning & Coordination Wing (WPC). Any additional bandwidth, if allotted subject to availability and justification, shall attract additional License fee as revenue share (typically 1% additional revenue share if Bandwidth allocated is up to 6.2 MHz + 6.2 MHz in place of 4.4 MHz + 4.4 MHz)."

- 3-

4~~28~~ 471

"18.3.3 The above spectrum charge is subject to unilateral review by WPC Wing from time to time which shall be binding on the licensee."

2.3 Existing Pricing Structure

2.3.1 The assignment of spectrum by WPC Wing to a telecom service provider (spectrum licensing) does not require payment of any upfront charges. Annual license fee (for the service licence) paid by telecom operators "does not include royalty fees payable to WPC Wing of Ministry of Communications for use of radio frequencies, which has to be paid separately by the licensee on the rates prescribed by the WPC Wing are as per procedure specified by it."

2.3.2 In the 2G bands – 800 MHz/ 900 MHz/ 1800 MHz – Telecom Service Providers have been provided spectrum at different times varying from 2 x 4.4 MHz to 2 x 10 MHz for GSM technology and 2 x 2.5 MHz to 2 x 5 MHz in CDMA technology. WPC Wing has, through various orders communicated the rates for various blocks of spectrum. These are as follows:

GSM

Spectrum Blocks	%age of AGR being charged
Upto 2 x 4.4 MHz	2%
Upto 2 x 6.2 MHz	3%
Upto 2 x 8 MHz	4%
Upto 2 x 10 MHz	4%
Upto 2 x 12.4 MHz	5% +
Upto 2 x 15 MHz	6% +

CDMA

Spectrum Blocks	%age of AGR being charged
Upto 2 x 5 MHz	2%
Upto 2 x 6.25 MHz	3%
Upto 2 x 10 MHz	4%
Upto 2 x 12.5 MHz	5% *
Upto 2 x 15 MHz	6% *

2. 3.3 In addition, charges have to be paid separately in respect of microwave spectrum used for point to point and point to multi-point radio links.

3 TRAI's Recommendations

DOT, vide its letter dated 13th April 2007, had sought TRAI's recommendations on the issue of determining the number of access providers in each service area and for reviewing the terms and conditions in the access provider license pertaining to substantial equity holding, transfer of licenses, mergers and acquisitions, permitting service providers to offer access services using combination of technology under the same license, roll-out obligations, etc. TRAI made its recommendations "Review of license terms and conditions and capping of number of access providers" on 28th August, 2007. While the report basically dwelt on the issues referred to the Authority, there were also some observations and recommendations on spectrum issues, including spectrum charges.

TRAI has recommended revenue share for spectrum charges as follows:

-4-

Spectrum	Current	Proposed
Upto 2x4.4 MHz	2%	No change
Upto 2x6.2 MHz/ 2x5 MHz	3%	No change
Upto 2x8 MHz	4%	No change
Upto 2x10 MHz	4%	5.00%
Upto 2x12.5 MHz	5%	6.00%
Upto 2x15 MHz	6%	7.00%
Beyond 2x15 MHz	No existing orders	8.00%

The TRAI recommendations regarding the "spectrum enhancement charge" at the time of additional spectrum allotment to licensees beyond 10MHz for GSM and 5 MHz for CDMA will be processed separately.

4. Revision of annual spectrum charges for mobile telecom services:

4.1 A Committee was constituted by Secretary, DOT, to examine the issue of spectrum valuation/ pricing has submitted its **Report on 7.1.2008**. The Committee has reportedly taken into account Hon'ble PM's observations regarding the need for **maximizing revenue from the telecom sector without creating entry barriers and compromising on growth.**

4.2 The issue of spectrum charges in terms of AGR and other issues of spectrum pricing have been covered in the Report of the Committee. The salient points are reproduced below:

4.2.1 Spectrum Fees Based on Users' Gross Income:

A fee can be charged based on a percentage of the gross income of a company. The value of the gross income used in the fee calculation must be directly related to the company's **use of the spectrum to avoid difficulty in the accounting and auditing processes.** This is somewhat similar to the method of AGR-based spectrum charges in use in India presently.

The approach suffers from a number of deficiencies, the more important ones being:

a) First, it can equitably apply only to such users as have a gross income directly linked to spectrum use and not to those users whose gross income results only indirectly from spectrum exploitation – as determining gross income may be difficult due to the complexity of company accounting and in addition determining how much of a users gross income is directly linked to spectrum use is virtually impossible, e.g., how much of a public utilities or telephone companies' gross income can be attributed to their use of microwave links in portions of their fixed network.

b) Second, such a fee does not necessarily promote efficient spectrum use or even equitable treatment of licensees because a user's gross income may not be directly related to the *value* of the spectrum. For example, two operators may have identical gross incomes, but one may be reaping large profits, while the second may be even operating at a loss.

c) Third, it *does not force* the licensee to use spectrum efficiently. Thus it may suppress spectrum usage, reduce growth of services, impair innovation and spectrum efficiency, and adversely affect international competitiveness.

– 5 – 427 ...

d) Fourth, under this system, an operator *not* using spectrum will actually pay *less* fees to government than one who's making better use of it and earning larger revenues. As a result, applications for spectrum may arise from the motive of *speculative hoarding* of spectrum.

e) Fifth, the operators may use different accounting policies/ treatments with a view to pay less spectrum charges to government.

4.2.2 The Committee notes with some concern that in India, where the charges are based on gross revenues *less* admissible deductions, large *inter-operator* variations are seen in the deductions claimed by them in relation to their Gross Revenues. During 2006-07, for example, the *private operators* in various Service Areas have successfully claimed such deductions ranging from 13% to 34% of their Gross Revenues, and are agitating in courts for obtaining more relief.

4.2.3 Areas of Concern In Present Charging Regime

a) A reference was made to the large variation in operators' claims for admissible deductions to arrive at AGR. In the face of the vociferous assertions made by the industry leaders about high spectrum costs, it also found it instructive to compare the amount of *spectrum charges* being paid by four leading UASL operators *vis-à-vis* the expenditures they make on items like *marketing, sales and publicity* and *network operations*.

b) The results of this limited exercise, taking the data furnished by the operators at face value, have been considered by the Committee. They bring out in a stark manner the large disparity that exists between the "high" cost of the *admittedly-most-crucial input of RF spectrum* (a 'public property' at that) on the one hand, and the above-mentioned expense heads on the other.

4.2.4 The Committee finds that whereas the *spectrum charges* ranging between 2.02% and 2.52% of their gross revenues in 2005-06 were considered a painful burden by the operators, they had *chosen* to spend 4.46% to 49.71% of the same revenues on *marketing-and-sales*, and from 8.10 % to 55.98 % on *network-operations*. **These data further convince the Committee that existing pricing regime needs to give way to one that gives the government (as a proxy for the public) full market value of the spectrum.**

4.2.5 The Committee is in full agreement with the view that frequency spectrum is 'public property'. In fact it recognizes that it is a limited resource having enormous economic value, and that for this reason it is in *public interest*:

a. That spectrum should be *priced* to reflect its *'real value'*, so that those licensed to use it are motivated to use it efficiently and also dissuaded from using it inefficiently.

b. That the government, as a *trustee* of this public property, gets the best price from entities authorized to use it, and uses the funds so generated to further the interests of the society (including, by aiding the relocation of government wireless usages to 'less congested' frequencies).

c. That this most vital resource – without which mobile service licenses would be no more than scraps of paper – is *not* handed over to a few *private operators* at rates considerably below par, since such a course of action amounts to an unfair transfer of public wealth to a limited number of persons at the cost of the public exchequer (society).

-6-

4.2.4 The Committee has recommended that the spectrum charges may be levied from Access Services licensees under UASL regime at a flat rate of 8% of AGR up to 5 MHz of subscriber Access spectrum, irrespective of the type of technology deployed and the quantum of spectrum held. For any additional spectrum, they may be charged extra @ 1% of AGR per MHz (*pro rata*). On this basis, the annual spectrum charges for 10 MHz spectrum would work out to 13% and for 15 MHz spectrum it would work out to 18%. **The Committee has also proposed that a minimum/ floor level of spectrum charges be also fixed, for which the details would be worked out separately.**

4.2.5 The present revenue share increases with the amount of spectrum, so as to ensure that the service providers should make use of various possible technological features for enhanced spectrum efficiency before they ask for additional spectrum. This principle is proposed to be continued. Also, one of the basic thrusts of revenue share regime was simplicity of its implementation. Hence, pro-rata revenue share (fraction of a percentage) for part of MHz of the spectrum, recommended by the Committee needs to be examined.

4.2.6 The Committee's recommendations regarding annual spectrum charges/ (revenue share) that spectrum charges may be levied from Access Services licensees under UASL regime at a flat rate of 8% of AGR up to 5 MHz of subscriber Access spectrum, irrespective of the type of technology deployed and the quantum of spectrum held, are submitted for kind consideration and approval by the Telecom Commission. For any additional spectrum the service providers may be charged extra @ 1% of AGR per MHz (*pro rata*). The concept of minimum/ floor level of spectrum charges (absolute amount) is also proposed for approval, for which the details would be worked out separately as indicated by the Committee.

5. Approval of Telecom Commission requested:

The kind approval of Telecom Commission is solicited for proposal in para 4.2.6 above.

This has the approval of Member (Technology) and Member (Finance), Telecom Commission.

(R. J. S. Kushvaha)
Joint Wireless Adviser

Annexure - VIII

The details of news items furnished by the DoT to the CAG Audit on 3.5.2010 pertaining to the fixation of cut-off date (25.09.2007)

Name of Newspaper /Media	**Date of Publication**	**Title / Caption**	**Extracts**
Business (Rediff India Abroad)	13.11.2007	DoT may issue LOIs to all applicants	In his letter to Prime Minister Manmohan Singh early this month, Raja had clarified that for spectrum allocation the process of first-come-first served would be followed. The government is also considering making September 25, the date on which it had announced October 1 as the deadline for filling applications for new licences, as the cut off date for issuing LOIs in the first phase. The procedure for the remaining applications would be decided at a later date. if any spectrum was left after processing the applications received upto September 25.
Business Standard	14.11.2007	DoT may issue letters for licences this week	According to Telecom Minister A. Raja's recent letter to Prime Minister Manmohan Singh, the 46 firms that have applied for spectrum are to be divided into two groups. The first includes those which applied before September 25, and will get the first priority.
Business Standard	12.12.2007	DoT seeks clarification from UASL applicants.	DoT has shot off a letter to all those who have applied for Unified Access Service License (UASL)

			before September 25, seeking clarifications on their Memorandum of Association. The move is being seen by the operators as a step closure to the issuance of Letters of Intent for the Licence to all eligible applicants.
Business Line	22.12.2007	Idea Spice resent DoT delay, say 'we applied first'	Since recent communication from DoT indicate that spectrum will be released based on the date of paying the entry fee, all the new players are clamouring to be the among the first to get an LOI.
Business Standard	24.12.2007	DoT wants redrafting of LOIs.	The note has pointed that 60 MHz of the 75 MHz for second generation (2G) services in 1,800 Band that is available with the DoT should be the basis for deciding the number of letters of intent that can be issued.
DNA	09.01.2008	LOI for 15 telecom operators ready	The cleared list includes Idea Cellular, Tata Teleservices, Reliance Communications, Unitech, HFCL, ShippingStop, DoT CoM, Datacom Solutions and Swan. Spice communications' application for pan-India operation is learnt to have been rejected over net-worth issues. Although real estate company Parsvnath's application for entry into telecom has been turned down as of now, as many as eight LOIs are being issued to Unitech group entities, sources said. Among the other new players, ShippingStop Dot Com and

			Datacom are also likely to get LOIs for pan-Inidia operation. Swan, in which Reliance Communication is learnt to have a stake, is set to get LOIs for 14 circles. Existing GSM service provider Idea Cellular (GSM) would get LOIs for the remaining seven circles-Kolkata, Chennai, Tamil Nadu, Punjab, West Bengal, Jammu & Kashmir, Orissa, Assam and North East. Idea currently operates in 11 circles and has LOI for another tow (Mumbai and Bihar). CDMA players Reliance Communications and Tata Teleservices would get LOIs for the remaining two and three circles respectively. While Reliance would get for Assam and North East. Tatas would be issued LOIs for Assam, North East and Jammu Kashmir. CDMA Player HFCL, which operates only in Punjab, is also learnt to be getting LOIs for the remaining 21 circles. The applications which have been rejected include those from Cheetah Corporate Services, Spice Communications and Parsvnath. Bycell Telecom's application is also not being entertained now.